SEASONS
an autobiography

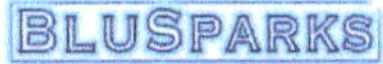

SEASONS

an autobiography

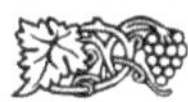

by Carla Carli Mazzucato

BluSparks

© 2021 by Carla Carli Mazzucato
All rights reserved.
edited by Paolo Mazzucato
No part of this publication may be reproduced, in
whole or in part, or digitally archived, or transmitted in
any form or by any method, electronically,
mechanically, by photocopy without the expressed,
written permission from the publisher.
Published by BluSparks - Tustin, CA

for information about permissions contact the publisher
at: http://www.blusparks.com

the text of this book was set in
Times New Roman
ISBN-13: 978-1-7379898-1-3

To My Family

CONTENTS

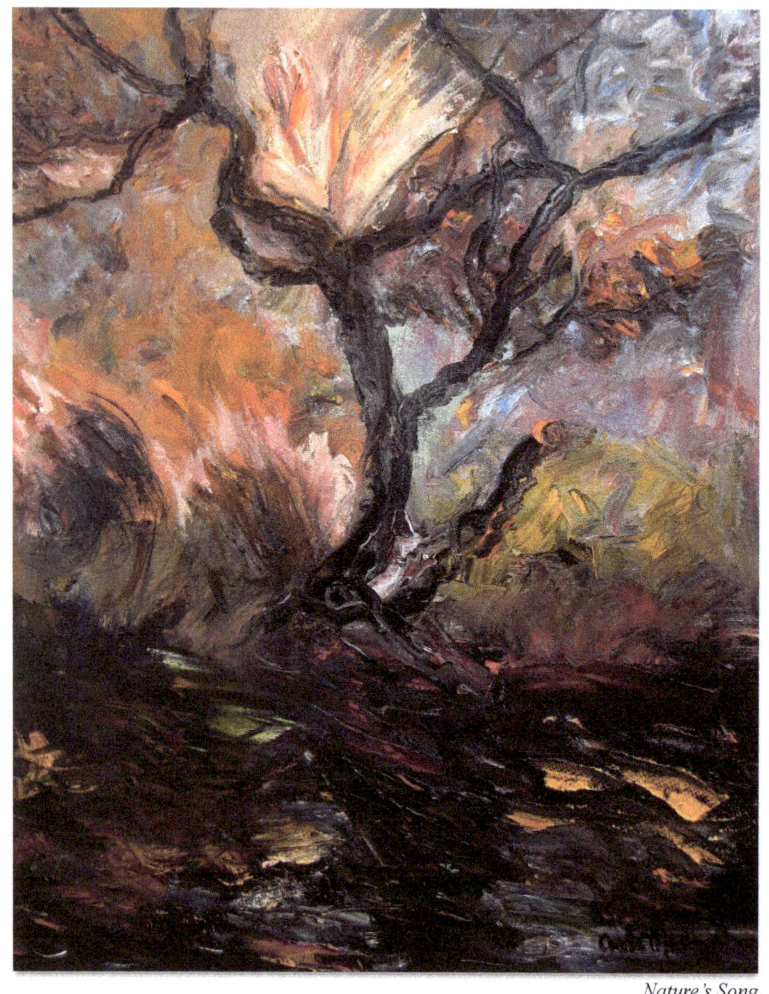

Nature's Song

FOREWORD

In life, as in nature, seasons mark our passage through time —from our beginning, our growth and transformation, and finally to our fading and vanishing.

The life of Carla Carli has wandered through various seasons, beginning with her childhood in Appiano, her years of study in Venice and Milano, and her later years of study in a new world, the United States. In America she traveled the country from the Atlantic coast to the Pacific Ocean in California where she made her home.

As an artist she has traveled as well, exhibiting her paintings in galleries and museums in Europe and America.

Her wandering however, has not solely been a geographic and artistic journey, it has also been a journey of the spirit. The colors of the seasons are like the cycle of her life, they suggest the pathos of her world in transition. She communicates her personal experiences without noting time or space, but taking us back to remember the sorrows and the joys of her past.

Dr. Edit Meraner

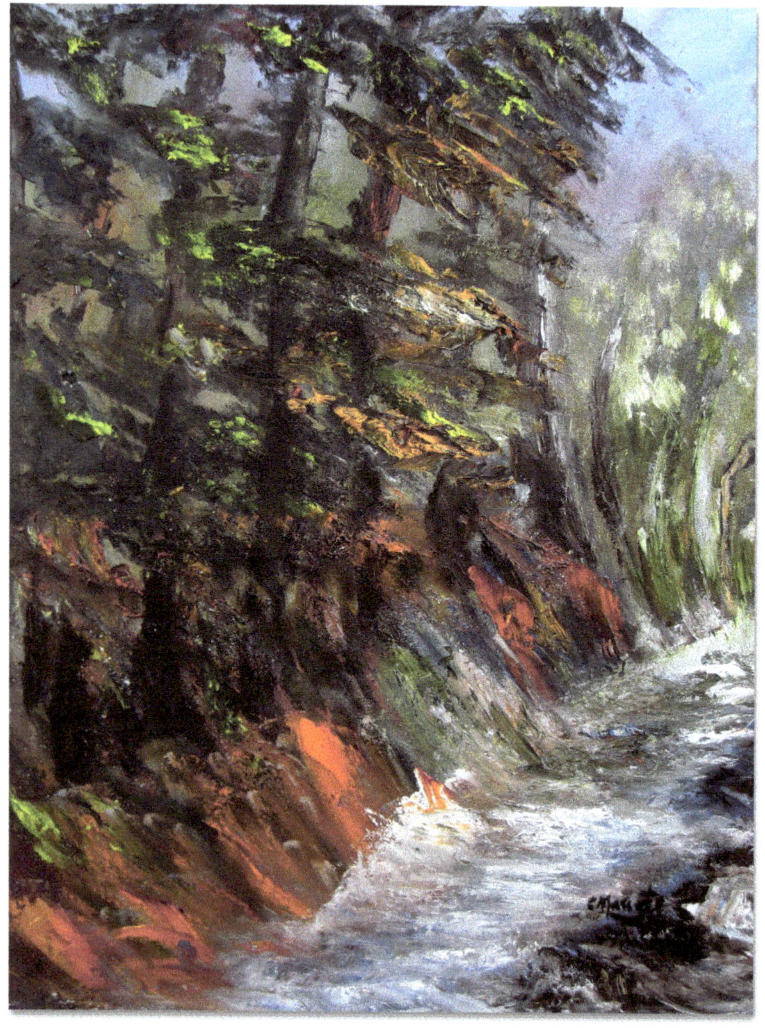

Ruscello

INTRODUCTION
by Carla Carli Mazzucato

I was born in autumn, when the grapes in my father's vineyard were ripe and ready for winemaking, and the apples from his orchard were picked and sent to the big fruit warehouses in town to be enjoyed throughout northern Italy or packed for export to southern Europe. It was the season of the harvest—the first season of my childhood—when I began my life, nurtured in love from my wonderful parents.

I grew up in a bilingual family. At home we spoke mostly Italian, but when I played with my many cousins in the big courtyard of our house in *Appiano,* or in the surrounding fields between our homes, I spoke the German dialect of the South Tyrol region which had been under Austrian rule up through the end of the First World War.

It was a beautiful place to grow, and I enjoyed the change of seasons—from summers spent in the sun and mountain air, to winters enjoyed down in the valley where great drifts of snow brought fun and games and the anticipation of our Christmas celebrations. But just as those seasons turned in a great circle, so did the seasons of my life.

Early spring was the time of my youth in Italy, while summer led me away to explore new lands and different people. From there, I spent many seasons in the United States of America, my adoptive country, where I married my husband, Giuseppe, and raised a family.

And as I reflect on the turning of each season, I remember moments of both struggle and great beauty from time spent in my native hometown, my new home in America, and all the places I have seen along the way.

My art gave me the opportunity to travel extensively and paint each new period with the light and color of different places, cultures and religions. And in each place where I have been, in the faces and lives of the many people I have met, I discovered the presence of God speaking to me through my own moods and emotions. It is a voice that I continue to interpret as I paint my life—the hopes, dreams and joys, as well as every moment of sadness.

I am roaming through time, from the early spring of my youth toward the fading light of autumn and winter. And when my time is complete, I will sense the silence of whatever season awaits beyond the mystery of this life.

What I have learned

Life is a union
of colors and form,
in a tapestry
of happy moments.

The best parts of my life
are the people I love,
the places I have seen,
and the memories
I have woven together along the way.

Carla Carli Mazzucato

PART I

CHILDHOOD

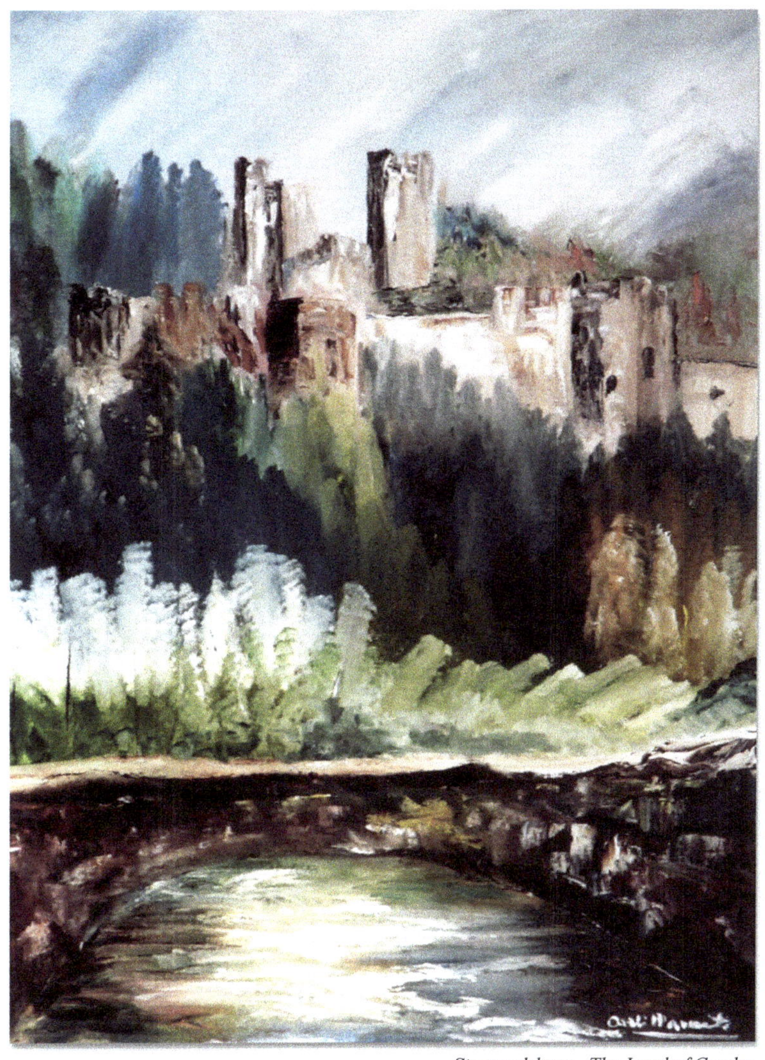

Sigmundskron - The Land of Castles

CHAPTER ONE

My Father

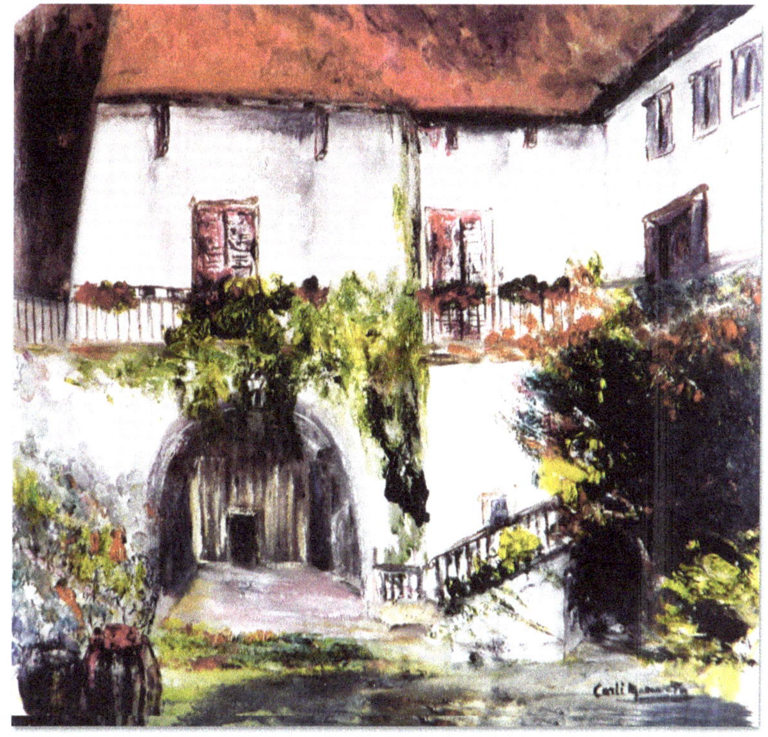

Courtyard of my Father's House

My baby room in my father's house,
Is where I learned to talk and pray;
Where love and happiness shined bright,
And many dreams set sail.

translated from a German children's song
"Es gibt ja nur ein Vaterhaus"

I was born on November 2, 1935, in my mother's bedroom, in my father's house, in the small town of *Appiano*, nestled in the Alps of northern Italy. Many nobles, of times past, had come to the region to purchase local estates together with the vineyards that rolled along the terraced foothills of the *Adige River Valley*. Then, when all the existing castles and residences were claimed, they began building new ones.

My father's house was one of these, built in the 1600's and once claimed as the noble summer residence of Count Emanuel Maria Thun, the Prince-Bishop of Trento. The Adige Valley was a beautiful place, fertile and green, dotted with these spectacular homes and castles, and rich with history and artistic tradition. And so it became known as the paradise of South Tyrol (*Südtirol*).

Emerging from the days of court and chivalry, medieval architecture set the style for the region, combining elements of late Gothic with Early Renaissance and Baroque. While I cannot know for sure how everything looked those many years ago, I do know that many of the buildings remain today, unchanged through time. Even the countryside must have been similar to how it is today with its fruited orchards filling the valley and lush vineyards reaching toward the sky.

"Tranquil" is perhaps the best word to describe the town of *Appiano* then. It was a simpler time, uncomplicated by the events that would unfold there in later years. Life ambled along, unhurried, content in the little things that filled each day with uneventful peace.

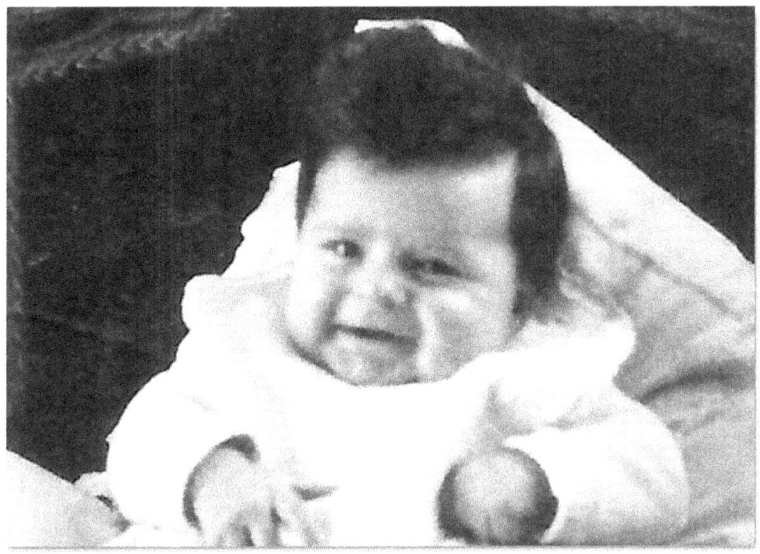

Carla Carli - 3 months

The event of my birth, however, was quite the big news in town, and brought with it certain traditional expectations for my father.

Vigilio Carli, my papà, was a well known and respected landowner in the region, who oversaw an expanse of orchards from which he established a successful business, exporting apples and other fruits to Austria and Yugoslavia. He was an educated man to whom people turned for advice on everything from financial matters to agricultural know-how. He had been the bank clerk for many years, and he was an authority on all matters of business for those who worked in agriculture. He was the founder of the *Kellereigenossenschaft* of *Appiano*, a wine-making collective for the whole region that joined local vineyards under one banner to produce wines for export.

So as the day of my birth approached, everyone in town had an interest in the news, because they knew that as a prominent landowner, Vigilio Carli needed a son.

As was the custom of *Appiano* and in all the *Südtirol* region, daughters were to receive a financial dowry when they were married, while the father's house and property would always pass to his male heir. If there was more than one son, then the estate would be divided, but the oldest son would always receive the house and the largest tract of land. It was, and still is, called the tradition of the *"maso chiuso"* which was set forth as a way of protecting a family's agricultural land from being so parceled off that it would become insufficient to sustain the livelihood of any one descendant and his family.

The birth of my sister, Lidia, born 18 months before me, was a joyous event, but now the town acknowledged that my father needed a male heir. In fact, they expected it. Papà may have wanted a son as well, but I, of course, was not one. So, it was big news.

Even so, Papà told everyone that he was just as happy with two heiresses. He never felt the need to march in step with all the prevailing customs that remained rigid and inflexible. He lived life according to his own sense of what was right and good. I think he simply decided that if he was only to have two children, then I would be his girl...and boy.

He called me his little *Finferle*, which for the longest time I thought was a type of mushroom, something small and always popping up unexpectedly. Years later, however, when I was an adult, I learned that the word actually referred to a small coin of five (or *fünf*) lire, something precious that you would always carry around in your pocket. And that was me.

My father took me everywhere he went. We took beautiful walks through the countryside, along quiet paths through town and up onto the hills above. He showed me the wooded timber trails in the mountains and the rushing streams and quiet lakes replenished from the mountain heights. It was through my father that I came to notice and appreciate the beauty in nature that surrounds us.

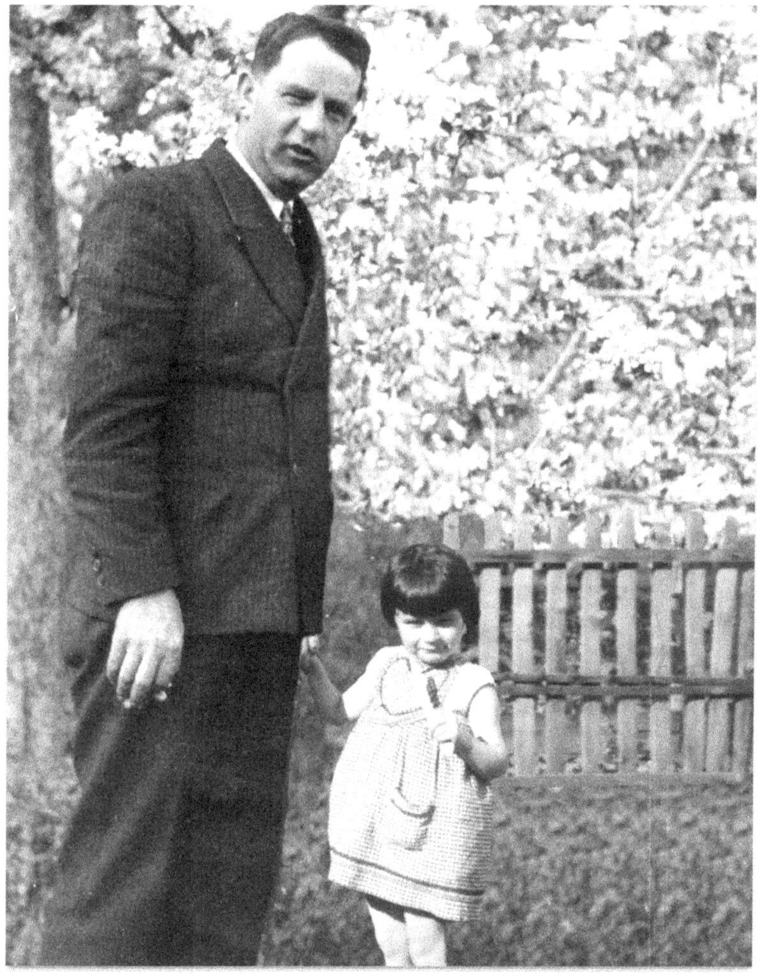

Vigilio and Carla Carli (c. 1937)

And he told me all the stories and fables that gave rise to the sense of mystery that I had about *my* valley. The castles, set high above the town of *Appiano*, enhanced that feeling as they towered majestically over the landscape. Built often over the ancient ruins of former strongholds from the time of Charlemagne, they sparked my interest and stirred my imagination with their many stories.

At the entrance of the valley, *Castel Firmiano* was the fortress that, years ago, had housed the garrison tasked with protecting the Archbishop of Trento when he came north. Then, in 1473, when Duke Sigismund sacked the fortress and rebuilt the castle, he had renamed it *Sigmundskron*, the crown of Sigmund.

Further in, *Castel d'Appiano* (*Hocheppan*) also held a commanding view of the valley. There, the local counts remained in power through the thirteenth century till they were defeated by the counts of Tyrol, who had claimed the region and first called it *Südtirol.*

Along with a love of the land and its stories, Papà had also passed along to me an unwavering sense of optimism with regard to the realities of life. Whatever traditions and expectations dictated, I learned to believe in kindness, commitment and hope as I made my way in the world. And this outlook, more than any house or inheritance which I would, in fact, eventually share with my sister *and* brother who came five and a half years after me, was the most valuable thing I ever received from my father.

My father's name was Vigilio, but he was always called Gilli. He was a late riser and always had a hard time falling asleep, so he often spent his evenings reading a book or playing guitar. In winter, he would always put a kettle on the kitchen fire to boil chestnuts because he did not like them broiled in the oven. But it was also because it was so cold outside.

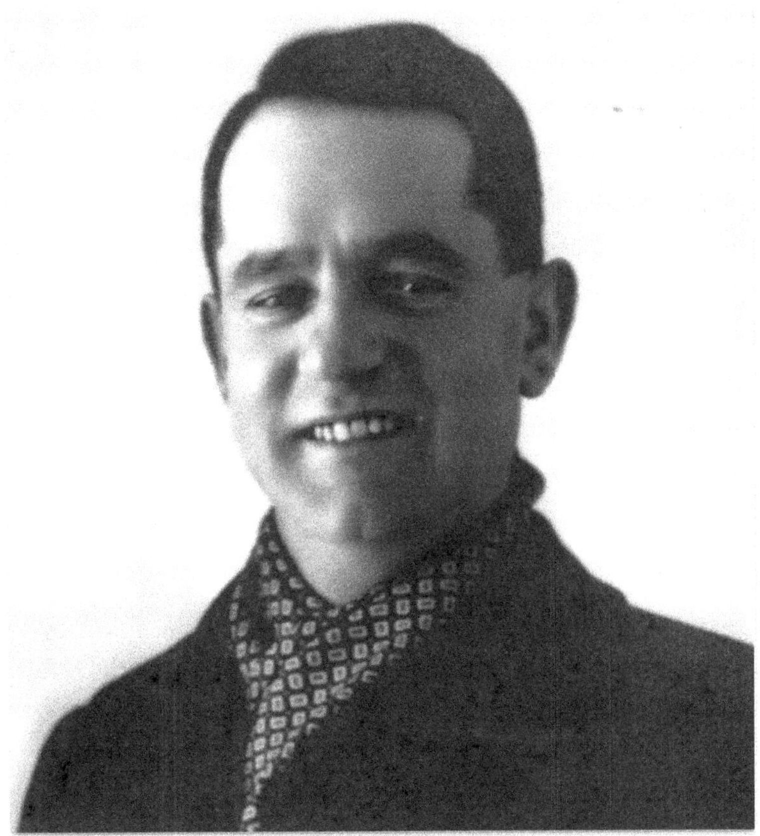

Vigilio Carli

Our house was built in 1680 and, as was typical for homes of that time, had no heat or bathrooms with running water. In the kitchen, though, where we all gathered around the fire, it was always warm.

On Friday evenings, the gathering would often include many of Papà's friends who came together around the kitchen table to play cards. I liked to stay up late and would creep into Papà's cozy arm chair in the corner to watch. The arm chair was where Papà would sit every morning to read the newspaper and every evening to read his book, but when he played cards, it was mine.

They played a card game, I remember, called *"Schnaps"* late into the evening, sometimes as late as midnight, and I would sit and stay for as long as I could keep my eyes open. It was wonderful to be allowed to fall asleep in that chair and listen to the fading voices of my father and his friends.

One friend, Mr. Gelmini, would always greet me and Lidia with a bow, and we would curtsy back as Mamma had taught us to do. Years later when I returned to Bolzano for my first art show at the *Galleria Domenicani*, he came to see me and reminisce about the past. He bought a watercolor with a smile…and a nostalgic bow. He passed away in the eighties, as did his wife. Their two sons opened a Café/Restaurant on *via Cappuccini* in *Appiano*.

Mr. Luis Dallapiazza was another friend of Papà. He was a kind and sincere man, but I remember that as a young girl I mostly thought that he was very loud. Though my father died many years before him, Mr. Dallapiazza cherished his memories of Gilli, who was, as he was fond of saying to everyone he met, a friend *"par-excellence."* He and his wife passed away leaving only a daughter, Rosetta, who tutored me in algebra when I was in high school. She married a gentleman from *Padova* and had two daughters.

Then there was Egon Kasper, who was so devoted to my father, that he would drive us wherever we needed to go after Papà became ill. In Papà's *"Balilla,"* Mr. Kaspar chauffeured Papà to all his doctor appointments as well as taking Lidia and me to our piano lessons in *Bolzano* every Saturday morning. I stumbled through my lessons, while Lidia, who became a gifted pianist, was always ready and prepared for hers.

Papà had many other friends, and he was known throughout *Appiano* for his kindness and generosity. He was a devoted son and a caring brother who became guardian to the children of his two sisters Maria and Kathy, when they were both widowed at an early age. He was always ready to help family and friends, which basically meant anyone who asked. Even years later, whenever I visited my hometown, I would meet people with fond memories and wonderful stories about Gilli, my father, Vigilio Carli, and those times long past.

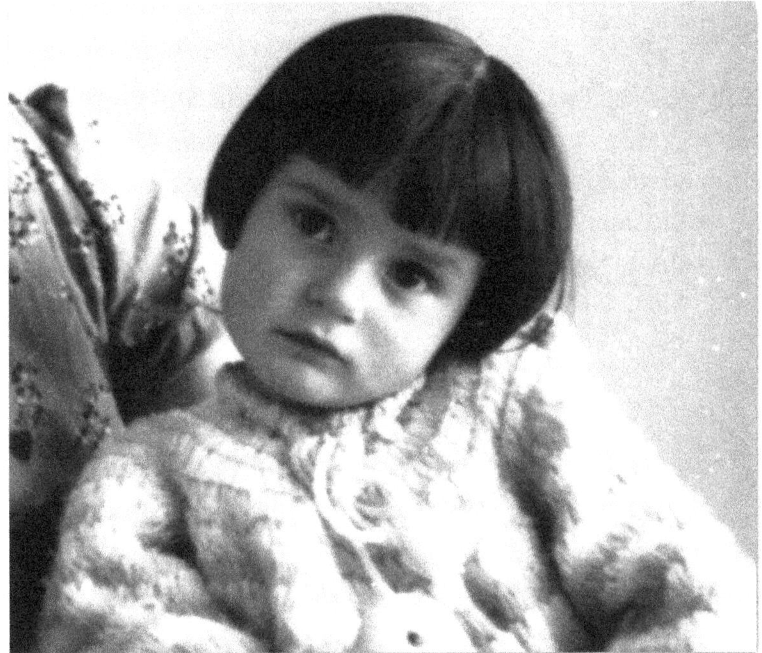

Carla Carli (c. 1938)

I rest on Papà's chair,
His voice so soft is fading,
His arms so warm embrace me,
As I drift to sleep and dream.

my rhyme from the evenings Papà played cards

My father used to take a nap in the afternoon. I knew when the time for napping came because he would wave his little finger to call me over to go rest with him. While I did not like to interrupt my day with a nap, I would always go since he promised that it would only be a quick five-minute rest. He would tip his hat low over his eyes to block out the daylight, and then he would lie still. I could never see if his eyes were closed or not, so after a few minutes, I would slowly rise to sneak away. After a few steps, I would hear his voice, *"Ciao Carla,"* and I then knew that he had not really been sleeping.

In the afternoon, Papà and I used to take many long walks. He had to oversee his many orchards and vineyards, and so I would accompany him. And every hike was always a fun adventure. As we walked between the different fields, he would munch on nuts that he had hidden in his pocket and wait for me to plead, "What about me? I want some too!" Then the guessing game began and he would empty his pockets until he would finally reveal the one with the handful of nuts that he would then share with me.

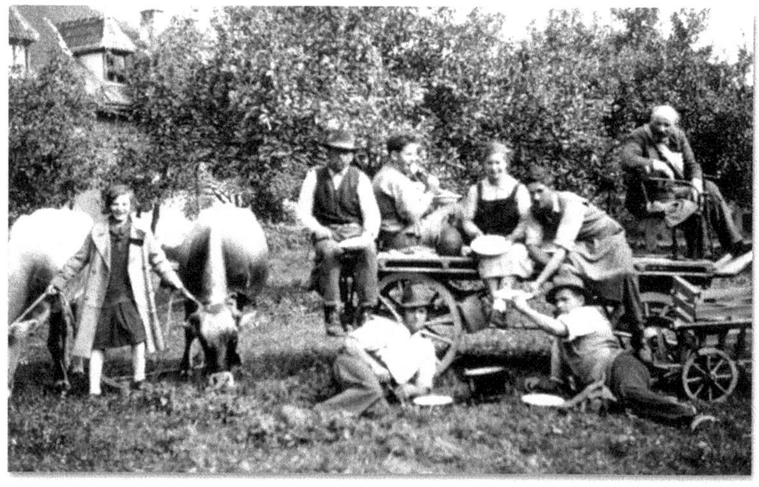

Orchard near Maria Rast

Papà's largest orchard was an expanse of pear and apple trees up near *Maria Rast,* a little church nestled in a grove of high poplar trees. Along the street to *Maria Rast* was a brook that ended at the church where there was a fountain. I used to throw a piece of bark into the brook and try to follow it all the way down to the fountain even though my "boat" would often get stuck somewhere along the way.

When we arrived, we would always sip some water at the fountain and then enter the church. It was like a little ritual. Inside was always so dark, and it smelled of incense still hanging in the air from an earlier service. The walls were covered in paintings, and I would sit on every bench to take a close look at all of them while Papà stayed at the entrance. He would remove his hat, his *"borsalino,"* and hold it before him for a moment of quiet reflection.

Then, after the short church visit, we got down to business. Together, we would check every apple and pear tree in the nearby orchard, and Papà would show me how to get rid of the worms hidden in the bark. He would also teach me how to estimate the value of the next harvest.

On the way back home we would always stop at the cemetery of *Appiano.* We would visit the family burial plot where both my grandparents were buried. Again, Papà would remove his hat and spend a few minutes to pray three Hail Mary's for his mother Maria Tapfer. She had died when I was only one year old, and I had no memory of her.

I did, however, remember my grandfather, Vigil Carli, because I was nine when *he* passed away. When he visited, he would sit with his legs crossed and bounce me up and down on his foot like a trotting horse and sing, "hopa, hopa, ho-pa-pa."

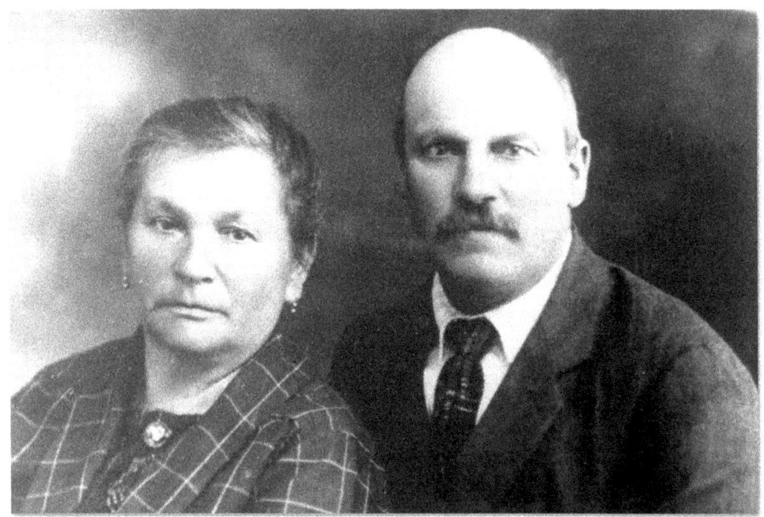

Maria Tapfer and Vigil Carli

On Sundays, Papà would often take me on another special outing to *Stroblhof,* a restaurant close to the wooded side of *Mount Penegal*, and the *Ice-Löcher* (*Buche di Ghiaccio* in Italian). The day usually began when he and his friends would go up to the town of *Predonico* to play *bocce* or a bowling game of *birilli.*

My reward for retrieving the *bocce* balls and resetting the *birilli* pins was a side trip afterwards to *Stroblhof* for a tasty dish of Tyroler *Schlagsahne*. It was a full dish of whipping cream topped with chocolate and cinnamon that was so delicious. Unfortunately, the last time I went to *Stroblhof, Schlagsahne* was no longer on the menu, only *gelato.*

Another place we visited often was *Monticolo*, a mountain lake nestled in the woods and surrounded by many hiking paths. My grandfather use to go there and return home with baskets full of mushrooms, among them, the small, yellow *finferli* that I mistook for my nickname for so many years.

Monticolo is also where I learned to swim when I was a teenager, though according to the pastor of our church, I had put myself in moral peril by doing so.

Back then, no young ladies went swimming in either of the two lakes in the woods around *Monticolo*. To do so was considered sinful, and we were told that the people in town would denounce us for such scandalous behavior.

A young teacher who had been hired at our school, however, didn't care for that nonsense. She was an "outsider" from *Trieste* by the Adriatic Sea. She was tall and young, around twenty years old, with blonde hair, blue eyes and a strong personality. It was a hot summer and she had no problem defying the pastor for a dip in the cool lake. Luckily, my mother agreed and allowed me to accompany this teacher to go swimming. Best summer ever.

In Autumn, Papà would take our dog, Fido, hunting, and just like Fido, I was always ready to go too. We both ran among the bushes to fetch the birds that Papà had shot down. Papà was not a great shot, but he and his hunting friend, Hies Ausserer, enjoyed the time outdoors, and so did I. The fresh air in the fields, the woods, and the walks in nature were all part of the wonder that filled the days of my youth.

When the winter season arrived, the foothills and mountains were quickly blanketed in snow. Every snowfall was a festive occasion, for me, my sister and my cousins. We would slide down the slope that started in the courtyard of my father's house, go through the vineyards and the orchards, and all the way to the railroad station of Appiano, a stretch of at least a hundred meters or so. It was great fun racing and then tumbling from our sleds onto the soft blanket of snow. We laughed and sang songs until the evening lights appeared.

We were sad to head home and leave our winter games, but the warm, yellow glow coming from all the windows of the houses in town was inviting and welcoming. Our kitchen would already be warm, and supper was waiting. Papà would often teach us some new songs or tell us stories from the German folklore he remembered from when he was young.

These were the happy times of my youth, seasons filled with discovery and laughter, a time that faded as the country marched into war.

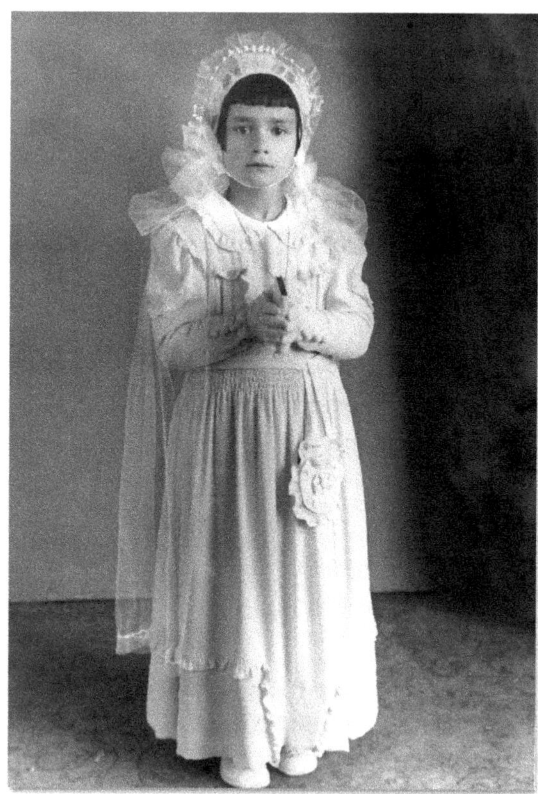

Carla Carli, first communion

Years of War

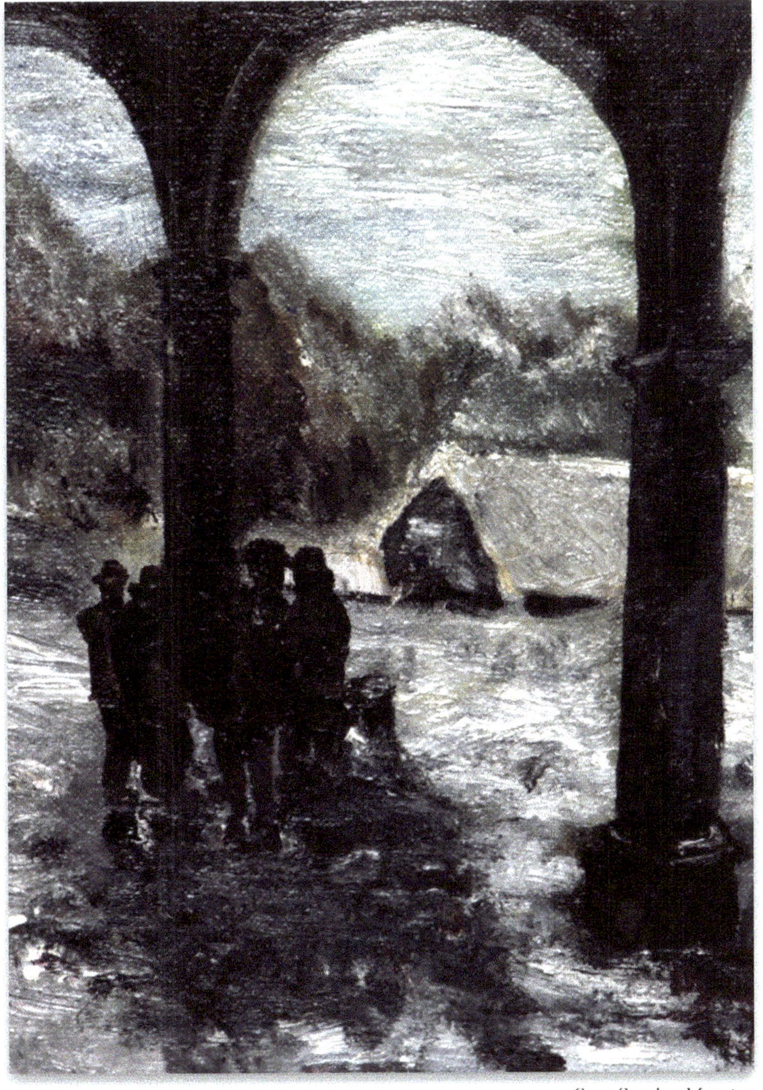

On a Sunday Morning

Italy entered World War II on June 10, 1940. I was not yet five years old, but the war would soon become a major turning point in my life.

Italian Prime Minister, Benito Mussolini, had delayed committing Italy to the war until France had fallen and Nazi Germany's victory seemed certain. I remember that my parents had told me that Italy had entered the war, but I did not really know what war meant. There was no difference in my daily life, and I had no direct experience with what was happening until the Allied bombardments reached northern Italy in 1942.

Though northern Italy was still held by German and Italian forces when American troops landed down in Sicily on July 10, 1943, the American forces had already begun the year before with daily bombing runs over the major northern cities of *Milano, Verona, Trento* and *Bolzano* to prepare for their northern invasion. They also targeted the most strategic bridges and routes connecting the cities to each other.

Appiano was situated along the *Adige River* which flowed south from the *Brenner Pass*, the primary route through the Alps to Austria and on to Germany. Consequently, we were often in the path of Allied bombers. Both the city of *Bolzano* and the bridge over the *Adige River* in the town of *Ora* were constantly targeted. *Ora* was less than thirteen kilometers (8 miles) away from my home in *Appiano*. *Bolzano* was only six and a half kilometers (4 miles).

It was a sunny day in May of 1942, when my father asked me to take our cow, Nella, from the stable to the nearby pasture. I was happy to go, and I led her, carefree, through the parallel rows of the vineyards toward the green of my father's orchard. I had created a wonderful world in my mind, with every tree in the orchard becoming a different room in a fantasy house. One was my bedroom, another the kitchen, and still another my cozy sitting room, depending how many branches I found within reach.

I loved to climb, and that day while Nella was grazing, I climbed high to see the blue mountains and green vineyards sloping along the sides of my valley. I watched the birds in the sky and listened to their faint chirping and the whispering sounds of flying insects and the occasional clang of a cow bell below. Those were the only noises in the spring air.

Suddenly, an awful, thundering sound broke the silence. It destroyed any sense of peace and tranquility, and while I had no idea what it was, I somehow knew that it was something terrible. I felt like running to one of the nearby houses to find a place to hide...but from what? The fields were empty, no one was about. I abandoned the cow, who didn't seem to mind at all. She continued grazing, undisturbed, as I ran home screaming and crying. I was afraid that something from above was crushing the earth, but I did not know what it was. It was the first bombardment of the city of *Bolzano*.

Many more of these frighting air raids followed. My father created a bomb shelter in our deep cellar, and I spent most of that spring and early summer hiding there in fear of the next bombing. It was the noise, more than anything, that kept me constantly on edge. I could not hide from the deep rumble of bombs, and I could not stop it.

My dear aunt, my *Zia* Maria Profanter, the sister of my father, used to come to the shelter with *Baldrian*, a natural relaxant to ease anxiety. I would take a few drops on a spoonful of sugar when the noise became too much to bear.

In addition to my *Zia* Maria and my family—my father, mother, sister Lidia and little brother Bruno—my mother's parents, Luigi Bella and his second wife Pia Bertolini joined us in the cellar as well. They all lived in separate quarters of our house, but when the bombs came, we would all huddle together in the deep darkness till the rumbling outside faded.

By that summer, a large bomb shelter had been built into the side of *Mount Penegal* which we could see from our kitchen window. And so, every morning at 9 o'clock, even before the air raid siren in town had sounded any alarm, my mother would take us up to the mountain refuge, and we would stay there all day until 6 in the evening.

I can still remember the uneasiness and the fear in the eyes of all the men, women and children who huddled in the cold and darkness of the shelter. Together with Lidia and my brother, Bruno, just one year old, I looked to my mother who was there to comfort us. I knew, though, that she was anxious and afraid as well, and so I felt alone.

My father didn't stay much in the mountain refuge; he had many responsibilities even during the war, and life had to go on. I suppose my greatest fear was that of losing him, losing his strength and optimism, the way he had of making me believe that everything would be fine.

The air raid sirens sounded often, but in the shelter covered by the earth of the mountain, the noise of the bombs was mostly muffled. And yet the deadened sound and tomblike atmosphere of the shelter imprinted on me so intensely that it affected my health in many unseen ways. Since that time, and still today, I have never felt comfortable in the darkness of tunnels or caverns beneath the earth.

By late summer, my father decided, for our health and safety, and especially for that of my mother, he would relocate us to the village of *Coredo* in the *Val Di Non* where my mother's sister, my *Zia* Idotta, and many relatives lived.

It was night when Papà woke me up, and we drove by car up through the *Mendola Pass*, to the other side of Mount Penegal, and into the valley. We arrived late in the night, and though I do not remember much of the trip, I vividly remember seeing the house on the hill in the small village of *Coredo* where we would be staying. After so much time inside the mountain, I was happy to be there, even though I was sad that Papà had to immediately go back. It was dangerous in *Appiano,* but he told us that in *Coredo* we would be safe. It was a nice house with ornate window frames and a beautiful front door, but it was somewhat isolated from the other homes in town which I thought made it look a bit somber.

Papà had rented the bottom floor of the two story villa, and it had only two rooms: one small kitchen and a bedroom. The bathroom was on the second floor and to reach it we would have to go outside and walk up two flights of stairs. Lidia and I were always uncomfortable using the long stairs, as was my mother, but not just because it was a long way up to go to the bathroom. Somehow, we thought it felt spooky.

When Mamma went to town, people would ask her how we were settling in…and if we had seen or heard anything unusual. It seemed an unusual question, but after a few such conversations in town, Mamma came home with the full story.

It seems that in that nice villa where we were staying, a man had murdered his young wife five years ago. And it was on those very stairs that we used to go up to the bathroom that the wife's bloody body was found. The man had been convicted and the house had been sold, but it was said that every year on the day that the wife had been killed, a dark bloodstain would appear on the steps.

Of course, now that we knew the story, the house was too scary for us and we were afraid to go inside. It took Mamma two weeks to find a new place for us to stay, a very small room on the other side of town. It was on the second floor of a large barn where the farmer use to store grain, and though we had to cross through the barn to reach the stairs to our small bedroom and bathroom, it was much better than climbing the spooky, outdoor staircase where bloodstains might suddenly appear!

Mamma was very thankful for the help she received from her new friends in town who found that place. There were few rooms left to rent because of all the people who had left the cities of *Bolzano* and *Trento* to escape the bombardments that seemed to happen almost every day by then.

I liked the new place. It was near the woods where a narrow trail through the pines and larch trees led to a small lake. In autumn Lidia and I would gather the fallen pine-cones and store them in the small hall at the top of the stairs of our "home," and later in the evening, we would use them to build a fire.

On our walks, we could see two castles on the nearby hill, the *Villa Mantovan* and the *Villa Rosa*, standing like two sentries guarding the village. While I knew there were no knights or soldiers there, they gave me the feeling of safety nevertheless. I felt protected, and surrounded by a new sense of security, like I was living in a land of heroic legends and fantasy.

And just like Cinderella, who lived in a grand house but had to do chores and go fetch milk, I too had to go with a large pail to buy milk every evening at the *Rizzi* Farm. The farm was tended by Beppino and Giorgio, the brothers of my uncle Ugo, who had married my mother's sister, Idotta. Giorgio was an engineer by trade, but had fled from *Milano* when the bombing had started. So, like him, we were all there as *"sfollati,"* refugees displaced by the war. And in this sanctuary, this land of legend, our families became quite close.

No legend would be complete, of course, without a princess, and the young Elena Rizzi, sister of Ugo, Beppino and Giorgio, definitely qualified. She had won a beauty contest in the city of *Stresa,* where a pageant was held every two years. Not only a great beauty, Elena had a special talent—she knew how to draw faces in different poses and with various expressions. Her completed drawings looked like the stylish images in beauty magazines, and I thought her pencil was like a magic wand, as magic as her ability to create her drawings on paper. "If only I could draw like that!" I would think to myself.

She drew a face for me in a little notebook and inscribed it with wishes for a glorious future in love, fortune and art! Many years later, I found that notebook in an old drawer along with other scribbles and writings I had kept from elementary school. The memory brought tears to my eyes, and I tucked the notebook back into the drawer of the nightstand in the attic of my father's house in *Appiano* for someone else to find someday.

Life in the village of *Coredo* was simple for Lidia and me. In the morning we went to school, and in the afternoon we played with friends. We created treasure hunts by burying colorful stones in the ground, and had fun with a game that involved knocking a can with a stone to see how far it would go. The game of "Hide and Seek" gave us the opportunity to roam about, and we enjoyed hiding and searching for each other in the fields and stables, behind trees and haystacks.

In the evening, *Coredo* was beautiful because many of the homes were built on the slopes of the valley, so when lights came on inside windows, the town lit up like a Christmas tree decorated with precious stones. On the top of the slope, the illuminated steeple of the church would peak through the trees, almost inviting the people to come and pray.

Every Sunday we would climb up the hill to go to the Sunday Mass. I liked to step along the little stony path among the chestnut trees, until the stones gave way to a staircase made of sturdy roots that led the rest of the way to the church. I felt the need to pray especially hard on those Sundays in *Coredo*, not only for peace in this time of war, but also with the hope that I would see my father again.

Though I had just turned seven years old, I had my strong convictions and ideas about how I could make a difference. I felt that I was fighting the war with prayers. I was convinced that by making little sacrifices, the Lord in heaven would listen to me. So on Sundays, after Mass, I would stay longer in church and pray extra, believing that this would prevent planes from dropping bombs in the valley, so that my Papà would be safe, and I would soon be able to return home to *Appiano*.

Then on every other day of the week, I would find some other kind of sacrifice that would help bring the war to an end. On one particular day, I was returning home with a large pail of milk, and I noted that the street of town was lined with many benches. I decided that to make my little contribution to the cause of peace, I would sit on every bench along the street as I walked home. I knew that this would not be easy for a young girl like me because I didn't like to sit still ever, but it was a "sacrifice" that I would make.

Well, my plan was working fine for a while, until I came to a place in the main part of town where men liked to gather and sit to loudly debate the news of the day. So now I would have to go to these men and ask if they would make room for me so I could sit on their bench. Surely, I thought, they would understand that ending the war was very important; after all, isn't that what they were always discussing anyways?

So I approached the first crowded bench, and with a faint voice I asked, "May I sit here?"

No reply.

"Please, let me sit here with my large pail of milk?"

No reply.

Finally, I raised my voice, loud and clear, so I would be heard. "I have to sit here with my heavy milk pail!"

At that, the men quieted down, and one asked me why I had to sit on the bench.

"I want to end the war!" I explained quite sincerely.

Of course, they all had a good laugh, as did the men sitting at the next bench and the next. I was embarrassed, and I suddenly thought that my "little sacrifice" might just be as ridiculous and futile as the war being fought, but I stood there, insistent…until one man finally moved over a bit to make room for me. I sat down quickly then jumped back up to continue my trip home. "Thank you," I said as I walked on.

I didn't know what my prayers and sacrifices would accomplish, but for my Papà, I had to try. And I believed it was all worth it.

Papà would only come up over the mountain once a month, arriving in *Coredo* after having walked for a day to get there. Traveling on the main roads was no longer safe, so Papà had discovered trails through the mountains that he could use to avoid open spaces. Soldiers, both German and Italian, patrolled the whole region now, and they needed no excuse to stop and detain you.

But when Papà arrived, our small room above the grain floor in the barn on the other side of town became a warm and cozy home again, filled with joy, jumping around, and a wonderful feast of whatever Papà had managed to bring to make the evening special. Papà would even come to school to greet our teachers, and spend the rest of his time with Mamma and with family. It was on those evenings, that I began to hope and believe that everything would be better again soon.

The war went on for two and a half more years. My memory of that time is hazy and vague. The constant anxiety and threat, not only from Allied bombs but also from German soldiers who began crossing into northern Italy from Europe in large numbers made everything seem twice as dangerous as before. The sequence of what happened during that time, however, will always be somewhat confused in my mind.

I remember that we came home from *Coredo*, and for a while we stayed in *Appiano*. German soldiers were everywhere in town, and even though Italy's King Vittorio Emanuele III had removed Mussolini from power on July

25 of 1943, and Italy had formally surrendered to the Allies on September 8, 1943, all of *Südtirol* was immediately annexed by Nazi Germany. So now, we were suddenly no longer Italy, but part of the "Fatherland." And yet, we weren't really.

About half the people in *Appiano* favored the Germans during this time of occupation, or at least behaved outwardly loyal to Hitler. The other half had to quietly witness and endure harassment and worse at the hands of these German loyalists and the Nazi soldiers occupying our town. They were brutish, everywhere in the streets, and they acted with no consequence if they decided that you were "too Italian" or not sufficiently loyal to Germany.

Going to school became a terrible ordeal for me and Lidia. Young boys who embraced the Nazi fervor threw stones at us as we passed because we were not "real" Germans. Italian partisans who formed a small armed resistance and hid up in the mountains were executed when they were found, and emboldened German soldiers took what they wanted and did as they pleased.

Our warm kitchen and living room, which had once been the gathering place for all our friends, was now taken over every weekend by Nazi soldiers with guns who drank and caroused late into the night. They forced my father to bring up wine from our cellar till they had their fill, while a soldier named Hugo pounded out loud German music on Lidia's and my piano.

My mother, who had always been full of fun and laughter during our family gatherings, was now constantly unnerved and fearful, and angry that my father allowed the soldiers into our home. But, of course, he had no choice. Refusing would have been immediately fatal. My mother could only take some small comfort in knowing that Lidia and I were still too young to be swept up to dance with the soldiers. She knew that other girls in town had not been as lucky.

Lidia, who was just nine, hid away in the back rooms of our house with Mamma, while I, not yet eight, and two-year-old Bruno were too young to fully understand what was going on. We watched from just outside the room, and, to amuse ourselves, we tossed little balls made from bits of rag onto the floor of the kitchen, to watch them get kicked about by the soldiers dancing boots.

So who was really in charge during this time? All I remember of life under Mussolini is the *"sabato fascista"* when all young students were required to report in the town square outside the school on Saturday morning to sing songs about the glory of Fascism and learn how to march. Failing to show up on time would result in severe punishment.

From the time when the Americans landed in Sicily on July 10, 1943, everything was in chaos. Mussolini failed to hold back the Americans, and Hitler refused to send troops to help him, so two weeks later, the king deposed Mussolini and had him arrested.

Then came the news from Rome that Marshall Pietro Badoglio had been appointed to replace Mussolini. Badoglio was a respected military leader, but he was opposed to Fascism and everything Mussolini had stood for. So the German soldiers didn't trust the Italian soldiers who were stationed at the *caserma* command post which was right across from the cemetery in *Appiano*. Everything seemed so tense and filled with suspicion and hatred.

The only ray of light for me in all this mess came from a little story that somehow gave me a bit of hope again—a love story:

During the month after Mussolini's arrest but before Italy surrendered to the Allies, the Italian soldiers stationed in *Appiano* decided to have a party to celebrate Badoglio's appointment. They wanted to buy cookies and cakes, so they sent a young Italian soldier, Guido Cesari, to the bakery.

The bakery, though, only made bread, so they sent him to my father's sister, my Aunt Kathy, who was an excellent pastry chef. Aunt Kathy agreed to the work. She baked and baked, and when it was all ready, young Guido arrived to pick up the sweets. That is when he met Aunt Kathy's daughter, my cousin Mara Chelodi who was eighteen years old. She was nice and smart…and very sweet. They said it was love at first sight.

Eventually, in better times, they got married, and after the war they settled in Switzerland. They lived there until Guido retired, then returned to Italy in 1994. It was then that I got to know them better, when they attended two exhibits of my art in Bologna and Prato, where they lived. They invited me to their home, and were wonderful hosts, and when I left, they gave me a book *"Come si mangia in Italia"* ("How we eat in Italy"). Life, like the seasons, seems to often turn in a circle—a book about "eating in Italy" for a love story that began with a cookie.

With Mussolini gone, and Badoglio in charge, things should have gotten better. But because the king delayed surrendering to the Allies for another month, Hitler was able to fortify Germany's position in northern Italy. By the time Italy finally declared war on Germany on October 8,

1943, Italian soldiers in our region were outnumbered by German soldiers, and they were quickly rounded up or forced to join the German army.

That is when the bombing ended, and it became something just as terrible. To rid the cities of the German troops still entrenched in northern Italy, Allied machine gunners now flew low over our streets and buildings, filling the valley with screaming airplanes and bullets in place of the low rumbling of bombs. The planes flew in quickly and were flying so low that we could see the markings on their wings from our windows.

On the day of *San Giuseppe*, March 19, 1944, I vividly remember the most terrifying *mitragliamento* (machine guns strafing) in Appiano. It was noon. Mamma and I were in the kitchen, and suddenly the roar of the planes split the sky and the bullets blasted all around us shattering the glass of every window in the house.

My mother yelled for me to duck under the sink as the planes raced past outside, then she called me to run with her down the stairs toward the cellars below. We had to be careful not to step on all the broken glass. We made it as far as the storage room downstairs before a blast shook open the door to the chimney flue and a cloud of black ash exploded above us and covered everything in darkness.

Eventually, even these days ended and passed away into memory. And yet, sometimes the noise of an airplane or a helicopter flying low in the sky overhead will bring me back to those moments that I would rather forget. There are, however, other moments from those dark times, little coincidences, that are like a tiny glimmer of light that I am happy to remember…

On that same day, when the machine guns shattered glass and sent me running to hide, a young man, nineteen years old, was arriving from Bolzano on a bicycle. Just as he was passing between the *Appiano* cemetery and the Italian military command post across the street, the planes and bullets came flying in. He quickly leaped from his bicycle and dove under a large truck parked at the side of the road. After the planes passed and all was quiet again, he came out from under the truck, only realizing then that it was a military vehicle filled with explosive munitions.

If the truck had been hit, things would have ended very differently for this young man…and for me as well. Because while I wouldn't meet him until seventeen years later, that man, Giuseppe Mazzucato, would become my husband, and when he told me the story of how he was, coincidentally, in Appiano on that day, he concluded that we must have been destined to be together. Even then, he explained, we were not far apart, in the same town, surviving the worst *mitragliamento* of the war on the feast day of *San Giuseppe*.

After that day, my father decided to move us again, this time up into the nearby hills of *Predonico*. It was where we had hiked before the war for his bowling games of *birilli* with friends, and since it was tucked up in the wooded area under the big mountain *Maccaion,* it would be much safer than being down in *Appiano*.

Papà had found a place we could stay, in the house of a Mr. Moretti, who worked an isolated farm with his family up high in the hills. Their farm stretched from the hills right up to the foot of the mountains that overlooked the valley, and we we could see the city of *Bolzano* and all of *Appiano* from there.

The farmhouse was on a slope so that the second floor was at the same level as the field out back, and we had a living room, a kitchen and bedroom to ourselves. Mr. Moretti lived on the first floor with his family—his wife, two grown up boys and three girls in their twenties. There was a stable beside the house with cows, oxen, pigs and chickens, and a herd of about twenty sheep, which was most unusual for *Appiano* and the surrounding areas.

Though the family did have a friendly dog, I was sad that there were no horses on the farm. My father kept two horses in our stable at home, Max and a mare named Liesl, and I enjoyed when I was allowed to guide Max from our orchard back to our stable. I was proud that my father trusted me with this task, and horses and dogs were always my favorite animals.

While we stayed in *Predonico,* I would often accompany one of Mr. Moretti's sons, Fernando, when he took the sheep to graze in the grassy field in the hills above the house. From there, I could look down into the valley, and search for my father's house. I could see the cemetery and military *caserme,* the streets leading to the *piazza* at the center of town where I had ofter walked. And not far from the tall steeple of our church, I could see the pale, yellow walls of my father's house, *Angerburg*—its impressive, arched entryway and solid wooden *portone,* or front gate.

Being able to see it there, so close…but remote, made me long even more for an end to the war when we would all return to our lives in our home, and I would once again play in the courtyard with my cousins and friends.

Evenings were dark on the hills of *Predonico.* There was no electricity, and the houses used dim carbide lamps when a little evening light was desired. But mostly, we children just went to bed early. The adults would sit on benches or on the steps at their front doors and talk late into the night. This tradition of evening chats was known as *filò,* and I would often fade to sleep while listening to the voices in the night air outside.

In the early morning, the voices were louder. Everyone in the Moretti family was awake and lively, ready to start the day's work. Housekeeping was quite a chore. My only task was to refill the lamp with calcium carbide and water to prepare it for the next evening, but the Moretti family had to feed all the animals, milk the cows, clean the stable, and make the bread. I liked to visit the room beside the house where the large bread oven was kept. When Mrs. Moretti baked her loaves of bread, the smells that filled the air were wonderful.

During this time, I would see my father every weekend. It was a pleasant and much easier walk for him to come to *Predonico*, than it had been when we were over the mountain in *Coredo*. It took him about one hour on the trail through the woods to reach us at the Moretti farm on the hill, and on Sunday our whole family would go to the small village-church together.

The church entrance had an arched portico where men from the village, and a few women, would gather after Mass to talk about the war. The image of these Sunday chats in the shadows of the church's portico, the ground outside dusted with snow, remained fixed in my memory. So much so that years later, when I had begun to paint, I revisited the scene on canvas in a painting I called "On a Sunday Morning."

Winter days were short, and our life was simple. We felt protected by the mountains and comforted by the tall chestnut trees, but down in the valley the dreaded *Gestapo,* the secret police of Nazi Germany, had set up their command and was actively rooting out partisans and Italian sympathizers.

By the spring of 1945, Nazi Germany was in full retreat from northern Italy. Soldiers were pouring through our valley, looting and stealing what they could as they tried to escape up into Switzerland.

Hitler had freed Mussolini a year and a half earlier, and had named him the leader of the contrived northern Italian *Republic of Salo*, but when Mussolini agreed to meet with Italian partisans in *Milano* on April 25, it was over for him. They seized Mussolini with his mistress Clara Petacci, and three days later executed them, while Hitler and his wife Eva Braun committed suicide on April 30. German forces in Italy surrendered on May 2, and with Germany's unconditional surrender on May 7, 1945, the war was finally over.

The war had passed, and I was anxious to return to my beloved home with my family to the life I remembered from before. But that dream would only last for two years.

My father had begun to lose his sight and started needing daily help. I would often accompany him to a place called *Thurnbach* where therapeutic baths with water infused with some sort of special leaves was offered as a healing remedy. Papà was a firm believer in the therapeutic quality of water and hoped that the treatments would help him regain his sight and restore his health. It did not work out that way. He went away to *Milano* to undergo surgery, where they discovered that he had a tumor on his brain. Papà died on the fifth of October, 1947, at the age of 48.

It was a month before my twelfth birthday when my father died, and I was lost. There was no way for me to fill the void. My heart ached and kept me silent. I was entering my adolescence—a new period in my life, and once again, I felt alone.

ADOLESCENCE

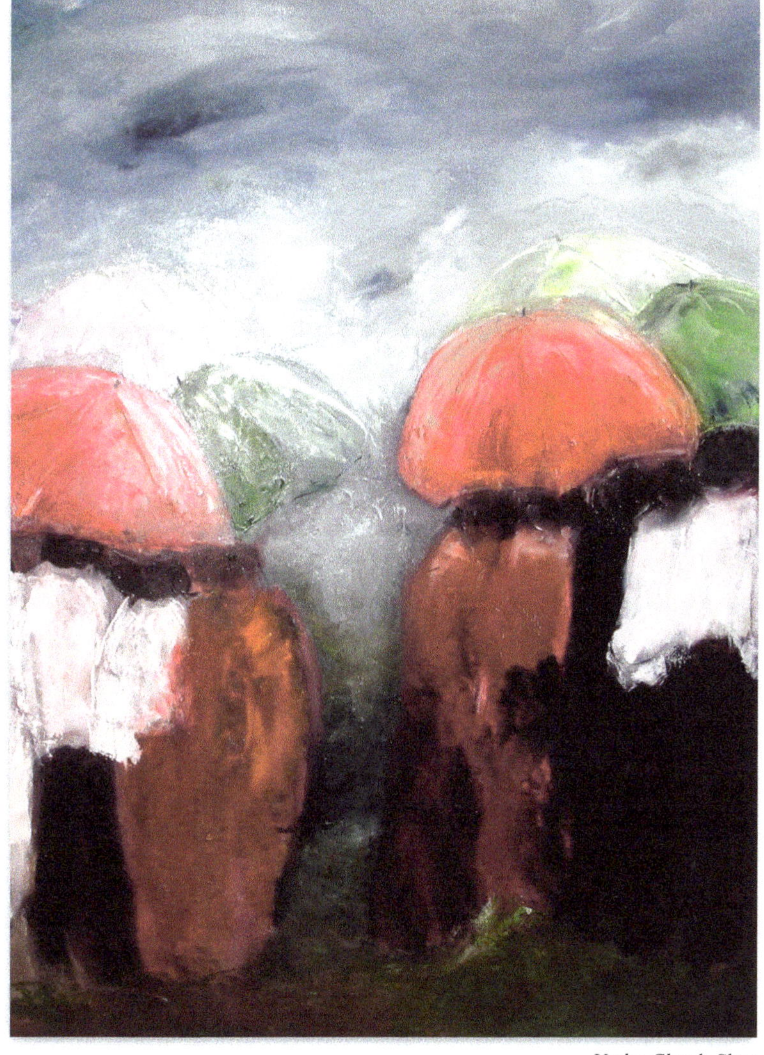

Under Cloudy Skies

36

CHAPTER THREE

My Mother

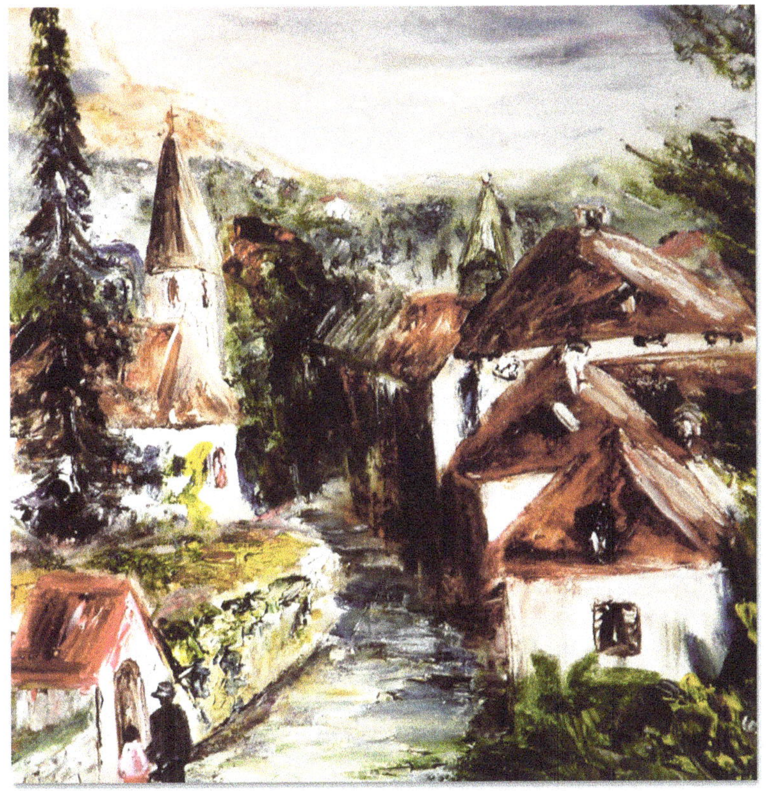

On the Street Where I Live

You cannot be like someone else,
You have to shine by your own light;
You cannot shine with another's light,
If I am someone else, who will be like me?

traditional saying

My mother was now the center of my life. I needed her love and her guidance, but that would not be easy for her. She was only 36 years old and already a widow with three children. She was alone and had to manage our fields and orchards as well as our big house that was in desperate need of repairs from all the bombardments and machine gun strikes it had withstood. The roof had holes in it. Walls and plaster were chipped from bullet hits.

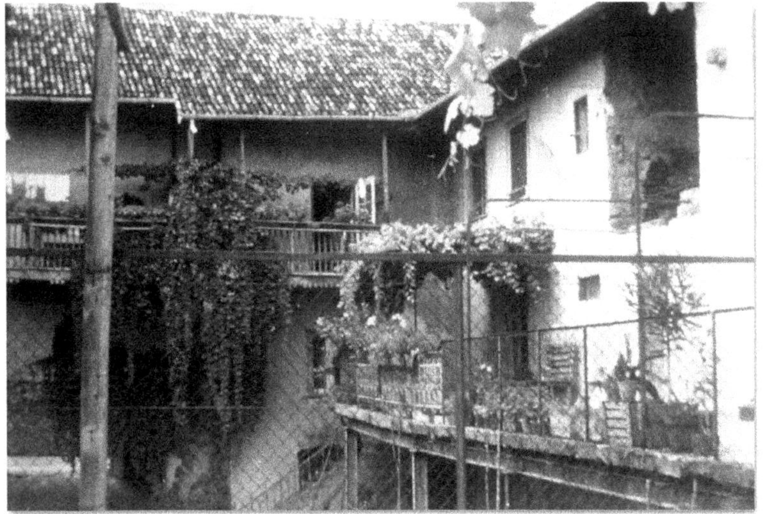

Our House - Angerburg

Papà had left the cultivation of his fields in the hands of a farmer by the name of Konrad Marini, who knew little about farming but was able to handle the manual labor in the fields. For his work, he would get half of the income from the harvest. The contract, which was typical for the times, was called a *mezzadria*.

Twice a year, we also received money from the *Kellereigenossenschaft* (the wine-making collective in *Appiano*) and with that, Mamma was able to pay for groceries at the *Delleman* store. She recorded all our expenses in her little note book, *il libretto,* and in February and November of each year, she would pay the bills. The income from the harvest was usually enough to cover expenses, but twice, when the money fell short, Mamma had to sell off certain fields that Papà owned in the valley near *Merano*.

My grandfather, Nonno Luigi Bella, the father of my mother, came to handle some of the many responsibilities we faced during this time, and remained with us for more than two years. He saw to it that our house was repaired and made sure that no one cheated or took advantage of us in my mother's grief. But more than providing his steady and astute business sense, Nonno Luigi helped to fill the void I felt. I looked up to him then, as I had my father, and he became a guiding influence in my life.

Times were difficult, but if they were desperate, my mother hid that from us children quite well. We never went hungry. The selection of food was limited, but Mamma was an extraordinary cook, and she always prepared meals with flavor.

I especially remember one occasion when she prepared a dish of meat with potatoes. It had been so long since we had tasted such a wonderful meal, and the house smelled so aromatic with all the spices and herbs, that we didn't stop to wonder how she had been able to find or afford meat at the butcher's shop. When we finally did ask she just told us to be quiet and be thankful. It wasn't until years later that we learned the truth about that meal…and the recently departed cat she had received from a neighbor down the street.

All during this time, I had so many questions about my future. I wondered about my education, about family and friends and how we would make it through the post-war period. I felt the need for love and acceptance. I pondered my own identity, who I was, and what I was meant to do with my life. I remember standing in front of a mirror and repeating my name again and again and feeling like my soul was coming through somewhere from a distant place. I needed to feel that I was *me*, that Carla was somebody and not just a soul wandering in a void of infinite space.

I felt so small and insignificant compared to my sister, Lidia. She was beautiful, skinny and tall and took care of her appearance. Every evening she would roll her hair in curlers so the next morning she would have the perfect hair-style. In school she was the smartest of the class, and she practiced her music daily, wanting to become a concert pianist with a distinguished career.

In contrast, I was a tomboy. I was much shorter than she was, and I thought I was fat. Where dresses seemed to fall gently over Lidia's form, they clung uncomfortably to my frame. I wore my hair in two braids, and my front teeth stuck out so that I could not even close my mouth.

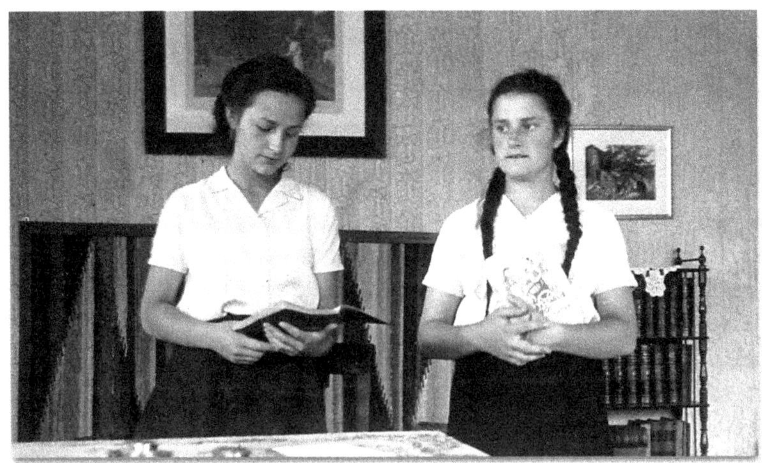

Lidia and Carla (c. 1947)

On top of that, I had no idea what I wanted to be in life. I certainly did not want to continue with piano lessons; my future was not in music. I considered becoming a school teacher. Or maybe I could set up a classroom somewhere in our big house and create a special program.

But somehow I seemed to know that remaining forever in Appiano was not for me. I wanted to travel and see other places. "Maybe I could become an airline stewardess and fly across the world," I wondered. Another thought I had was to become the manager of Papà's fruit export business, but the war had devastated much of the landscape, and other, savvy farmers had taken over what market was left, so that was not possible anymore.

While I was thinking and dreaming of my future, I happened to see that a film from America was playing at a local movie theater in Bolzano. I decided to go and see it. "Little Women" was a 1949 film based on the novel by Louisa May Alcott. The part of Josephine, or "Jo," was played by June Alison, with Elisabeth Taylor, Margaret O'Brien and Janet Leigh in the other parts.

After seeing that film, I came home certain that I could find where I might belong. Like me, the character Jo was a tomboy. She was assertive and confident, and dreamed of becoming a writer. She had spirit and drive, and loved to be on stage playing the fictional characters she had created in her writing. And she did not care to be in love with any boy. She was the inspiration I needed, and made me think of the stories my mother had told me of her dreams and ambitions in her youth.

Anna Bella, my mother, was born in Trento, January 9, 1911, the first daughter of Luigi Bella and Carlotta Menapace de Tasullo. Carlotta had left her hometown of

Rallo in *Val di Non* to become a lady in waiting to the Baroness Tschiderer in Vienna. The Baroness was the sister of the archbishop of Trento.

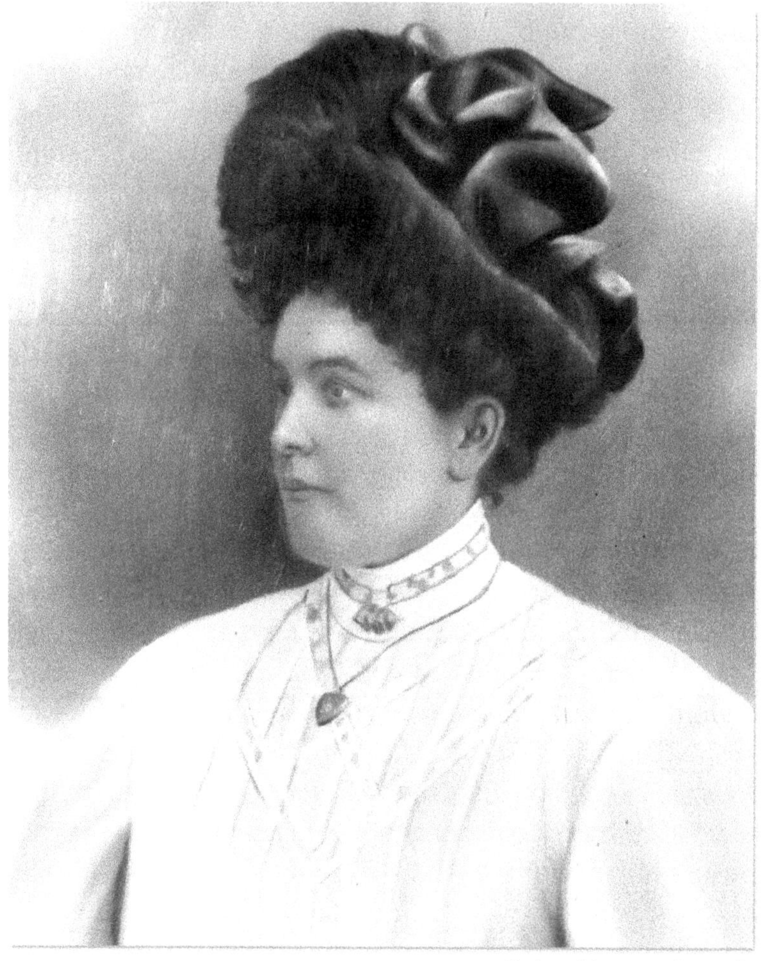

Carlotta Menapace de Tasullo

Into this high society came my grandfather, Luigi Bella. They met and married, and two years after my mother was born, they had a second daughter.

Sadly though, Carlotta died in 1919, during her third pregnancy, and left Luigi a widower with two young daughters: my mother Anna (Annetta), at eight years old, and her sister Ida (Idotta) two years younger.

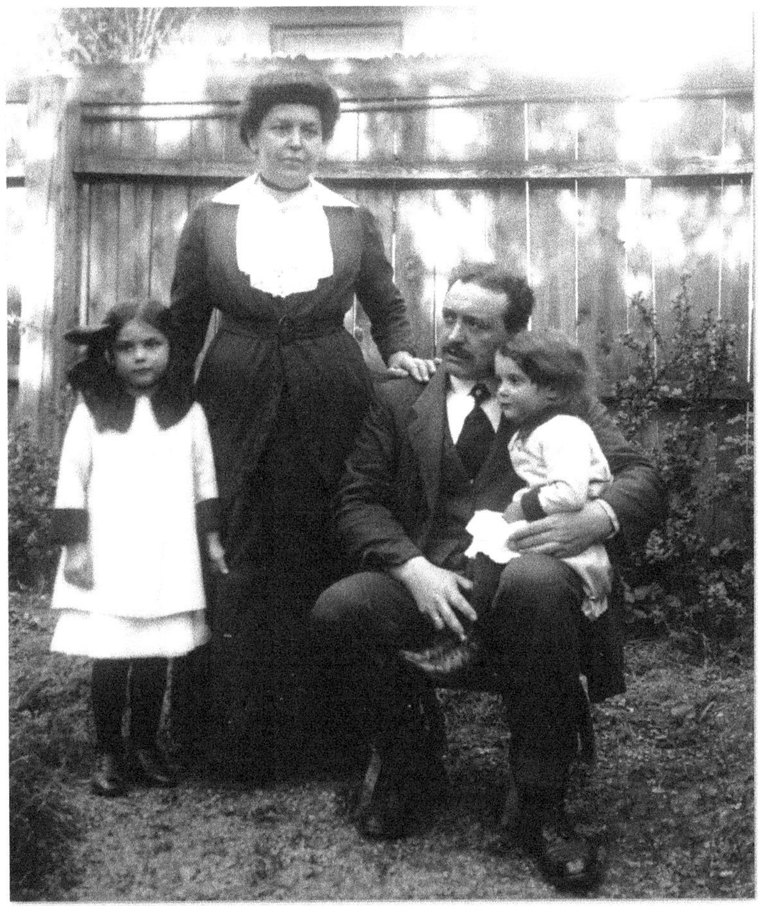

Anna, Carlotta, Luigi and Ida Bella

At the age of fifteen, my mother became a student at the prestigious school, *Le Dame Inglesi* of *Rovereto*. The nuns of this private school were known to teach drama and literature to prominent girls, and since my mother was the daughter of Carlotta Menapace de Tasullo, she was one.

I remember listening with admiration when Mamma recited lines of famous plays like <u>*Macbeth*</u>, <u>*La Partita a Scacchi*</u> of Giacosa, and the <u>*Cantiche d'Inferno*</u> of Dante Alighieri. She was fantastic. She remembered lines of poetry and knew how to bring drama to the interpretation of all the plays she knew by heart. She was also able to sketch the scenes of the plays she had studied, and then paint them with watercolors. She had become a teacher and had just begun at the school in *Appiano* when she met my father.

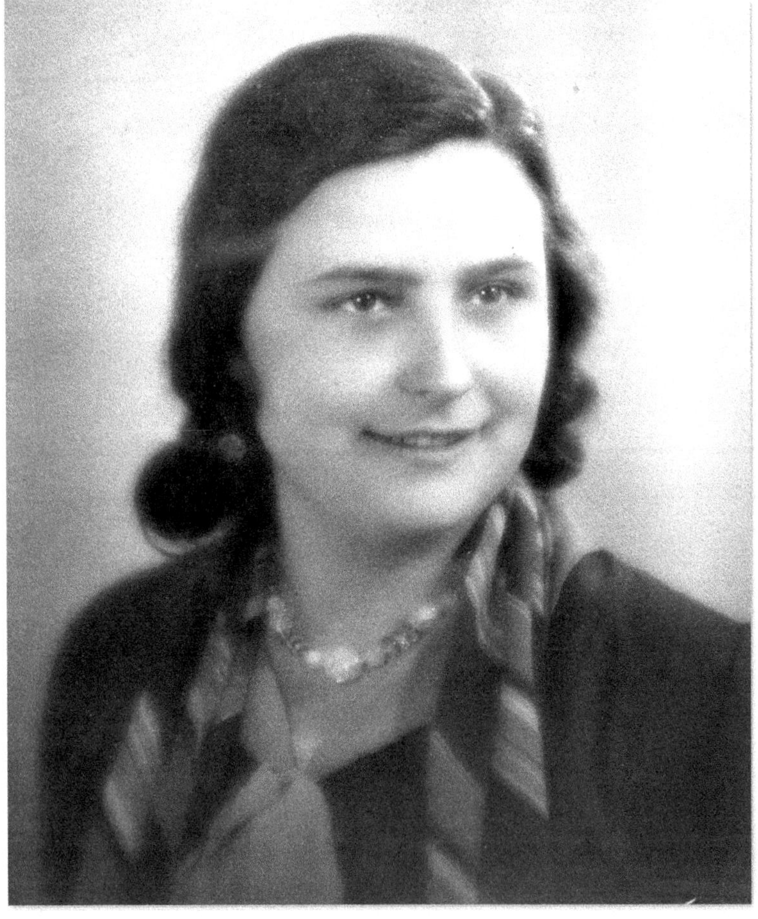

Anna Bella

I loved to hear the romantic story of how they met. In my mind, it was as dramatic and momentous as the story in the <u>*Iliad*</u> of Homer, when Prince Paris of Troy presented Aphrodite with a golden apple so that he could leave Sparta with the beautiful Helen…and spark the Trojan War. While, in my parent's case, there was no Greek goddess…or war, there was an apple, and true love.

It started when why mother and her friend, both teachers in *Appiano*, found a room to rent in my father's house. They both thought my father was charming and quite handsome, and they often greeted him at the Bank in the *piazza* where he worked. He seemed to like them, but they were never sure which of them he preferred. Then, on a sunny day in October, he came to their door holding a large, red, juicy apple he had picked from his harvest, and offered it to…Annetta. He had chosen my mother to invite to a harvest dance.

Vigilio Carli and Anna Bella were married on March 21, 1933. They honeymooned in Rome before returning to Appiano to start their life together.

Because she had been a teacher and a lover of literature, art and drama, my mother was always called upon whenever there was an important visitor in town. When a magistrate was scheduled to appear, she would design and prepare a poster to announce the arrival. If a Bishop was passing through, she would write a poem to honor the occasion.

Doctor Hans Nicolussi, the physician of Appiano, would also call on my mother when he needed assistance performing small medical procedures in his office. She had always had an interest in medicine and would have been an excellent physician or nurse. She spent many hours visiting sick children and people who were confined to bed, drawing pictures for them or telling stories to make them laugh.

She also befriended many people of authority in town, and though she never studied the German language, she learned to speak the dialect spoken in *Appiano*. Although her grammar was not always correct, she was not embarrassed at all by her mistakes. In fact, many in town found her so wonderfully charming, that they adopted her "grammar-free" way of speaking. Mamma would often spend hours chatting and laughing with her dearest friend, Bianca Dellagiacoma, inventing new words in German, Italian or both. It was all part of her boundless humor.

Our house was always open to everyone, from friends and relatives, to visitors and street vendors of all kind. Everyone knew of my mother's great congeniality and warmth, and while a salesperson might arrive to sell fabrics, carpets, kitchen utensils or fresh fish on Fridays, they all ended up staying to share a bite or some pleasant conversation. Mamma's hospitality was never ending.

It was no surprise, therefore, when my mother received a special visit from a distant cousin that lived in Paris, France.

Antonia Bertolini was the daughter of a brother of Pia Bertolini, the widow from *Rovereto* that my grandfather, Luigi Bella, had married after his wife, Carlotta Menapace, had died during childbirth. Pia's full name was Pia Modesta Amabile Bella Magagna Bertolini, which literally translates as *pious, modest, lovable, beautiful…* and, as if to prove that her parents had a sense of humor… *magagna,* or "defect."

Well, her niece Antonia had immigrated to France where she had studied music and become a singer. Shocked by the depravity of the Parisian nightlife, however, she had entered the convent and become a nun. After twelve years, though, she became disenchanted with the nuns she had joined, and decided to form her own religious order which she vowed would be more charitable and less rigid.

Unfortunately, her plan was discovered, and she was expelled from the convent. So she abandoned the church and went back to music and a secular life.

During her younger years, however, she had developed an interest in palmistry and astrology, and had learned how to analyze the shape of hands, and interpret what their lines and mounds represented. Using her studied insights, she began counseling the many, young girls in Paris that had taken to life on the streets and had lost hope in life. Through palmistry she gained their trust and helped them consider other possibilities for themselves.

Her charitable work through her new profession brought her some recognition and acclaim in France where palmistry was considered a reputable science from the time of Desbarrolles and d'Arpentigny.

So when Antonia visited my mother in Italy, her arrival created quite a commotion. Many came to have a hand reading. Girls my age, curious about love, listened to every word, suggestion and prediction that Antonia would offer. Older people in town were perhaps more skeptical, but some would eventually sit for a hand reading.

Her knowledge and skill was so impressive that I began to read with interest various books on palmistry as well, studying theories and techniques used in India, France and Italy.

My mother's sister, Ida, also visited often. She had married Ugo Rizzi, and their children Paolo and Anna had been the constant playmates of me, Bruno and Lidia when we were young. It was so wonderful growing up so close with our cousins, and I loved my *Zia* Idotta and thought she was so well read and brilliant.

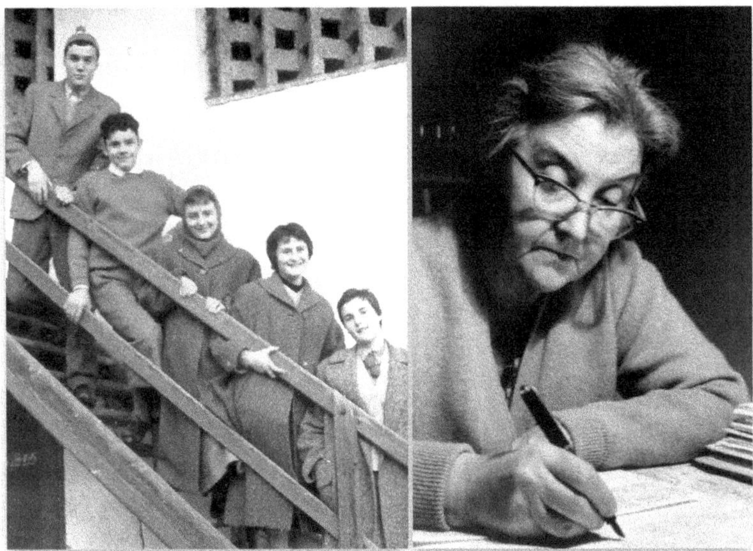

Paolo Rizzi, Bruno, Lidia, Carla, Anna Rizzi   Zia Idotta

I was fifteen, and I had just finished three years of study at the *Giardino di Maria*, a school run by the Cistercian nuns whose convent was located on a hill in the *San Paolo* section of *Appiano*. Like my mother, I enjoyed literature and drama, and I was thrilled to be part of a little theater group we had formed to perform plays in the chapel hall. I still remember my part in the many dramas we staged under the direction of my mother, with piano music accompaniment provided by my sister, Lidia.

I felt so excited after every performance. Acting in front of an audience made me feel important, and I loved when people would congratulate me afterwards by saying that I was just like my mother, a "second Annetta." I wondered: Was I really a girl with talent like my mother? Would I live out her early dreams and ambitions, learn to recite famous plays, and become a prominent figure like *her* mother, my grandmother, Carlotta Menapace de Tasullo? And would anyone ever bring *me* an apple?

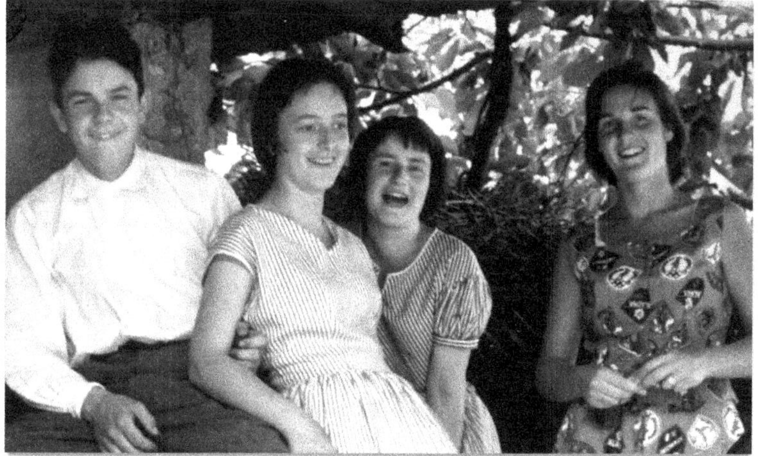

Bruno, Lidia, Carla and Anna Rizzi (c. 1950)

In the summer months, I used to go with a group of my friends up into the mountains where the air was cool and clear. We would sing mountain songs, talk about life and laugh together. There were some handsome young boys that seemed attracted to my confidence and spontaneity, but I kept my feelings to myself. That seemed only to intrigue them more. Of course, there was one boy in particular that I might have liked during that time, which made falling in love with anyone else difficult, but I still had hopes for a different life in a wider world, so I kept many of those secrets quiet and hidden deep in my heart.

50

CHAPTER FOUR

Nonno Luigi Bella

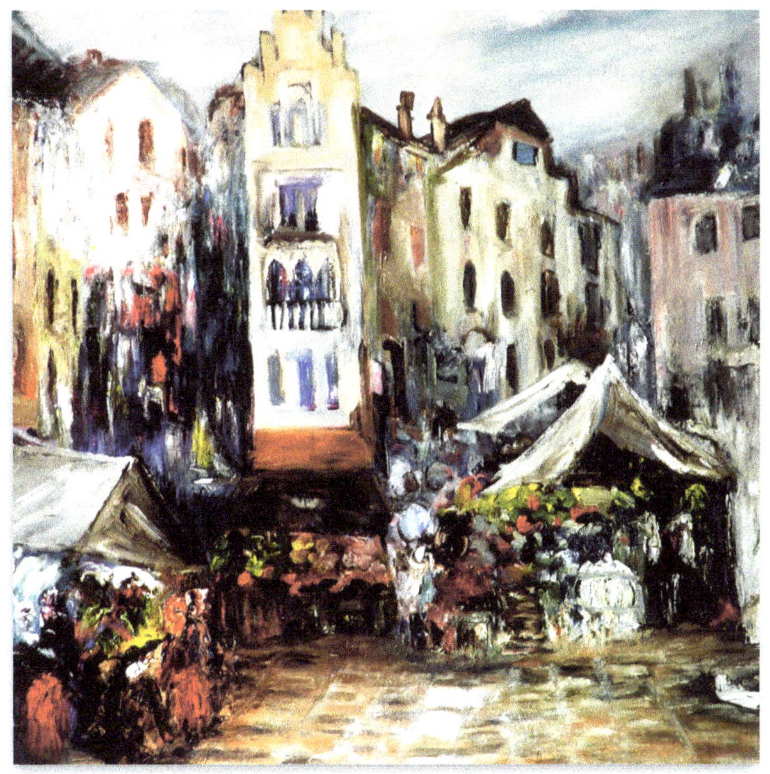

Market in Bolzano

*To accomplish great things we must not only act,
But also dream; not only plan, but also believe.*

Anatole France

Before I could explore the dreams and ambitions I might have had, I was sent to go live with my grandfather, Nonno Luigi Bella, when he moved to his apartment in *Bolzano* on via Zara.

I was enrolled in the *Scuola Tecnica Commerciale* to study and receive a diploma in bookkeeping. It had been decided that a future as a public accountant, a *Computista Commerciale,* would be much more practical for a girl like me. It was far from what I wanted, and nothing like what my mother had studied at her prestigious *Le Dame Inglesi* school of *Rovereto*, but in post-war Italy, things were different, and possibilities were limited.

After my three years at *Giardino di Maria* in *San Paolo*, I had a good foundation in math and business. But I felt that I was in the wrong place. All the other students in the *Scuola Tecnica* were so different from me. Their main concern was to finish school and get a job, while I was drawn toward literature and languages, Latin and Greek, toward a career that embraced the humanities and art.

My Nonno Luigi was a "Renaissance man, " and I admired him greatly. He was tall and he spoke, and even walked, with authority. I never saw him laugh, but he often smiled at me, at people, and at the world. He came into my life at such an important time. He was there for me when Papà was no longer, and he became such an influence in my life.

Nonno Luigi always followed the news of the day and he recorded his thoughts and opinions regarding the news in his diary. He filled so many notebooks with the events of his life, during the two years I stayed with him in

Bolzano, and I know that I was frequently the subject of his writing.

I believe his favorite time of day was in the evening hours, when we were still sitting at the kitchen table after supper, and I was busy studying. Nonno would be writing in his diary, his right leg gently bouncing and his foot tapping on the floor. He was always so absorbed in his writing that sometimes, lost in thought, he would reach out across the table without looking up to sneak some sugar from the sugar bowl and mistakenly end up with a pinch of salt in his mouth. I would laugh. He would smile. His leg would stop bouncing, then he would dip his pen into the ink tank and continue writing.

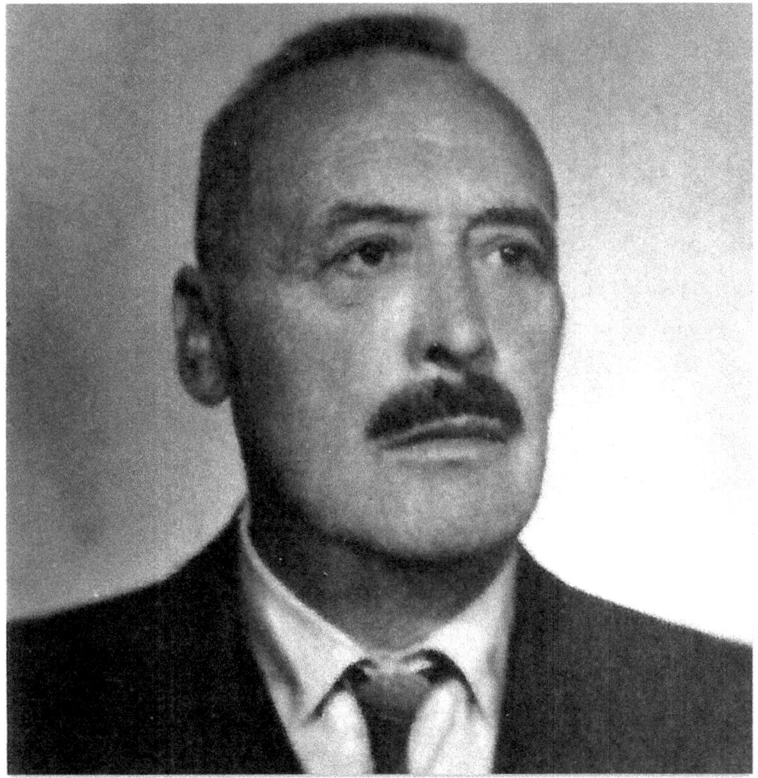

Luigi Bella

He got upset when I confided in him that I did not understand chemistry or that I was afraid I would probably get bad grades on the exam. Then, he would sit with me patiently and explain every formula, from the beginning of the book through any chapter that might appear on the exam until I understood it better. It was the same approach he took for all the subjects I was studying. He knew them all, and I was amazed at his vast knowledge, especially when it came to Civil Law.

He had a little, blue, law book that he always carried with him, and many people that had a business often sought his help when they needed legal advice or had to resolve a problem with the Government. He had the authoritative appearance of a man that could not be fooled, and he suffered no fools in return. He was respected for his intelligence, was inquisitive by nature, and was kind and generous with all the people that asked for his help.

He spoke four languages—Italian, German, French and some English—which was useful in his post as the director of the European Railroad in Italy and Austria. To him, there was nothing greater than curiosity and the acquisition of knowledge, and it was this ethic and his deep affection for me that gave me the confidence and the desire to study and learn for the rest of my life.

When I concluded my *Computista Commerciale* studies in *Bolzano*, Nonno decided to move back to his large house in *Trento* which he had purchased years earlier. I moved back home to *Appiano* but found few employment opportunities in my small town. Lidia had found some work, and lived there with my mother, but Bruno had entered the Catholic Seminary in *Trento*, to prepare himself for the priesthood.

Nonno Luigi thought that I should come to *Trento* as well, and that I might have a better chance at finding work in the big city. So, off I went again to stay with Nonno, where I would live for the next two years.

Nonno's home at *via Brennero 31*, was a tall building with ten separate apartments on five floors. I thought it was a beautiful palace, but it needed repairs and reconstruction after the war. I had my own space in Nonno's apartment on the third floor, and across the hall was a separate apartment where Nonno's sisters, Ida and Dorothea (Retti), lived. His other sister, Massimiliana (Maxi) had passed away before I ever met her.

At home, we had always affectionately called Ida and Retti *le vecchie zie,* the old aunts, because they were both in their sixties by then.

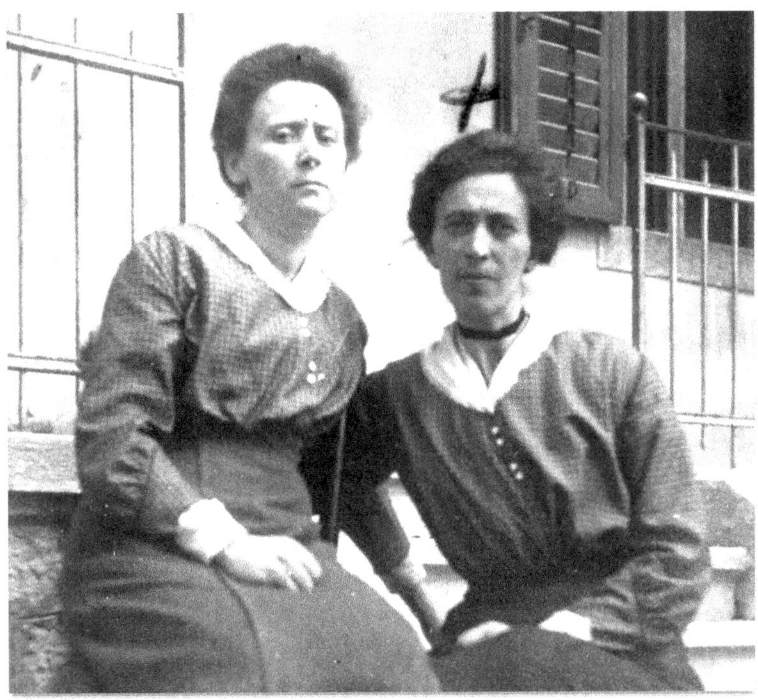

Zia Ida and Zia Massimiliana (Maxi) Bella

I loved *Zia* Retti very much, and remembered how I had stayed with her for about a month during the time that my mother was pregnant with my brother, Bruno. I was only five years old then, and I didn't understand why I had been sent away, but *Zia* Retti made me feel welcome and always found games for me to play. And on nights when I missed my mother and began crying for attention, she would patiently take me into the kitchen where I would calm myself by scooping and weighing grains of rice on the kitchen scales for hours until we both fell asleep.

When daytime arrived, I tried her patience again, because I never wanted to stay inside the house, up high on the top floors where I felt lost in the sky. Out back, there was a large garden full of flowers and vegetables and two big trees filled with *cachi*, or persimmons, my favorite fruit.

Now, at seventeen years of age, I was back and looking for a job. I did not find one, though, so instead I enrolled in two language courses, German and French, at the *liceo Prati* school in the center of the city.

Nonno was absolutely happy that I was eager to learn and follow in his linguistic footsteps, particularly with my choice of French. He searched through all his books to find the French version of the classic <u>Orlando Furioso</u> by Ariosto, so that we could study it together.

Nonno also took me to the theater, the *Teatro Sociale* in Trento, to see Verdi's <u>Rigoletto</u>. It was my first time at the opera to see a production and hear Verdi's music, and with that, I began to study all the libretti of the various operas by Verdi so that I could sing the most famous arias.

I also loved very much going to see movies, especially those from the United States, but Nonno strongly disliked cinema and only appreciated performances at the opera and…the circus. I was *not* interested in the circus, and even though I was happy to share my enjoyment of the opera with Nonno, I felt I had to keep my passion for movies a secret.

When the film <u>Gone with the Wind</u> arrived in the theater in *Trento,* I concocted a story so that I could go to see it by myself, knowing that Nonno would be against the idea. I told him that I was going to read and spend time at the park, but at some point during the three hour movie, it began to rain heavily outside. When I returned home, I lied and told him that I had met a friend and went to her house to stay dry until it the rain had stopped. Nonno said nothing, but I am sure he did not believe me, and for that I felt guilty for quite some time.

Trento was a marvelous city with so many places to visit every day. I used to spend time in *piazza Dante*, near the railroad station where a large statue of Dante Alighieri sits at the center. The figure is posed with his finger pointing north, a political reminder to the Austrian people that *Trento* is part of Italy. The irredentist patriots, Cesare Battisti and Fabio Filzi, were vocal in their belief that Italian portions of the Austro-Hungarian Empire should be united with Italy, and their executions are part of *Trento's* rich history.

Zia Retti's son, Aldo, who also lived with her and *Zia* Ida, used to take me exploring in the city of *Trento* every Sunday, and explain to me the history of all the various places we visited. I discovered the meaning of every monument and the importance of every church, *piazza* and famous building rising in the shadow of the opulent *Castel del Buon Consiglio*. Trento was (and still is) quite beautiful.

Around every corner and beneath every arch, I saw the old city come alive. I remember arriving in the evening at the *Piazza del Duomo* and standing before the domed cathedral and the spectacular fountain of Neptune, and becoming enchanted by the city. The lights on the buildings, the water, the stars in the sky above, every stone seemed to be whispering to me about stories of old times. It was a feeling that I hoped would last forever.

Of course, some feelings I prefer to forget. I was excited to try new things during this time, and since curly hairstyles were suddenly fashionable, I decided to have my long braids cut and styled with a permanent. I had made the decision, and I entered the hair salon with a confident smile, but when I left later, I had tears in my eyes.

What a disaster! I looked at my red, square face in the mirror, surrounded by all those curls…and I missed my braids. I thought that I would have to skip going to class for at least a week, or maybe through Christmas. I was just miserable.

Despite the occasional "misery," I was really quite happy. I felt that I was entering a wider world with new experiences, and seeing, perhaps for the first time, the promise of new possibilities for my life. I looked with great hope toward where I might be going, while pondering with great interest the place from where I had come.

Trento & Some Family History

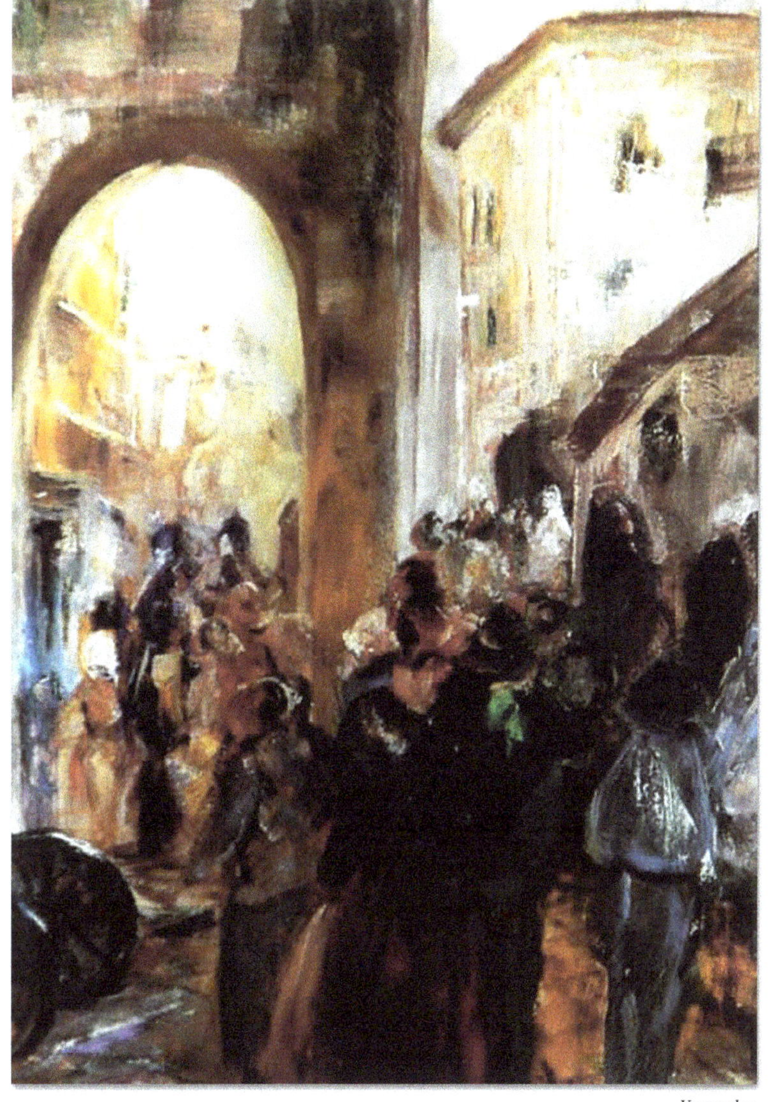

Yesterday

During the time of the Roman Empire, *Trento* was at an important juncture on the road between Rome and Austria. Trento was the only fortified city along the ancient Via Claudia Augusta between *Verona* and Augusta Vindelicorum (present day Augsburg), the capital of the Roman imperial province of Raetia.

To ensure free passage through the area, so vital to his political interests, the Holy Roman Emperor Conrad II, in 1027, appointed the prince-bishops of *Trento* to rule the area locally, establishing the city as a seat of great religious influence and secular power.

It is no small coincidence, therefore, that centuries later, the city was chosen by Pope Paul III, at the suggestion of then Emperor Charles V, as the site for the *Council of Trent* (1545-1563) to reform the Catholic Church in response to the Protestant Reformation.

Trento was an important city, and in 1796, Napoleon wanted it for France, so he invaded the region and claimed it in his *Department of Alto Adige* and part of his *Kingdom of Italy*. By 1815, however, Trento was annexed by the German-speaking *County of Tyrol,* a province of Austria administered from Innsbruck.

After a century of Austrian occupation, the First World War broke out in 1914, and *Trento* was called to fight for Emperor Joseph I of Austria. But with the end of the war and the Treaty of Saint-Germain in 1919, *Trento* and *Alto Adige,* all the way up to the *Brenner Pass,* was made part of Italy again.

The *Trentino-Alto Adige/Südtirol* region, where I was born, was given special autonomy through an agreement included in the *Treaty of Versailles,* and while that arrangement was greatly reduced under Mussolini's Fascist government, the northern Italian border and the region's autonomy was reconfirmed after World War II (1939-45).

All this regional history played an important part in my own story, even though when I was young I didn't fully understand it.

My grandfather and his sisters in *Trento* spoke Italian, of course, but they also spoke perfect German. Others, in certain Alpine areas, spoke the ancient language of Ladin, derived from pre-Roman Latin populations; and there are German dialects that survive today in remote areas like the one spoken in the *Valle dei Mòcheni* and in *Lavarone*.

My great grandfather, Giovanni Bella, had married Monika Fichtner in Munich-Germany. She gave birth to three girls by the name of Massimiliana (Maxi), Dorothea (Retti), Ida, and a son, my *nonno* Luigi.

Maxi died very young, Ida stayed single, and Retti married a widower by the name of Parmesani who had two children, Costante and Olga, from his first marriage. Aldo was from his second marriage with Retti.

My *nonno* Luigi was born in Weilheim, Germany, on March 8, 1883. He met Carlotta from *Rallo*, in *Val di Non*, and she was part of the very large Menapace de Tasullo family. She married my *nonno* when she was eighteen, and they settled in *Trento,* where soon after they had two daughters: my mother Anna (Annetta), born on January 9, 1911, and Ida (Idotta), on December 8, 1912.

This "family history" happened while the *Trentino* region was still part of the Austrian Empire. In a land that was passed back and forth between the Romans and Austrians, the French and then finally the Italians, I was happy to discover the culture and history etched on every corner in *Trento*. After spending my youth in my small town of *Appiano*, *Trento* seemed like a vast, new world to explore. And I would have stayed there with Nonno for as long as it took to absorb every bit of it.

But once again, autumn became winter. Nonno Luigi's health took a turn, and while his sister Ida and his second wife Pia took good care of him, his heart began to fail. A Doctor Carlucci visited him twice a week, and some days Nonno felt well enough to spend time with me reading <u>Orlando Furioso</u> in French or telling me the stories of his life. His voice was soft, his legs resting quietly, his diary unopened on the table beside him.

On a cold December day, the streets covered with snow, *Zia* Ida checked Nonno's vital signs. It was cold in the apartment, but I was relieved knowing that my mother was coming from *Appiano* by train to see her father and stay with us for a few days. Nonno never left his bed anymore; his legs were swollen and his breathing shallow. He needed to rest his head on three pillows.

When my mother, his Annetta, arrived, Nonno looked happy. I imagined that maybe he was feeling that he had completed his mission in life. As we all stood by his bedside, he smiled faintly and raised his hands as if to give us all a final blessing. He knew that his death was close, but he had prepared for it and was at peace.

Nonno died in *Trento* at 70 years of age, on December 15, 1953.

The Path Ahead

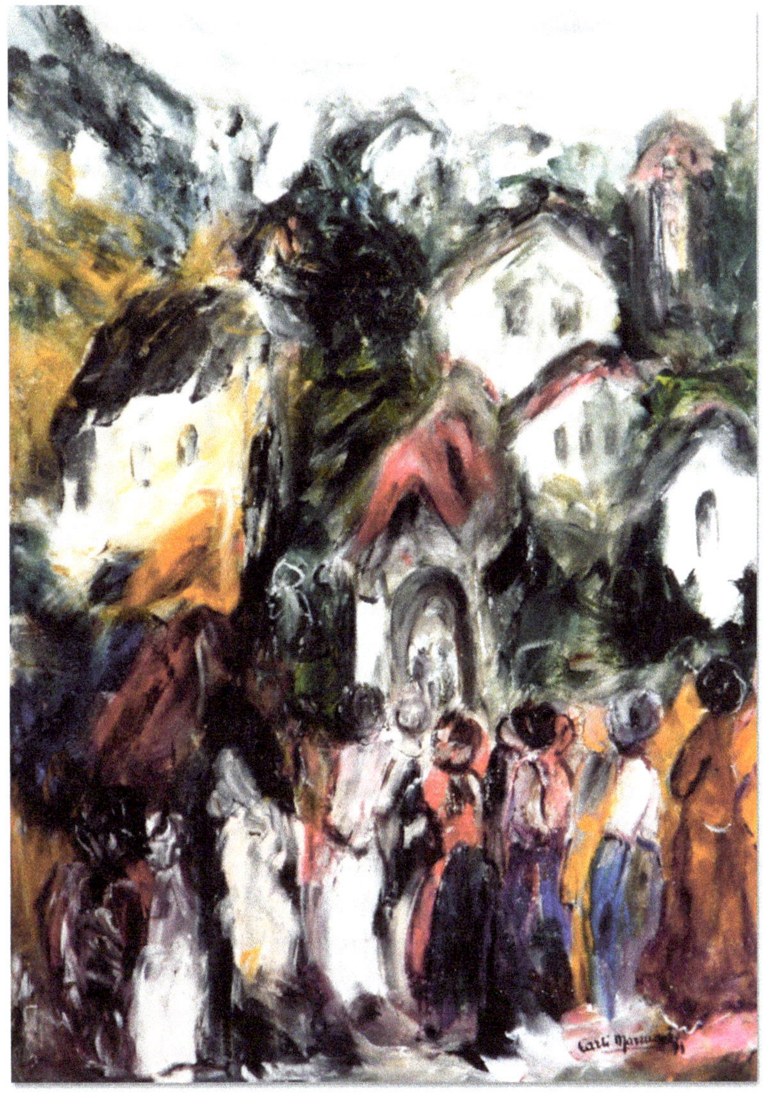

Along the Village Road

Faith and Love are the most important elements for a young girl of eighteen. They both touch the spirit, and become the language to express what she has in her heart.

Catholicism, the religious faith in which I was raised, was very important in my life. In my early years, I learned to speak with God in my prayers, and to listen to the many beautiful stories about Jesus.

As a child with my parents, I would go to church on Sundays, and attend catechism lessons in school during the week. The pastor of our church was very nice, and I liked how he explained the stories of the Bible through the large sacred pictures on the wall. The art always made a profound impression on me.

Later on, I joined the children's choir, and I loved to remain after Mass to hear the organ music and to smell the incense still drifting through the empty church. Religion, especially at that time of my life, gave me a sense of identity and security. I never doubted the existence of God, and I knew that in my life I would grow in faith as I continued on my path.

During my adolescence, I became interested in reading religious histories, and learning about myths and sacred symbols. I knew though, that with Nonno's passing, my time of studying would be over, so I never imagined I would get the chance to pursue those interests.

It was at the funeral of my *nonno* that I met don Luigi Borghesi, the pastor in a small village in *Val di Non*. He was the nephew of my late grandmother, Carlotta Menapace de Tasullo, the first wife of my Nonno Luigi. My mother was his cousin, and though she hadn't seen him in many years, they had been childhood companions, and she was pleased to renew their friendship when he came to Nonno's funeral with many other relatives from *Val di Non*.

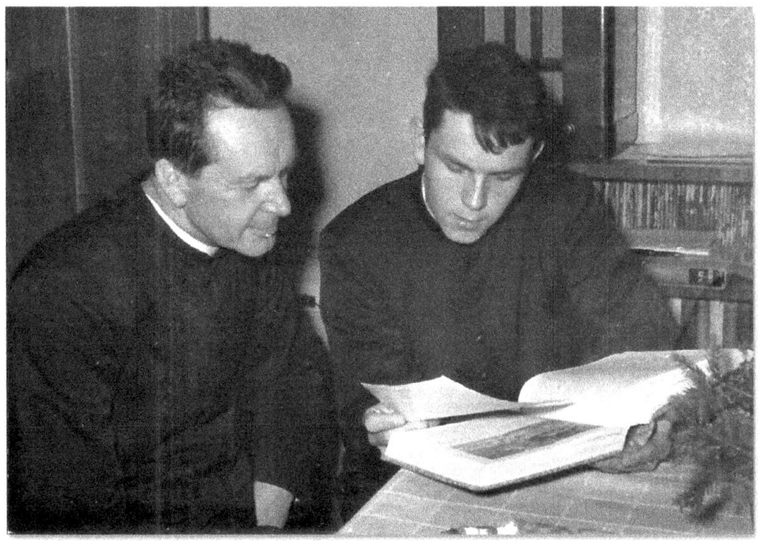

Don Luigi Borghesi and Bruno Carli

As they reminisced about the past, I considered my future. I would be moving back to *Appiano* after my two years in *Bolzano* and two years in *Trento,* but I wasn't sure what I was going to do with myself. Don Luigi had mentioned that his housekeeper would be going on vacation in summer and asked my mother if she knew anyone who could help... And so, once again, I was sent off, this time to the parish of don Luigi Borghesi in *Val di Non.*

I was quite happy to go, actually. While there was some cooking and cleaning among my daily duties, don Luigi also involved me in many more elevated activities. It was a splendid occasion for me to delve into a different life and get to know the ways of the church. I felt so special to be able to walk up the steps of the altar and to see the inner workings of the church up close. I could visit the sacristy, learn about all the various holy implements, and see that part of the church I had only ever seen from a distant pew.

I was more in touch with a spiritual life that I had never truly experienced before. Don Luigi introduced me to daily meditation, various religious readings, and his manner of presenting catechism. He narrated the gospel in such simple and common terms that made it seem more current and relevant.

He was a humble man, and he was embraced by all in his parish as a good father. He knew he was no great theologian or church philosopher, but he accepted his mission to be a true and honest servant to his parish, and to beautify the architecture of every church to which he was sent.

At the church of *Romallo,* I saw the new altar he had commissioned. He oversaw the construction of new pews for the choir in the church of *Spormaggiore*, and the hand-carved, wooden entrance door of *S.Michele all'Adige.* He helped get church bells placed and stained glass windows installed. He even helped with repairs of a bell tower in one church. To me he gave the gift of a wonderful example of kindness and generosity as well as his copy of a book, <u>*Intimità Divina*</u> for my daily meditation.

Another chance encounter during this time that had a great impact on my life was with an elderly woman named Madam Zita Filippi. She was an elegant woman of Russian descent who had married a gentleman from Trento who lived in a rented castle in *Appiano.*

Madam Zita spent her days outside on the beautiful grounds of the castle, painting the landscape scenes filled with colorful flowers. She had also painted the walls of the chapel at our church which is where she met and got to know my mother.

One day we had been invited to visit the castle where she lived, and I saw Madam Zita's wonderful art. "If only I could paint like that!" I would think to myself. I wondered if being an artist was even a possibility I could consider. I had studied to be a public accountant. Was that my path now? I would have liked to pursue what I felt in my heart, but I knew that what was required of me would be something much more practical.

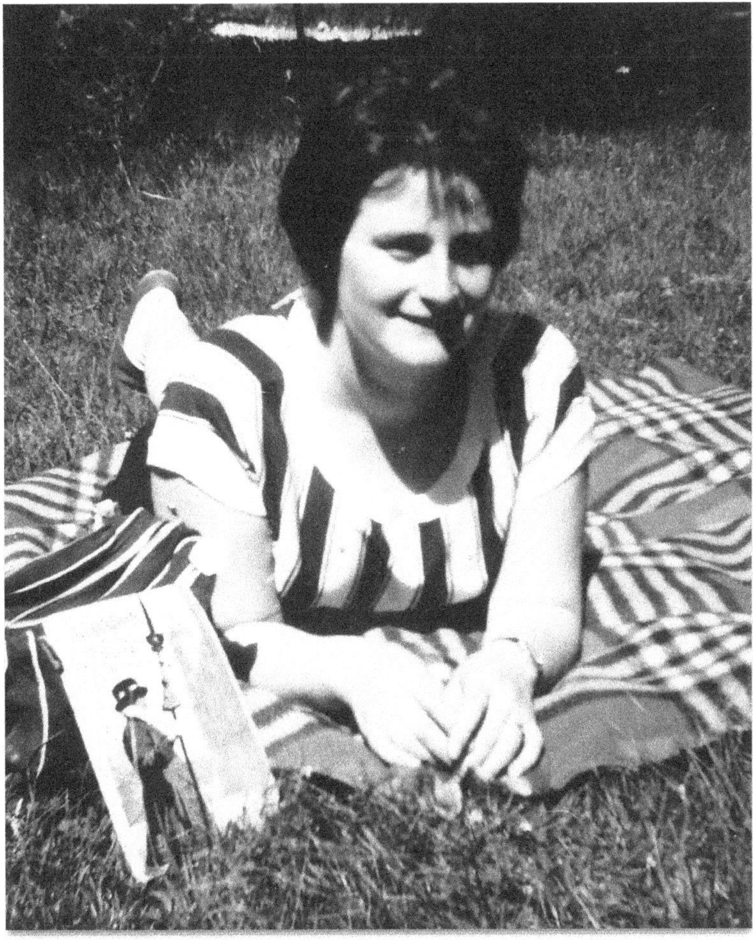

Carla Carli (c. 1954)

CHAPTER SEVEN

Perseverance

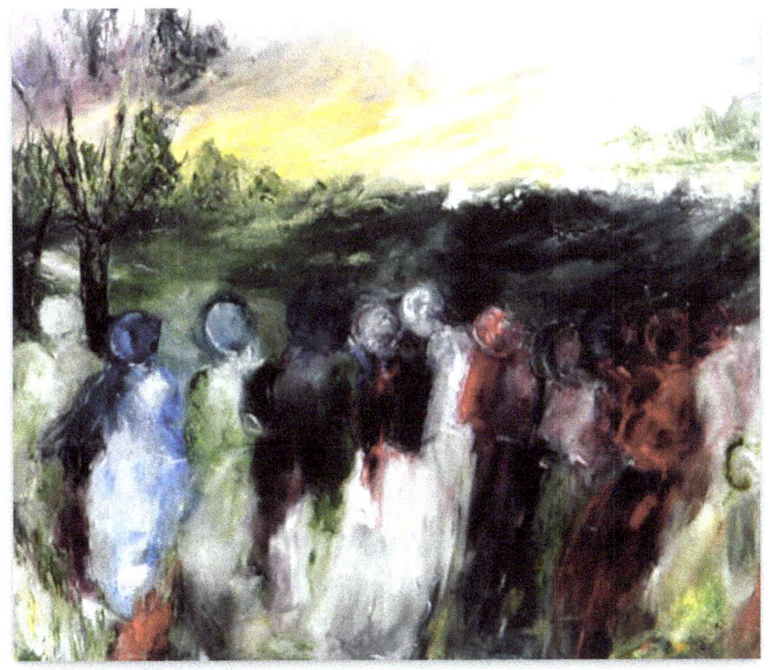

My Green Valley

If you persevere…you have a real opportunity to achieve something. Sure, there will be storms along the way. And you might not reach your goal right away. But if you do your best and keep a true compass, you'll get there.

Edward M. Kennedy, <u>True Compass: A Memoir</u>

69

After my summer in *Val di Non* with don Luigi, I returned home with the realization that I needed to find a job to provide my mother with some extra income to sustain our family. Lidia was working at the City Hall in *Appiano* but was also enrolled at the *Conservatorio di Musica* in *Bolzano* pursuing her degree in music. My brother, Bruno, was still in the seminary, the *Seminario Maggiore,* in *Trento,* studying for his priesthood. I wondered what I could do.

Mr. Otto Kucera was the owner of a lumber company in Bolzano called *Forest*. He had also been a friend of my father, and he was happy to offer me a position at *Forest* as a bookkeeper. I took the job gratefully.

The days were long and tedious. I started at eight in the morning and finished in the evening at seven, but there was not really enough accounting work to keep me busy all day. The company transported lumber from Austria to various Italian cities, but business from the days after the war ended had been slow.

Mr. Kucera stayed in *Austria* most of the time, while I worked in the *Bolzano* office with Mr. Schnidder from Berlin who only spoke German. I took dictation, then had to translate all the letters into Italian. When evening came, I was exhausted and happy to take the train back to *Appiano*, and hope for a better tomorrow.

On the train I always saw a number of friends who also worked in the city, and that made the hard day seem better. Bruno Cemin, Larry Trentini, Romeo Soppelsa and Marco Marchesi were always there, and my friends Ines Cemin, Sonia Pallaoro, Olinda Martini, Erica Tatz completed the group. The train ride always seemed so short because we played games or told jokes the whole way, and we never seemed to have enough time to finish.

Even though I enjoyed taking the train to and from Bolzano, I did not stay too long at the *Forest* Company. Lidia left her job because she had to go to a hospital in *Feltre* to be treated for a thyroid condition. So, I applied for her position at the city hall in *Appiano*. It was another job that I did not like, or really want, but my mother thought is was a prestigious job and so close to home, so I accepted the opportunity.

But the passion for learning that Nonno Luigi had instilled in me made me decide to see about furthering my studies to pursue a different career, one that was more in tune with my own interests and dreams—a career in the arts.

My early years in school, at the *Scuola Tecnica Commerciale*, involved mostly listening to the lectures of teachers with little or no participation from me, and every teacher had their own way of testing their students. I still have memories, and panic-dreams of the way Professor Leoni quizzed us in mathematics and physics. For every lesson, he would select two students names from a box, and then, in front of the whole class, we would be interrogated and asked to solve a formula written on the blackboard.

Since neither math nor physics was my forte, I was always humiliated by Prof. Leoni. He liked to proclaim that I was dumb like a goose by drawing out the vowel sound in my name and calling me o-o-cha-car-li. (*ocha* means goose in Italian).

Not quite the same but still dreadful, was when my accounting teacher, Professor Esposito, would make us write all the errors we had made on our exams on the blackboard to show everyone how stupid we had been.

But now that I had decided that I wanted a career outside of numbers and accounting, I would have to see about going back and completing the course of study in the *Liceo Classico* for liberal arts. But I had no idea if I could do it.

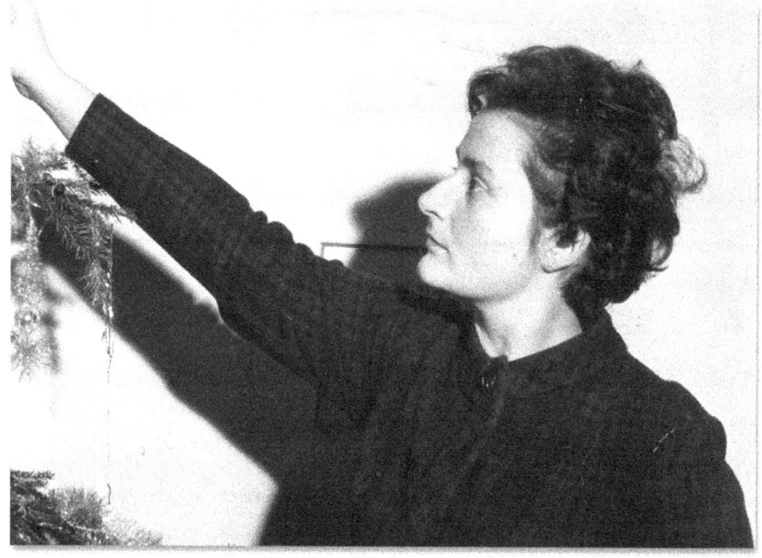

Carla Carli (c. 1955)

Since I had attended the *Scuola Tecnica Commerciale* for accounting, and not the *Liceo Classico,* I had to complete all the new curriculum independently and try to compress five years worth of studies into two so that I could complete the required courses, be tested, and get a new diploma. Then hopefully, I would be able to attend a University and major in Classical Studies.

With the help of Mother Sofia, a nun I had known for years who had taught me during my time at *Giardino di Maria*, I began to study Latin and Greek. My evenings were now spent up in the attic of my home, studying by candlelight, where I wouldn't be disturbed by anyone.

When I finally could enroll in the *Liceo Classico*, I was one of twenty or so students that had transferred over from different schools, and I knew that as much as I had studied, I was far behind every other student.

Professor Paduano, a young man in his thirties, was the Greek language teacher. He seemed easygoing, and it seemed that the first day of class would be more of a review. He sat back in his chair behind his desk and scanned his class list to select a student to evaluate and see how much Greek we knew. And of course…he picked me.

My heart sank, thinking that here, yet again, I would be humiliated in front of my new class in my new school. My proficiency in Greek was poor and certainly below the level of all the students who had been studying the language for years in their "classical" studies. I had only learned what I could…over one summer.

So, I stood, as courageously as I could, and asked if he could give me one month before he called on me in class. Prof. Paduano looked surprised, but then, after rechecking his class list, he must have seen that I had basically taught myself with no formal instruction, because without another word, he nodded and called on someone else. I sat, my face red with embarrassment, but by the next month I had studied and prepared myself for his questions.

Professor Lidia Menapace was my Latin and Literature teacher. I liked her very much. She was a short woman with a round face and bright, vibrant eyes that gave me confidence. She was a superb lecturer, and very involved in the politics of Italy at that time.

Her lectures in class were unique—comparing the words of poets from the time they lived to current events happening in the world. I loved the *cantiche* of Dante, and the romantic poems of Giacomo Leopardi and Giosuè Carducci. When she passed away, December 7, 2020, much was written about her professional life and her involvement in the Italian political scene.

Professor Pastore taught philosophy. He was in his sixties, tall with white hair, and was a philosopher himself, wandering along talking to himself out loud, lost in thought. In his left hand, he carried a stack of ruffled papers and a well-read book, in his right, a wooden cane as he walked slowly, never in a rush.

He was a nice man, always with a gentle smile on his friendly face, that created a perfect learning environment for his students, even if sometimes he forgot to test us entirely until the end of the semester. I came to love philosophy, and later in life revisited what I had first learned through Prof. Pastore when I continued my studies and explored comparative religions.

I spent all my free time buried in my books, and though my final exam, the *maturità classica,* was extremely difficult, I knew afterwards that my Nonno Luigi would have been happy for me. The strain I put on my brain, though, had lingering effects, and even years later, I would have nightmares that I still had to prepare for my exam.

A good teacher can have a lasting influence on every student with whom they interact. They open new windows to new ideas and possibilities and guide them in discovering a subject that might lead to a career that brings fulfillment and joy. Now I finally felt that I was on my way to something better. I would continue on and devote myself to my studies and focus on my goals…with no distractions.

But distractions always seem to come about. I was at the age where most girls were getting married, and so it happened that a few marriage proposals came my way too.

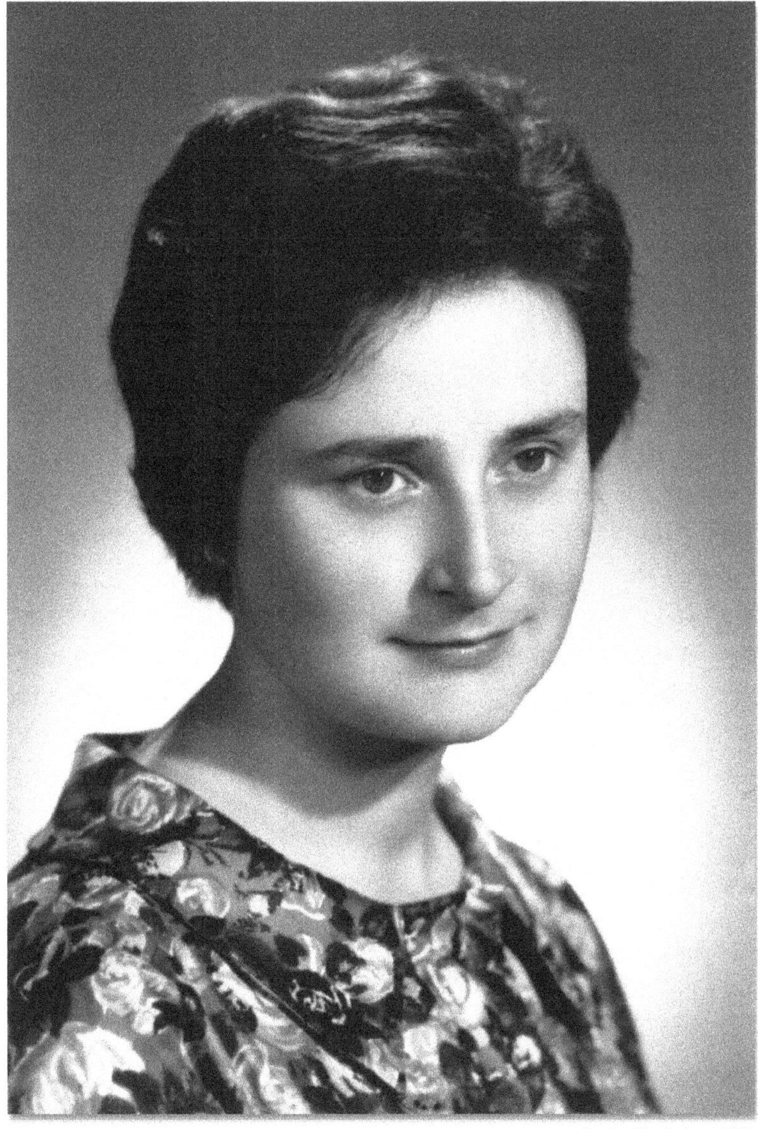

Carla Carli (c. 1957)

Bruno Cemin was the first of my friends to ask for my hand. I was a bit surprised, but I had no interest in marriage. I was busy and independent and…too young to get engaged and make such commitments. And besides, I still secretly had someone else in my heart.

When another friend, Marcello Giuliani, proposed, I again had to explain that I had other plans for myself. Marcello went on to become a successful merchant in *Appiano*, while Bruno moved to Switzerland to work in architecture until he retired to his hometown in the Italian Alps near *Passo Rolle* where he passed away.

One more unusual proposal came a few years later when a young man living in Trenton, New Jersey, in the United States, had asked his aunt in Italy to find him a suitable wife. She had to be Italian, young and educated, and, of course, physically attractive, and…he would require a photo for consideration. The poor aunt asked my sister Lidia for a photo of me, and while, I must confess, I enjoyed the attention and the thought of traveling far away, even to America, the whole thing seemed too strange. The man was a pharmacist and I would have had to arrive in New Jersey for the wedding having never met him in person. Lidia and I laughed together about it. What an adventure it could be…NO! We decided the pharmacist from New Jersey would have to go looking somewhere else.

After having finished my *maturità classica* exams, I was ready and eager to continue my studies. I registered at the *Ca'Foscari* Academy in Venice, but I had to continue working, so I would have to attend…from home.

The few times I went to Venice for my exams, I stayed as a guest with an elderly couple that lived in *Corte del Milione,* in the house that was once the home of Marco Polo. In the thirteen century, Marco Polo had gone to China and served for 17 years in the court of the Emperor Kublai Khan. I couldn't help but feel that I too was an adventurer and explorer in a strange new place. And just as Marco Polo had written his book, <u>*Il Milione,*</u> about his voyage, I continued to keep notes of my adventure in my diary.

One scary adventure that happened during the days I spent at the Academy was not from nightmares of preparing for my exams, but rather from the hazing of first year students by the older ones. It was an unpleasant university tradition in which sometimes dangerous pranks were played on students.

After I finished my exam, I was planning to go to visit the basilica of *Santa Maria Gloriosa dei Frari* to see the famous masterpiece *Assumption* of the Venetian artist Tiziano. I had searched for the church the day before but had gotten lost in the maze of *calli,* the alleyways of Venice. The next day, when I left the exam building, a group of older students began following me. I had no idea what they were planning to do to me, but I ran. I was lost again, not knowing which way to turn in the maze of Venice, and I was quite scared. Suddenly I emerged into a *piazza* and ended up in front of a church. It was the *Basilica dei Frari,* the place I couldn't find the day before. I quickly entered and lost my pursuers.

Despite all the plans and preparations I made for my studies and my life, one is never really prepared for what the future has in store. We had all begun to notice that Mamma had become more and more withdrawn and sad during this time.

Since Papà's death, she was lonely, and she missed all the family members and friends she had lost during the war and in the years after. Now they lived only in her memories. Her sense of joy had faded, and the usual charm and brilliance she had when sharing her stories had faded into memory as well.

It was August 19, 1959 when Mamma died in the hospital. She was only 48 years old. Her death was caused by complications after a surgery for a hernia.

Lidia and I were there with her all night before she died. She was sharp and clear-minded and talkative until the very end, complimenting the doctor on how well he had performed her operation. She thanked him with a sense of peace; she was ready to die, and told him not to use any further measures to prolong her life. I think she felt that she had suffered enough.

Afterwards, many people offered their condolences to Lidia and me—the usual sentiments about how death is part of human existence and an integral part of life, but…I felt numb with grief and once again, extremely alone in this world of continuous suffering.

To believe that 'death can give meaning to our existence' is a difficult idea to accept, and to experience it again first-hand as a life lesson, is even harder. I remained in deep mourning for almost a year, and had to learn how to accept the pain, sorrow, and everlasting separation from someone so dear, gone much too soon, with renewed courage instead of fear.

Why restless, why cast down, my soul?
Hope still; and thou shalt sing
The praise of Him who is thy God,
Thy health's eternal spring.

Psalm 42

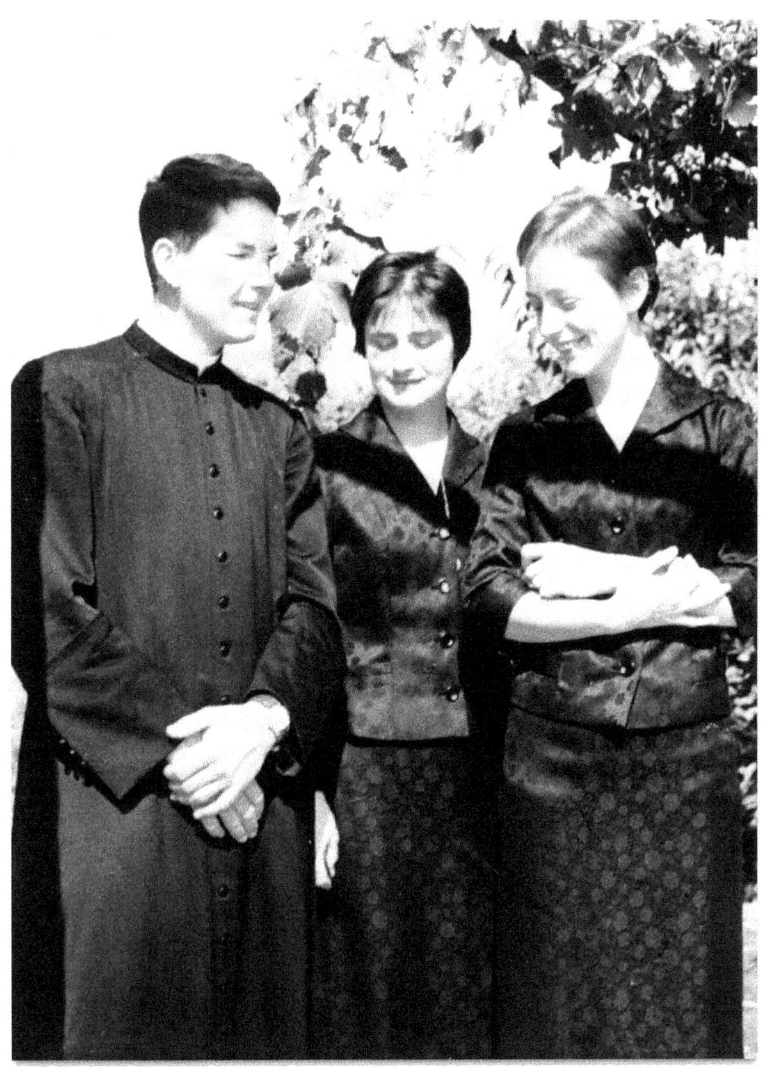

Bruno, Carla and Lidia (1959)

CHAPTER EIGHT

Giuseppe

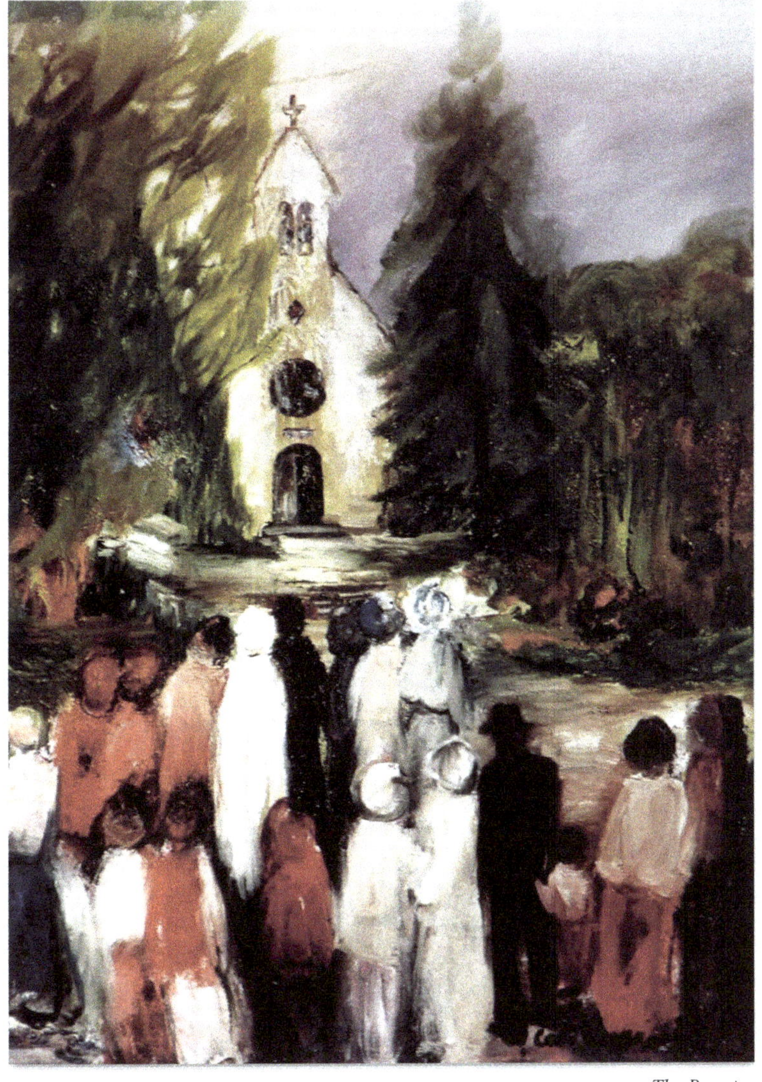

The Promise

If time heals all pain, then I could say that in time, I started to become myself again. I smiled even though I was sad, I laughed though I cried too. I remembered, however, the example of my father—to approach life with kindness, commitment and above all, hope.

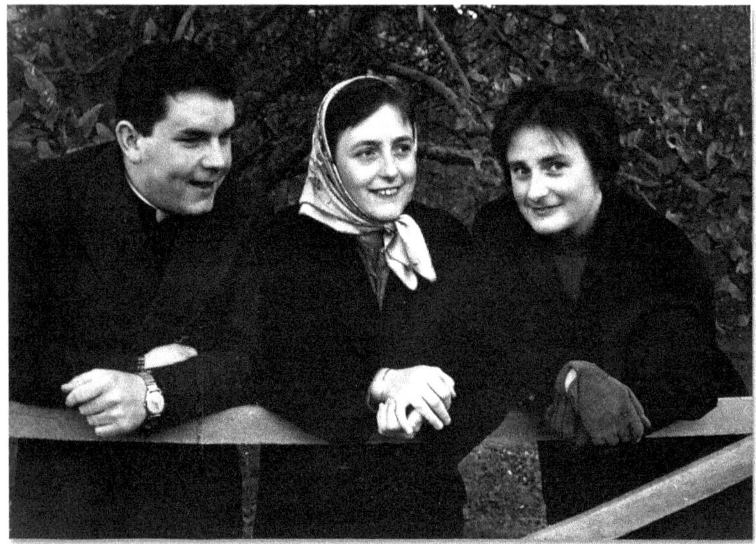

Bruno, Lidia and Carla (c.1960)

After completing my exams at the *Ca' Foscari* in Venice, I transferred my studies to the *Università Cattolica* in Milan. Attending class in *Milano*, however, would not be possible because I needed to continue working in my job at the City Hall of *Appiano*. I needed to find someone willing to help me study from home if I wanted to continue my education.

Benito Mazzucato, a classmate who was also studying at the university, agreed to share his semester notes from the classes we were taking together so that I could prepare for my final exams in each subject. His family was living nearby in *Bolzano,* so he would often stop in *Appiano* to help me study.

Then, on a wintery day of December in 1960, while Benito and I were busy preparing for our upcoming exams, my brother Bruno, who was home from the seminary, came into the living room to inform us that Benito's brother had arrived to give Benito a ride back home to Bolzano in his car.

I was surprised to hear that Benito's brother had a car. It wasn't common back then. And I was even more surprised to learn that Benito's brother had come to Italy from Chicago, in the United States, to be home for Christmas.

Giuseppe Mazzucato was waiting in the kitchen with Lidia and Peiga Pingerra, a dear, old family friend who had lived in separate quarters in our house since our childhood. He was sitting at the table, completely at ease, as Benito greeted his brother and introduced me. I didn't imagine that I made any impression at all.

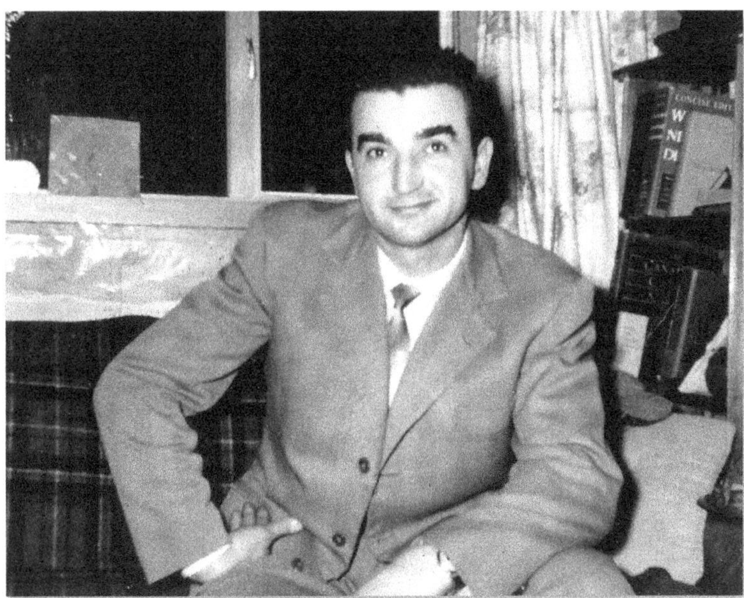

Giuseppe Mazzucato (c. 1960)

My appearance, at the time, was…not the best. I was still in mourning from my mother's passing and dressed in black as was the custom. My hair was short, messy and certainly not styled, and I still had buck teeth. And since I had never used makeup in my life, I was simply very plain looking.

Yet later, what I would be told by the handsome, young man now sitting there in my kitchen, was that when he saw me, my eyes were so sparkling and my voice so pleasant, that his heart jumped, and he thought to himself that he had finally found the girl he had been looking for. "I found her," he said softly to himself.

A few days after that "introduction," I was at work and looking through the local newspaper when I saw the front page news with a picture of a car accident—a large American car, a Pontiac, had been hit by a little, Italian Fiat in a narrow street of Bolzano. The driver of the American car was Giuseppe Mazzucato.

Since I was standing in the receiving room of the *Appiano* City Hall, the only place where the employees could use a telephone, I immediately picked up the phone and called Benito. His youngest of three sisters, Ottelma, answered and told me that everybody was fine, and that Giuseppe was out seeing to the repairs of his car.

Days later, I was busy at work again when Mr. Moscon, the man in charge of receiving and relaying city communications around town, usually by bicycle, came to get me in the office where I worked. He was always teasing me because I was the youngest in the office and, in his mind, in danger of ending up old and single like the other women who worked there.

But that morning, he hurried into the room happy to announce that the voice of a young "sweetheart" was waiting for me on the phone in his receiving room…finally.

Giuseppe had phoned to thank me for calling to check on him, and he asked, quite politely, if he could come to visit me when his car was fixed. Of course, I was happy that he should come, and told him that any evening after six would be fine.

A few days later he drove to town in his big car with his sister Ottelma. We all enjoyed an evening of songs and music, Lidia at the piano while I sang. It was a wonderful time of togetherness, like those gatherings I remembered from what seemed long ago now, when my mother and father welcomed friends to gather around our table. The cold, wintery day, had suddenly became so warm and tender, and I wondered…was this love?

After that first visit, I asked our old friend, *Signora* Pingerra, to sit by the telephone at home while I was at work so that I wouldn't miss any calls in case Giuseppe called again. And he did call.

Even though there was so much snow that winter, Giuseppe took me on many rides in his car to neighboring towns and places like *Merano, Renon, Ortisei, Soprabolzano* and even up the mountains of *Passo Sella.* We went south to *Trento* to visit Bruno, who was back at the seminary, and while there, told him that Giuseppe and I were now engaged.

On a beautiful diamond ring of white gold, Giuseppe had inscribed his name and the date, January 28, 1961. And I had promised that in one year's time, I would take my first flight ever to come visit him in Chicago. He would be waiting for me and would introduce me to America, and then, if I liked it there, we would be married.

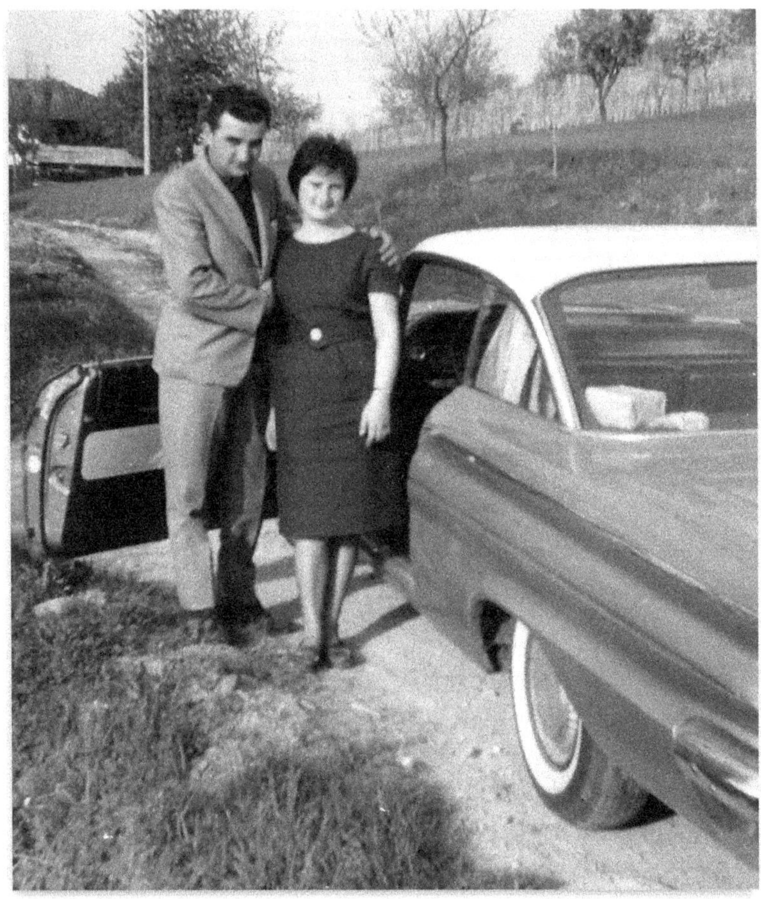

Giuseppe and Carla (1961)

That spring, Giuseppe's sister, Ottelma, married her fiancé, Remo Gaiba, who was finishing his military service in *Bolzano* before returning to his home in *Bologna*. Giuseppe made sure that everything needed for the wedding was provided. It was his way of showing his love for his family as well as offering a final farewell to all the friends who had gathered.

Later that April, Giuseppe was booked for passage back to the United States on the ship, the *Leonardo da Vinci,* en route from *Genova* to New York.

I was full of emotion during the trip down to the port in *Genova*. Benito and I accompanied Giuseppe there, where his American car was loaded back onto the ship, and he then departed on the sea.

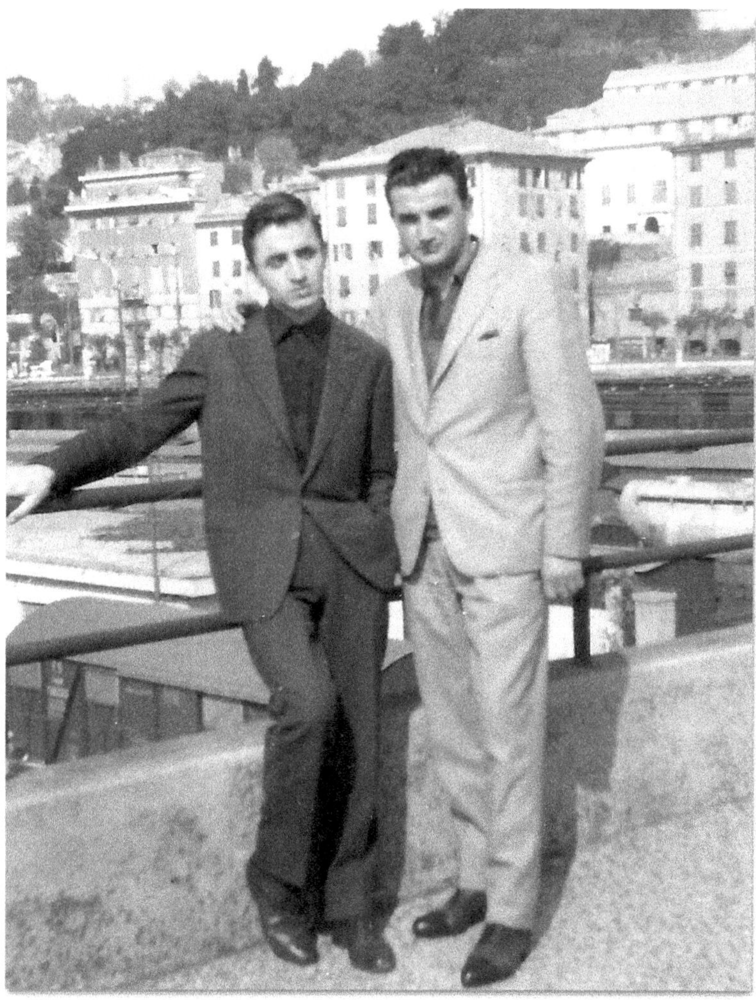

Benito and Giuseppe Mazzucato (1961)

I had never felt like this before, joy and sadness together. Could it be that I was so full of love in such a short time? I had only known Giuseppe for five months, and while my promise to visit next year still provided an opening for me to change my mind, I was ready, I thought, to follow him across the ocean.

I was alone as I traveled on the train back to my small, Alpine town of *Appiano,* and quietly, I cried all the way there.

Giuseppe and I corresponded by mail continuously over the next year, and I remember how he used to fold his letters to me diagonally so they couldn't be read through the parchment-thin airmail envelopes. His sentiments were very sweet and always seemed to end with a sincere hope that I wouldn't change my mind during our time apart.

But any anxiety that I felt melted into a smile that next spring when I said goodbye to friends and family in *Appiano* and traveled to the airport in *Milano* with my brother and sister to depart for a new shore.

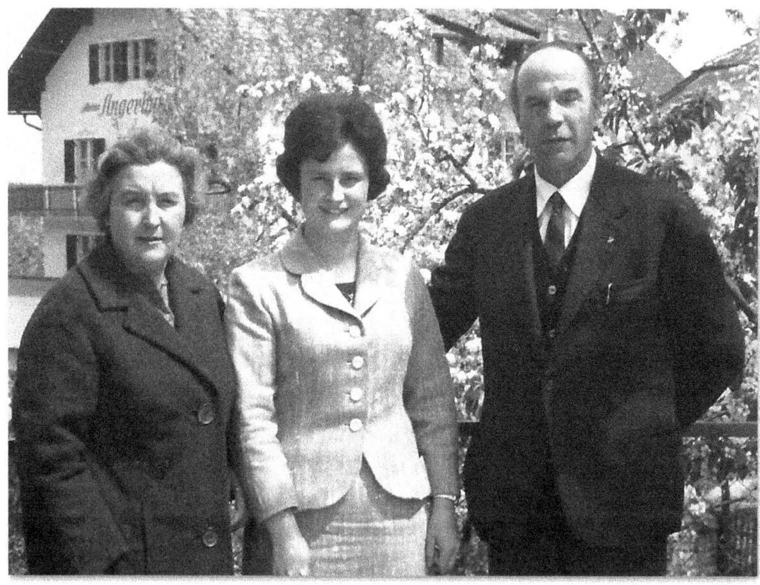

Zia Idotta, Carla, Zio Ugo Rizzi (1962)

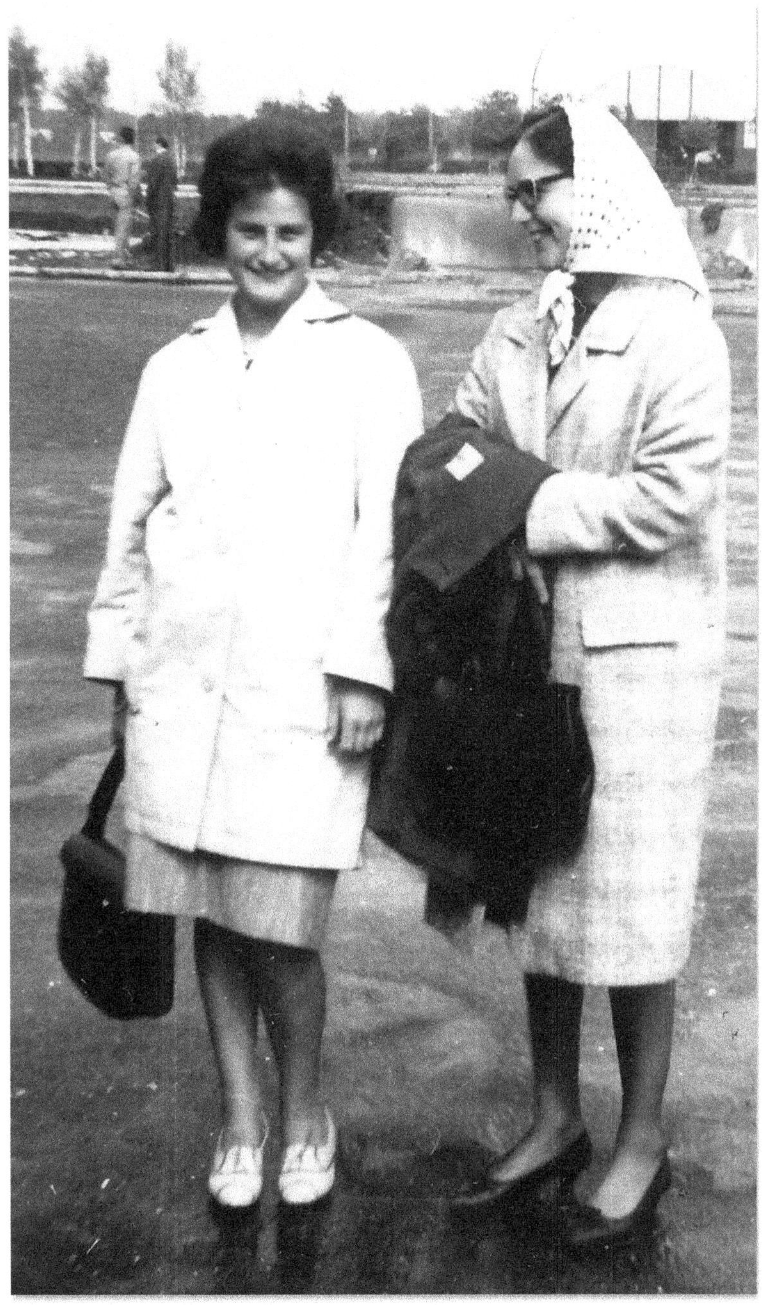

Carla and Lidia (1962)

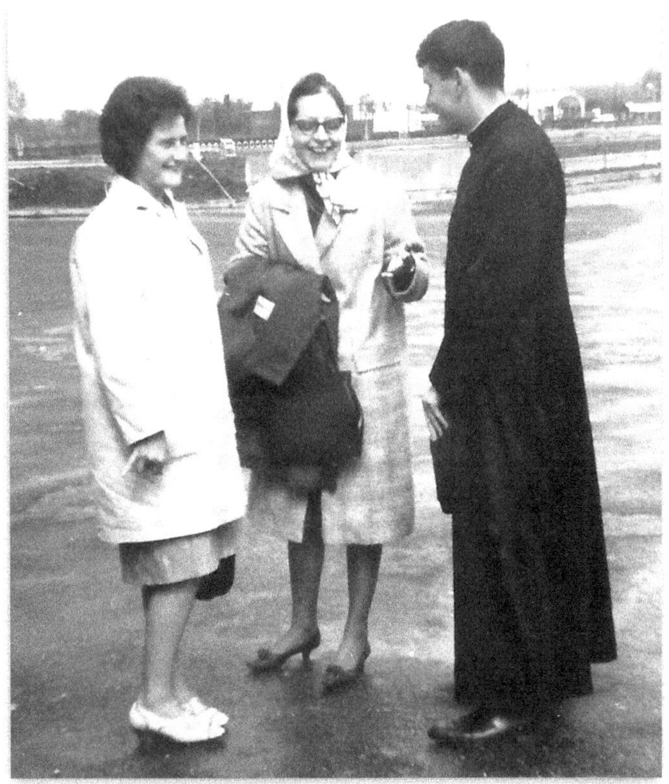

Carla, Lidia and Bruno Carli (1962)

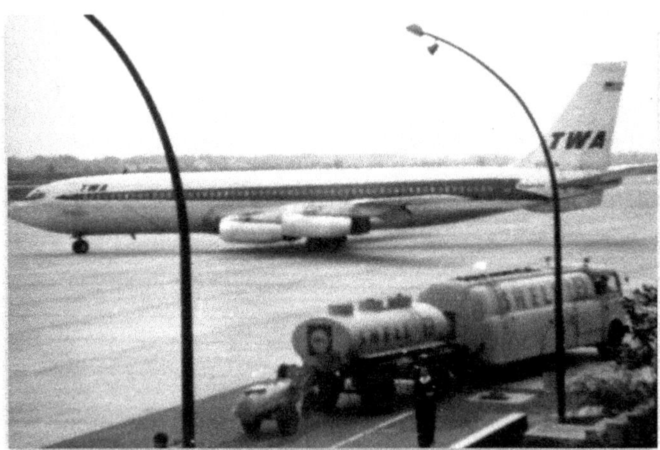

Flight to the United States (1962)

A NEW SHORE

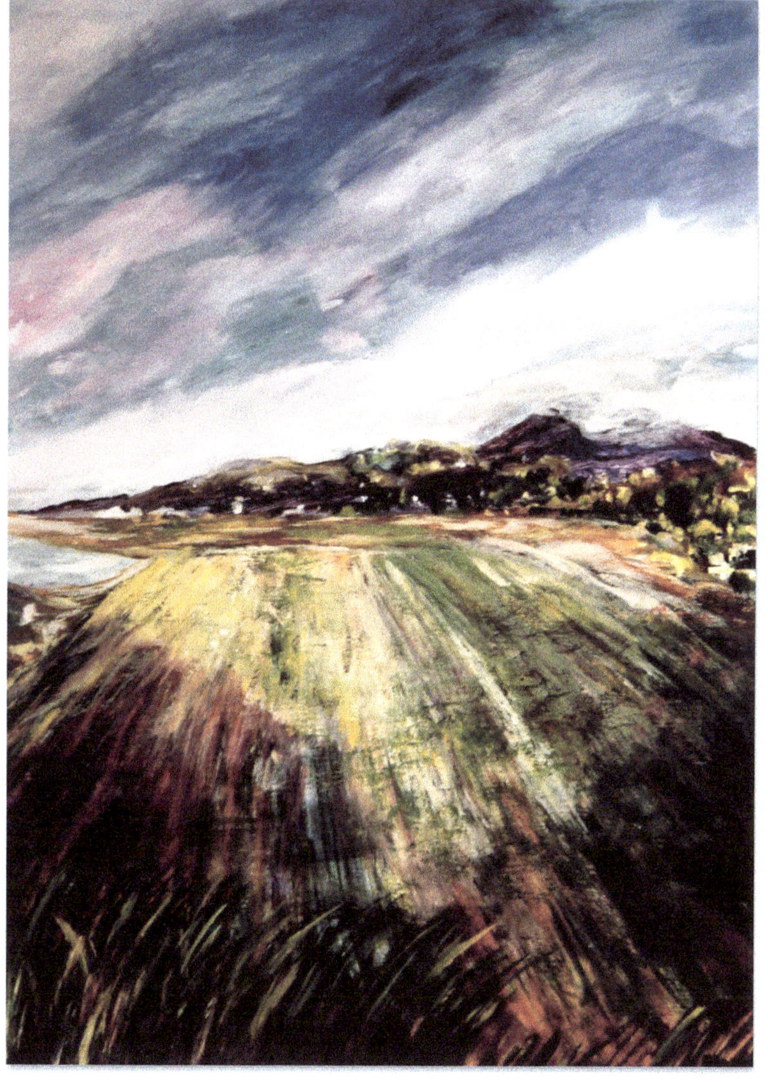

Blue Sky

Life in Chicago

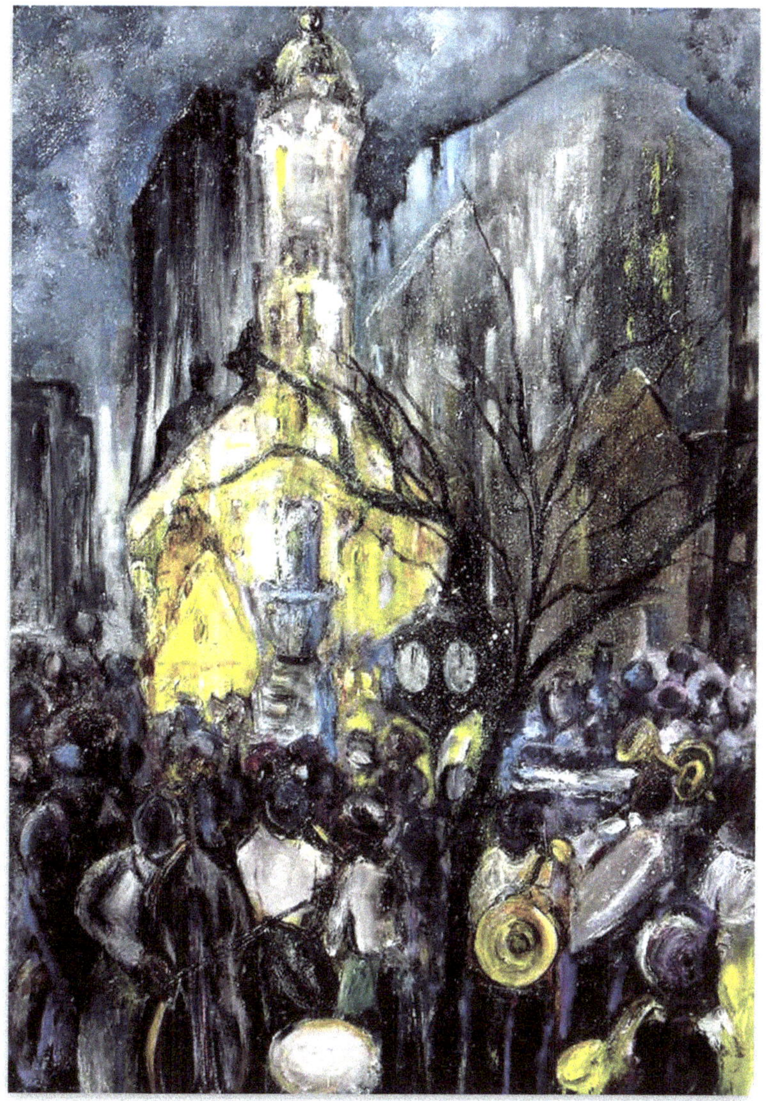

Chicago Blues

Be strong to hope, O Heart!
Though day is bright,
The stars can only shine
In the dark night.
Be strong, O Heart of mine,
Look towards the light!

Adelaide Anne Proctor

It was May 4, 1962, and from high above in the blue sky, I saw the wide, flat Midwest of the United States as my TWA flight from Milano descended toward Chicago below. It was my very first flight, and though I was nervous, I was excited too. A year had passed since my uncertain farewell to Giuseppe had taken place, and now I found myself returning to him, but leaving behind my family, my home and country. It would be a big adventure in a new land where I would start a new life.

Giuseppe had provided the plane ticket for me to join him, and I was happy to be traveling to see him again, but I was restless during the long flight and very thirsty. The airplane hostess asked me what I would like to drink and started naming a list of choices that confused me, but when I heard Coca-Cola, a drink that was also sold in Italy, I gladly said yes.

The flight had stopped first in New York, and not understanding that my luggage would automatically be sent onward to Chicago, I had desperately tried to explain to the flight attendant, in my broken English, that my suitcase was lost. Luckily a fellow passenger spoke German and was able to explain to me that all my things would be waiting for me when the plane landed in Chicago.

I still remember the astonishing sight of the blazing, orange sun on the western horizon over the Chicago

O'Hare Airport runway. I had always seen sunsets over the towering mountains in the Alps where the light would duck behind the peaks and fade into night from high above, so seeing the sun so close to the earth was a spectacular sight.

I felt as if the earth were expanding before my eyes, just like my heart was inside me. I gazed at the land beyond the airport, the highways and the streets, the houses so small by comparison, surrounded by a sea of green trees. I was ready to begin.

Giuseppe had lost some weight in the year we were apart, but my heart was light and I felt almost breathless when I saw his most wonderful smile as I exited the plane. He had a swirl of black hair sweeping past his forehead in the breeze as I saw him, and I thought he looked even more handsome than when I had last seen him.

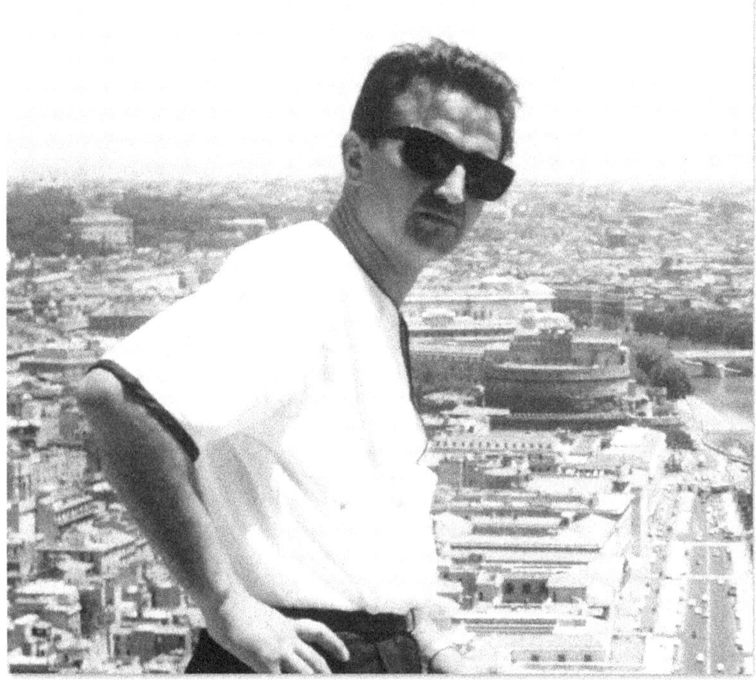

Giuseppe (c. 1962)

He had arranged for me to stay with the Boccagni family whom I had met the year before in Italy. They had a home in Steger, about thirty miles from Chicago, and Giuseppe had wanted to make sure I would be comfortable staying with them once I arrived and until our wedding.

I thought they were wonderful. Osvaldo and Franca Boccagni welcomed me as if I were their own daughter and had prepared a special dinner with Italian wine for that first night. Because I was still so thirsty from the long trip, Osvaldo kept refilling my glass, and though I was certainly happy, I think I may have become…a little too happy as I celebrated my new life.

Osvaldo and Franca had four children: Enzo and Oriana, who went to school every morning, and Marisa and Janie, their two youngest who stayed home with their mother.

Franca was a marvelous seamstress and was always busy making dresses for her daughters, while I only knew how to hem my skirts. But I was eager to learn, so Franca happily taught me. I used to tell her that she had the hands of a magical fairy, which made her smile.

Giuseppe had a rented room in a house on Phillips Road, not far away, but because he worked the evening shift at Osvaldo's machine shop, I had time to myself every morning before he would arrive to see me.

I would often take walks along the wide, tree-lined streets of Steger and admire all the neat, little houses with their front and back gardens called "yards." Though none of the homes had fences, I had the sense that the whole city was very orderly and well planned…and quiet. I wondered, "Are all hours of the day so calm?"

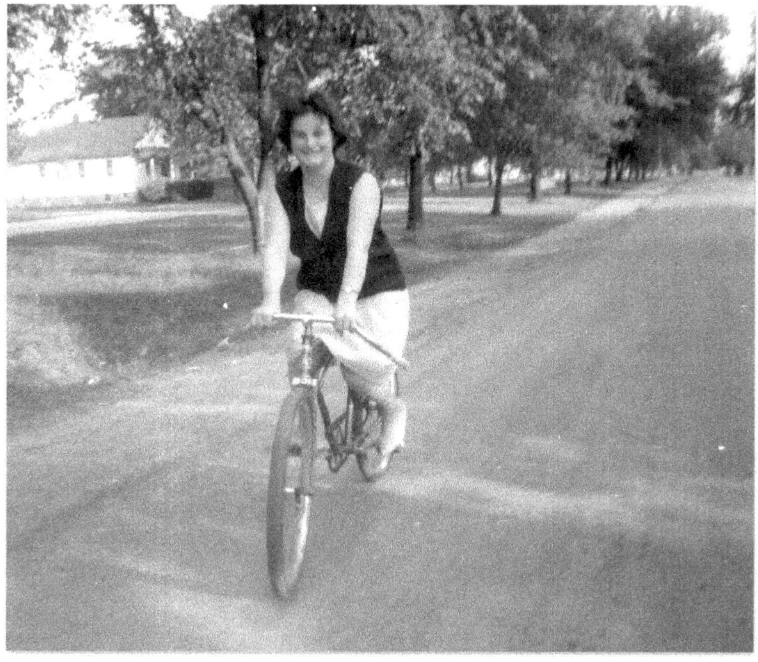

Carla, biking in Steger (1962)

It seemed to me a quiet village with green trees and green lawns, no central town square and no traffic noise, but I felt welcomed and secure. I told myself that I would love this new land.

People in the streets greeted each other quite casually by their first names and smiled at me with a warm, "Good Morning," or "Hello," even if they didn't know me. People were spontaneous and friendly, and English rolled off the tongues of children playing on sidewalks and on lawns, making me eager to learn the language better myself. I was becoming confident and ready to assimilate this new culture.

Giuseppe knew that I was writing to my family every day because I was missing them, so he began to introduce me to his friends and co-workers. They were mostly Italian immigrants too: Gino and Maria Luisa Beatrici, Silvio and Carmela Ciscato, Mario and Anna Sauro, Luigi and Jeanine Fiorelli, Cesare and Hermine Salvatori, Al and Julia Lobbia, Ernest and Maria Dalle Molle…

Every weekend I met Giuseppe's friends, and I quickly realized how appreciated and respected he was. He was a good man, honest and hard-working, and I was looking forward to beginning our life together.

There were about twenty couples from among Giuseppe's co-workers that were invited to our wedding. They all called him by his American nickname, Joe, because it was short and easy to pronounce. I started using it too because I found it cute.

His friend from *Padova*, Silvio Ciscato, and many of his friends who knew him back in Italy called him Bepi instead. He answered to them all. Of course, the only name that never changed was the one I would soon take for myself: Mazzucato.

My Wedding

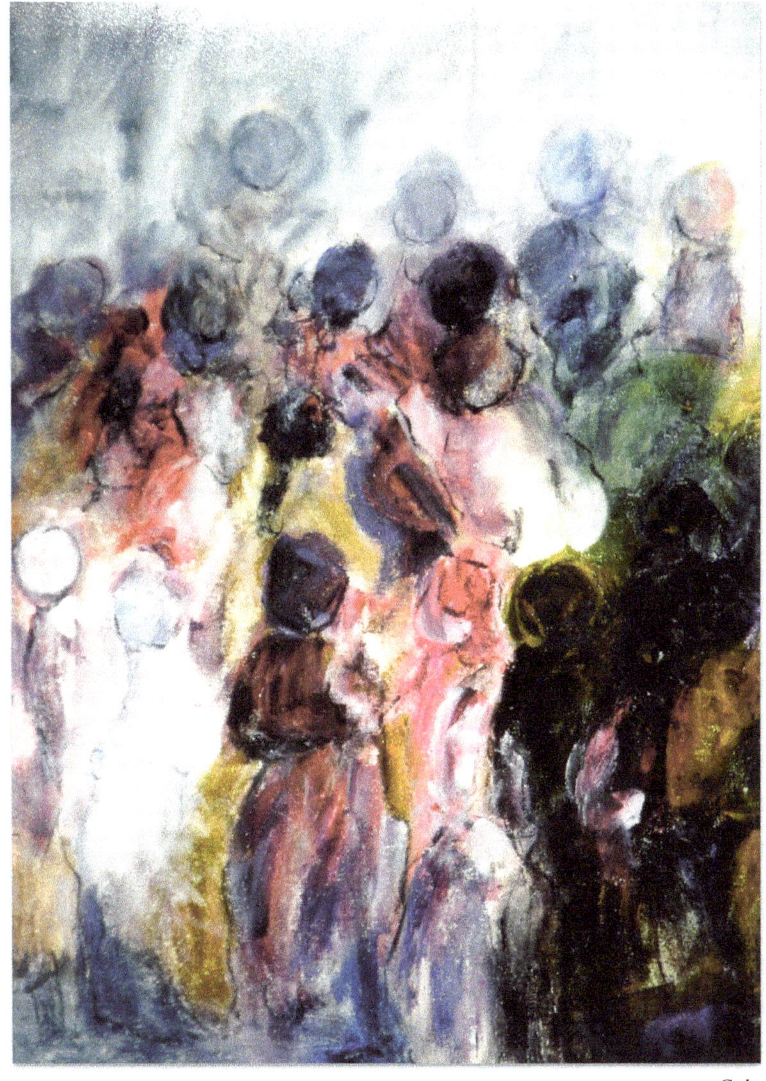

Gala

Before our wedding, there were a few appointments we had to make. Most important was our visit to the city clerk of Cook County, Chicago, to apply for our marriage license. I also had to report my arrival and wedding plans at the immigration office. A visit to a doctor for a medical examination was then required to screen out immigrants who might be ill or infected with diseases.

There was a short time, during my first weeks in Chicago, where I felt that there might really be something wrong with my health. The weather was hot and very humid and I often felt that I couldn't breath.

Joe had wondered if perhaps I had changed my mind and was looking for a way out. He told me that he would make arrangements for me to return if that is what I wanted, but I assured him that my feelings toward him had not changed. Seeing his smile actually helped me adjust to the heat, and soon everything was back on schedule.

Since I had arrived initially on a student visa, I also needed to find an immigration lawyer to prepare and present all the documents I would need so that I could remain in the United States.

Mr. Ciambrone was the lawyer that was recommended to us. He was Italian, connected with the right people, and his office was conveniently close in Steger, but he was unusually expensive. We understood, though, that it was the cost of doing business, and Joe was ready to pay him what was required to take care of everything.

Most of the offices I visited during that time were located in the center of Chicago, where I saw, for the first time, the skyscrapers that I had only seen on postcards before then. Somehow, I had expected to find them everywhere, as if the city landscapes of all the tall buildings from my imagination would stretch across the whole United States. I think that such a big change from the small town life I had known till then would have been a big shock. So I was happy that I had first been greeted by the neat, little houses along the streets in Steger.

After some time spent searching, Joe and I found a small, two-room apartment on the upper floor of a house in Chicago Heights at 1221 Wilson Ave. It belonged to Ennio and Olga Mazzoco, the couple that lived on the first floor. It was a quiet neighborhood, and while I had never lived in a small apartment before, it would become our first home together after the wedding, so for me, it was close to heaven.

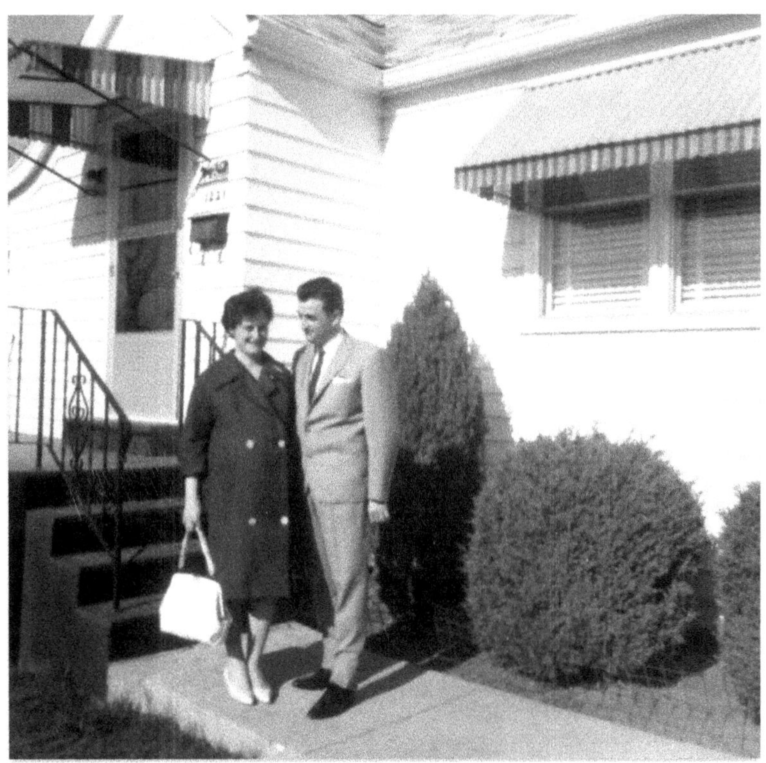

House in Chicago Heights

On June 16, 1962, in the church of St.Anthony of Padua in Roseland, just west of Chicago, I walked the aisle accompanied by Osvaldo Boccagni, proudly standing in for my father. Franca joined me at the altar where Joe was waiting with his *compare*, his best man, Gino Beatrici.

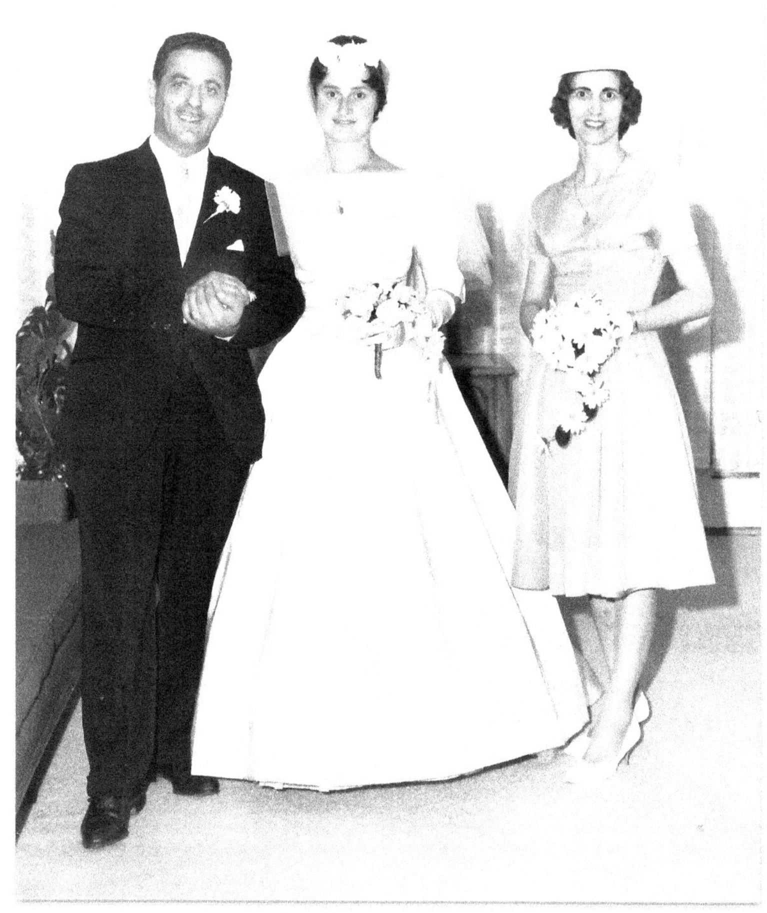

Osvaldo and Franca Boccagni with Carla (16 June, 1962)

All the preparations had been handled, and though I was far away from my country of birth, alone among all these people I barely knew, I felt confident as I settled at Joe's side, ready to begin my new life. I remember Joe's face, his eyes were shining and happy as I gave him my solemn promise of love.

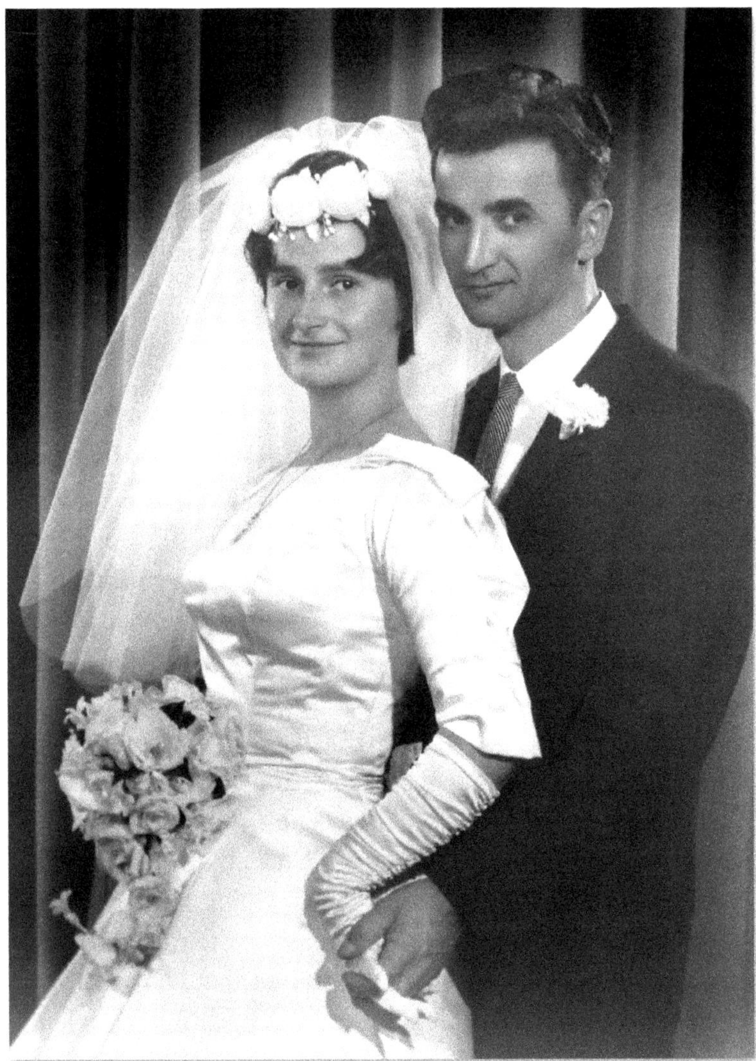

Carla and Giuseppe Mazzucato (June 16, 1962)

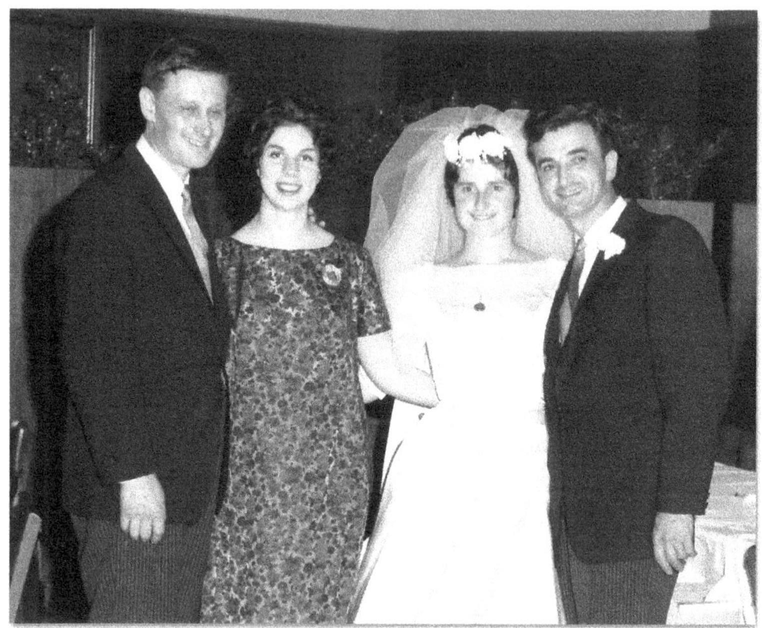

Gino and Maria Luisa Beatrici, Carla and Giuseppe Mazzucato (1962)

For our honeymoon, we took a week-long trip to Niagara Falls. When we returned, Joe went back to work, and I began my life as a young, married woman, ready to embrace this new culture. I learned English with lessons I received from Sister Janet, a Dominican nun that was a teacher at the High School in Chicago Heights. Every morning, I walked to a park near our apartment to study under the cool shade of a large tree there.

I was also within walking distance of the house of Jeanine Fiorelli, and that of Anna Sauro, who both became good friends. Anna had come from Europe during her high school years and was of Polish and German descent, so we would speak German and sing songs together to pass the time. She also liked to sew and knit and had learned, from her father, to paint ceramic, Tyroler figurines in the style of Hummel.

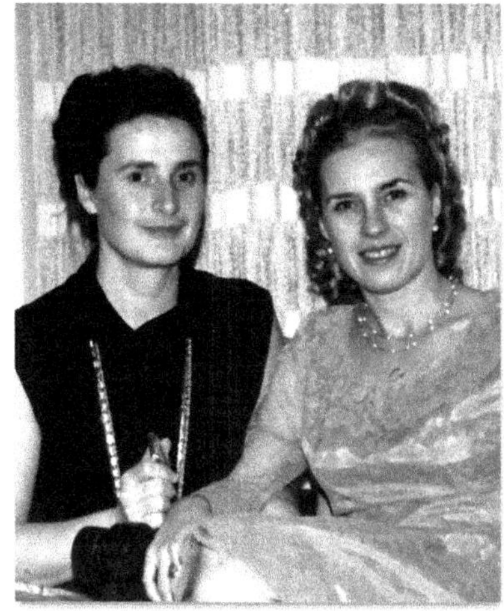
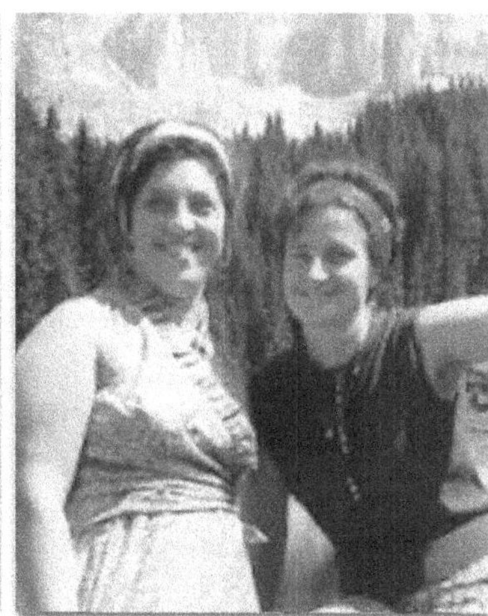

Carla and Anna Sauro   *Jeanine Fiorelli and Carla*

On weekends, Joe and I would always visit the Boccagni family, and almost every Sunday we drove to Roseland to go to Mass and then spent the rest of the day with Gino and Maria Louisa Beatrici.

Maria Louisa knew everything there was to know about the city of Chicago, and loved to make plans for our Sundays together. We went to concerts in Grant Park, to the ballet, the cinema and different museums. We even attended a performance by Luciano Pavarotti in Hyde Park.

I was so happy to be able to see so many new and interesting things, and to have such wonderful friends. Maria Louisa was so kind and brilliant, with a lively personality and intelligent curiosity. She became my true and beloved friend, and I spent many hours with her as I embraced my new life in America.

I remember that she liked to point out that she was born on May 29, the same day as President John F. Kennedy. She was so proud that we had such a good and respected leader in Washington D.C., and though I was not even a citizen, I realized that I was proud too. It was indeed a good time to be in America!

By July, we were quite settled in our place in Chicago Heights, but it was still missing those personal touches that would transform it completely into my new home.

I had left Italy with very few personal things, only what I could fit in my one suitcase, so my sister, Lidia, had packed a large steamer trunk that would be shipped with all my wedding gifts, clothing, linen sheets that my mother had embroidered years ago, my books and notebooks from my studies…and bundles of old photographs of my family and friends. I was happy when we received the news that the *Montrose*, the ship from Italy, would soon be arriving in Detroit.

Joe left for Detroit early in the morning, a five hour drive from Chicago, and when he returned later that evening, I hurried out to see my cherished belongings. But all he had was unthinkable news. The *Montrose*, with all its cargo including my trunk, had sunk to the bottom of the Detroit River.

I didn't believe him at first. I was sure he was joking, and I asked him to stop. But it was true! It was as if all my past, with a single, blunt blow, was gone. It seemed as if I were being taught a hard lesson about not growing attached to material things. I was being told not to look back but to focus forward instead. But how could I?

Motherhood

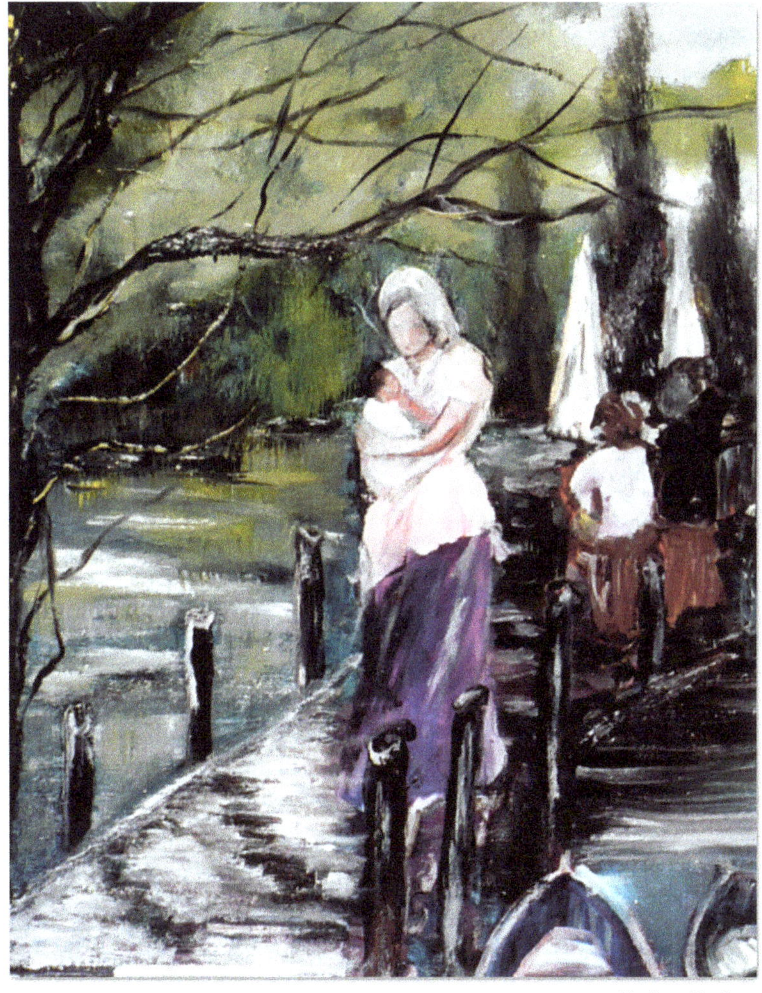

Endless Rocking

Like looking to the seasons ahead—summer to autumn, then winter to spring—*forward* is always where hope is found. My life was full of joy again when I learned the wonderful news that I was expecting, and my first child would arrive that next spring.

The sadness I had felt for the lost things from my past was suddenly replaced by immense joy. I felt certain again of the direction my life was taking, like I was fulfilling my destiny, and I looked forward as I busied myself with all the preparations for the event.

Joe celebrated the news in his own, quiet way— becoming even more tender and loving as he saw my happiness.

In my seventh month, though, joy almost took a dark turn. I began bleeding, and for a week I had to stay at the Hospital of St. Francis in Blue Island, worrying that I might loose my baby. I was afraid, with lingering anxiety about being there, since both of my parents had passed away in Italian hospitals. But I had no choice. I had to stay.

I received the best care by the doctors and nurses, and the lady next to my bed, who had given birth to five boys and was now hoping to give birth to a new girl, gave me courage. She put me at ease with her "knowhow," and assured me that it would all turn out fine. Then she gave birth…to another boy. She wished me well as she left and smiled as if to say, she'd be back to try again.

Soon after, it was my turn.

On April 27, 1963, at 5 pm in Blue Island, Illinois, I gave birth to a beautiful and sweet, seven-pound girl. She was twenty inches long and had a full head of dark hair. She opened her eyes wide to greet me and I thought how she looked so much like her father. Even Olga Mazzoco, our landlord, used to call her "little Joe." We named her after her two grandmothers: Anna, the name of my mother, and Virginia the name of Joe's mother.

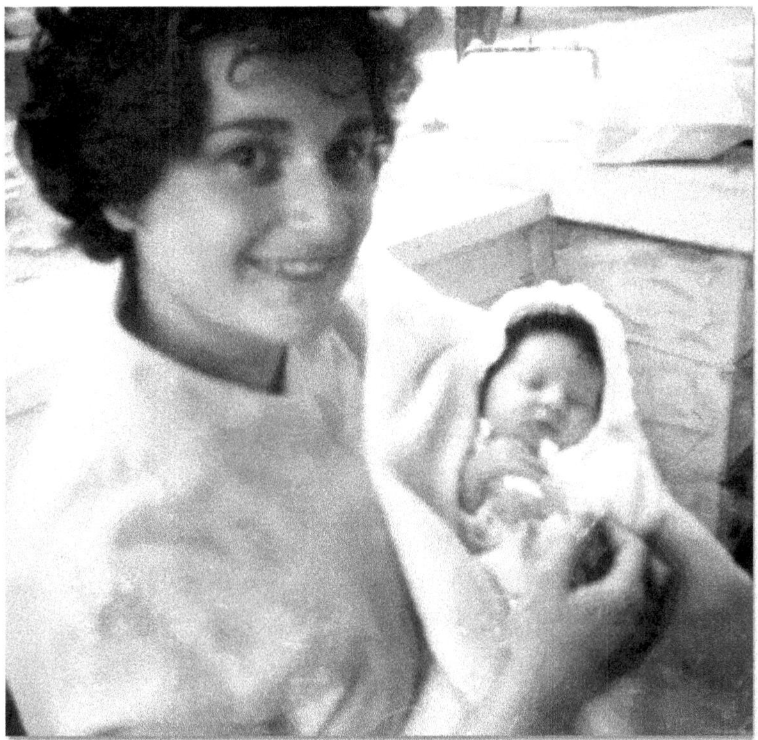

Carla and Anna Virginia Mazzucato (April 1963)

A new child in the family changes your life. Now, my time for reading and studying was limited, and instead I spent more time watching Anna and snapping pictures with our new Kodak Instamatic camera.

I felt a little lost from not having my mother or even my sister close to me, and not being able to show them my baby, but Dr. Sesking, the pediatrician, put me at ease on our first visit by telling me that Anna was "just perfect." She was healthy, and for me, alone as I was in a new world, that was everything.

Another expression that was new to me—one that I would hear often from that point on—was that my baby was a "cutie-pie." I thought that was just wonderful too.

While I was full of joy at home, however, the world outside was being shaken. I was occupied with the events taking place in my immediate circle of experience—caring for Anna, adjusting to a new place, a new language, new friends, a new life. The political unrest that was reported daily on the news seemed distant and unclear. Most of what was happening went practically unnoticed by me…until November 22, 1963.

On that day, the terrible news of the assassination of President John F. Kennedy shook the whole world. Throughout the country, time seemed to stand still, and in that moment, everything changed.

Mr. and Mrs. Mazzocco and all our neighbors huddled in the street, most of them crying in disbelief. Maria Louisa, so proud of her shared birthday with President Kennedy, was stunned silent. Joe was at work when the news was broadcast, and I was alone with my thoughts. I could only embrace my young baby to feel some measure of comfort. The unbelievable had happened. It felt like a family member had been killed, and a dark cloud had settled over the country. It was a sorrow felt around the world.

Kennedy's short presidency had been all about courage and intelligence, with a youthful energy and style that made the future seem exciting and full of potential. Through him, there was grace in the country's leadership.

The president loved poetry and used it often in his speeches. He wrote: "When power leads man toward arrogance, poetry reminds him of his limitations. When power narrows the area of man's concern, poetry reminds him of the richness and diversity of existence. When power corrupts, poetry cleanses."

Less than a month before his assassination, in remarks made at Amherst College, President Kennedy spoke of how he, like the great poet, Robert Frost, believed that "our national strength matters, but the spirit which informs and controls our strength matters just as much." He believed that a "great artist is…a solitary figure," and art was a "form of truth" that must "nourish the roots of our culture," because in serving that "vision of truth, the artist best serves his nation."

I couldn't have known then how these words would eventually play out in my own life, but in the death of President Kennedy, I felt that a great force for change and for good in America was extinguished, and I could only turn inward to my little family for comfort.

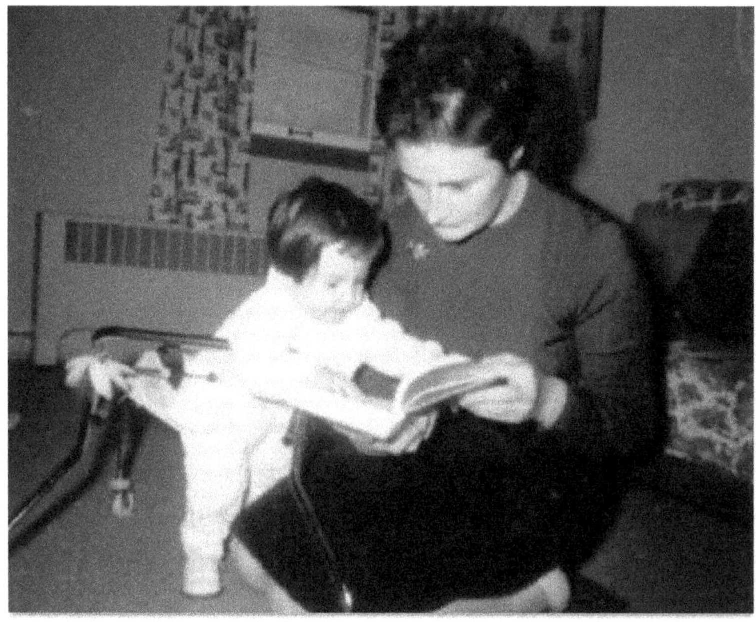

Anna and Carla (1964)

Anna took her first steps at eleven months old, and from then on she was never still for very long. She wandered everywhere. Soon, she learned how to go faster. She waited for her papà to kneel down so she could climb onto his back. Then he would be her *cavallino*, her little horse, and she could ride around the living room. He was devoted to his little girl even if he had to crawl on the floor after a long day at work.

During Anna's second year, she began to sing and dance when we played her two favorite albums—*Eine kleine Nachtmusik* by Mozart, and *The Sound of Music*—on our new record player. As expressive as she was with me and her father, though, she was quite shy around other people.

On one occasion, when we had taken her to a party at the home of the Dalle Molle family, the many people gathered inside the house frightened her, and Joe had to walk with her outside for the entire evening, which, of course, he was quite happy to do.

In the following years, I had to leave Anna twice when I was rushed to the hospital. I had two consecutive miscarriages after Anna, and it definitely affected her…and me.

She was too young to understand what had happened, what I was going through, and why I had left her with Franca Boccagni both times, but she felt abandoned and offended. After the second time, she even refused to embrace me when I returned home.

It was a terrible feeling for me to have twice lost a child, and then to have my daughter resentful, but without my mother to help me through my own fears and feelings of guilt, I had to suffer in silence.

Joe tried to comfort me as best he could, making sure that I knew he loved me and was quite happy even with our little family, but it would take a while before I could get past the fear that our little family would remain just that.

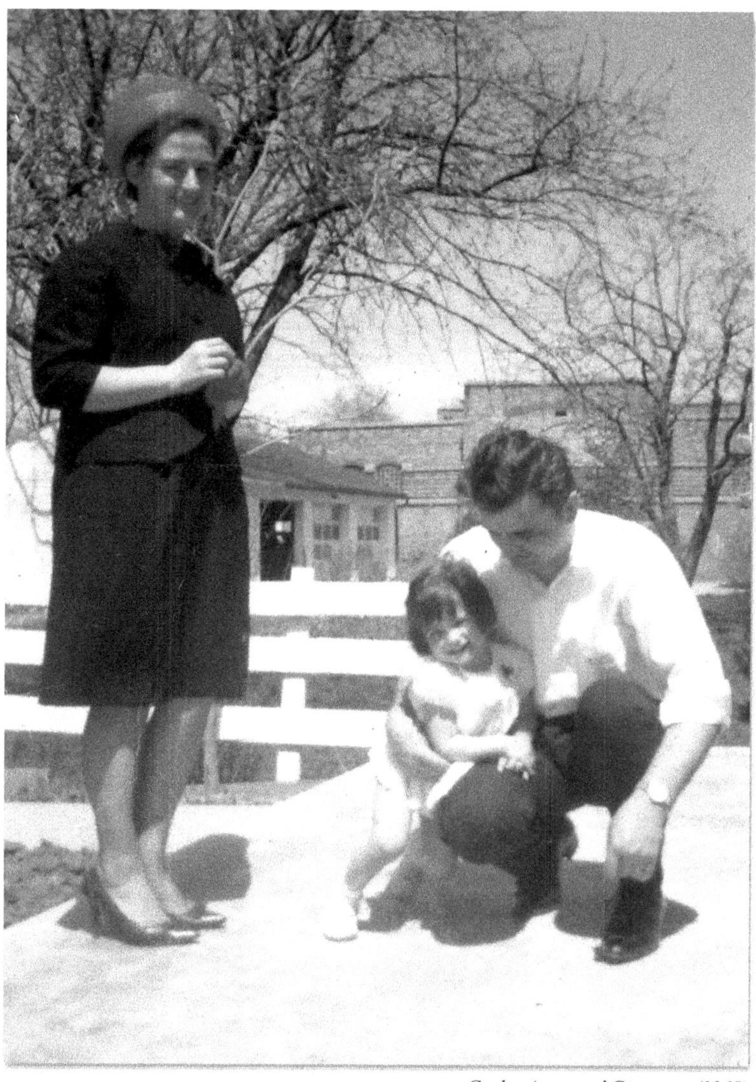

Carla, Anna and Giuseppe (1965)

114

Into the West

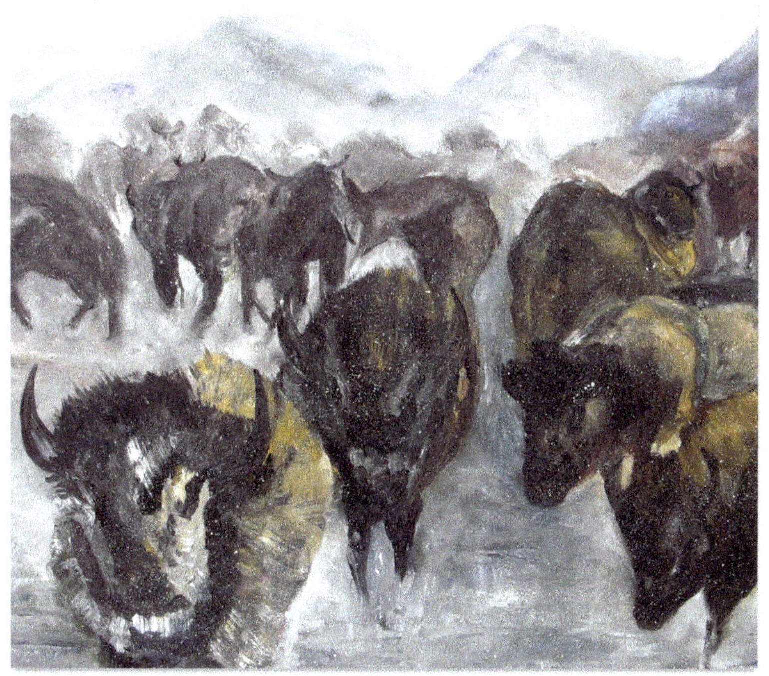

Where Buffalo Roam

I stand at the shore of a changing world,
where every stone turned can reveal a new life.
And I do touch the earth
every moment of each day.

from the poem "Every Stone," pvm

In the Summer of 1964, Joe decided a change of scenery would be nice and decided to take us for a long trip along the great and vast American highways to go and see the West. He had never been there, but he had promised me that he would take me to see the mountains that I missed so much.

First, he planned to drive west to the Black Hills of South Dakota to see Mount Rushmore. Then, onward and further west and south to cross through the Rocky Mountains in Colorado.

In the back seat of the car he made a sort of bed for Anna. She loved to travel short stretches to go to church on Sundays, or go shopping or to the beach, but this would be a long ride, and after driving the long hours of the first day of the trip, she was worn out and wouldn't stop crying until she felt asleep. I felt so bad, and wanted Joe to stop the car, but he had planned the entire trip and needed to keep to his schedule.

There was not much to see while driving West, a blazing sun and a never ending road in front of us. It wasn't the lush and Alpine landscape I was used to. I realized then how incredibly vast the United States was. It was a land where the horizon stretched out further before you with every mile traveled—wide prairie below and infinite, blue sky above. It was silent and empty between the small towns that would suddenly appear along the highway to embrace you and define a moment of space with something intimate and familiar then disappear again as the road went on.

We drove through the Badlands National Park and finally saw the Black Hills of South Dakota. They were shrubby, rolling hills, not mountains like those in my mind. What was very interesting, though, was seeing, for the first time, herds of bison roaming the plains as they moved like waves over the pastureland.

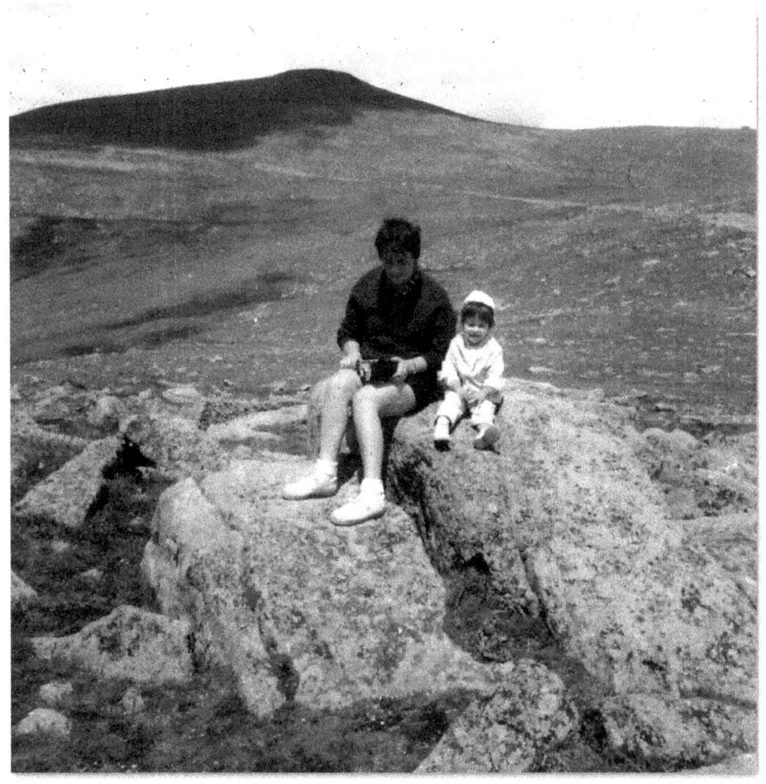

Carla and Anna (1964)

In Rapid City, we spent our first night in a motel near a spot in the Black Hills where we were told that Crazy Horse and Sitting Bull, great chiefs of the native Sioux tribes, had led a series of uprisings in 1876 and achieved a great victory at the Battle of Little Big Horn.

The Lakota, or Western Sioux, and the Teton Dakota tribes, that united under Sitting Bull, were hunters and warriors who followed the buffalo herds and had signed a treaty that granted them rights to the sacred Black

Hills. But when gold was discovered in the territory, white settlers forced them out. In 1890, in the Battle of Wounded Knee, the U.S. army massacred over three hundred Sioux.

Here was a history that I knew nothing about, and yet it was another sad example of war that I knew too well. It was the last, big fight between Native Americans and the U.S. government, and we saw many monuments and places to mark and record the sad events from that time in history.

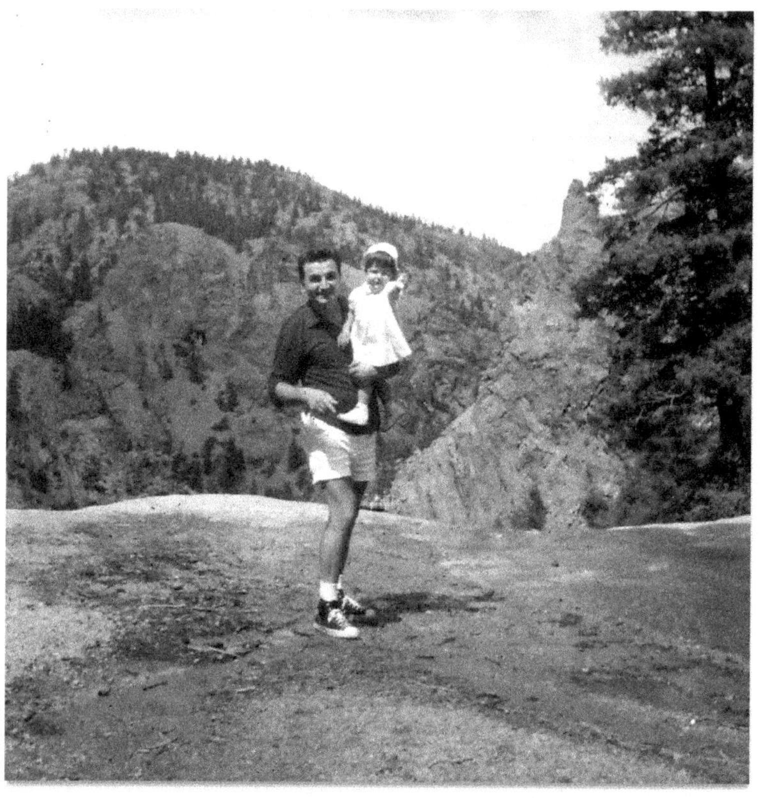

Giuseppe and Anna (1964)

The Mount Rushmore National Memorial is the world's largest sculpture. I remember arriving before the mountain onto which the majestic heads of four American Presidents—George Washington, Thomas Jefferson,

Theodore Roosevelt, and Abraham Lincoln—were carved. It was stunning. The white granite shined in the blazing sun, and the four faces gazed out quietly over the landscape.

We were greeted there by a Native American dressed in traditional Sioux clothing, a feather tucked into his long hair. He was sitting alone, smoking a long pipe, and willing to take a picture with us. Knowing now the history of the contested land of the Black Hills, the memory is tainted with a note of sadness, but at the time, it was a fascinating encounter.

Anna, however, did not think so. She was still shy around other people, and while she watched from a distance, she was not quite ready to embrace the unknown.

We passed through the state of Wyoming under a blanket of clouds. At one point, I remember hearing a rumbling noise that seemed to be getting closer as we drove along. Suddenly, the cloak of fog thinned, and we saw a large herd of buffalo descending along the prairie to the side of the road. It was a beautiful and powerful image.

Eventually, we reached the state of Colorado and drove up into the Rocky Mountains. They were so different from the Alps I loved. They were rugged and desolate— peaks covered by trees, but no walking trails to reach the tops. In fact, we drove through most of the National Park without ever setting foot on the ground.

We ended up in Colorado Springs where we rented a cottage to stay for few days. At Seven Falls, there was a beautiful series of waterfalls inside a large canyon between two towering rocks called the Pillars of Hercules.

Impressive as it was, Anna was more fascinated with the small squirrels that liked to come close to the visitors looking for a nut or two.

We drove to the top of Pikes Peak, the highest summit in that part, over 14,000 feet, where the air was cool and dry. I thought it was breathtaking, but while I was standing and waiting for Joe to take a picture, I saw a young gentleman actually lose his breath and faint because of the thin air at the high altitude.

The following day we visited the Garden of the Gods where the mountains of sandstone were raised by movements in the earth and sculpted by the wind and water into intricate formations that tower hundreds of feet in the air. The mountains, shaded in orange and red, are sacred to the Native American Ute people, whose oral tradition holds that man was first created among the rocks in the "garden."

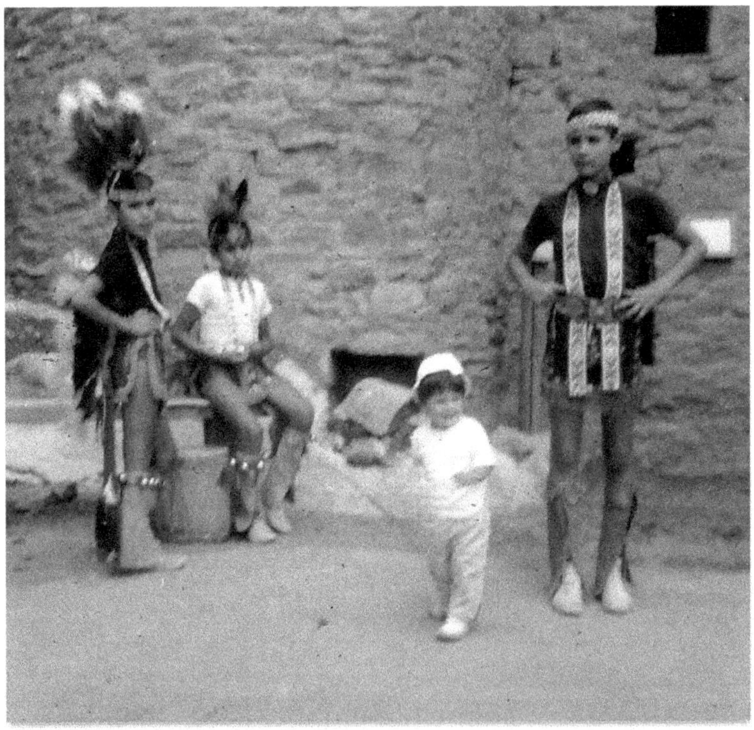

Anna and Native American dancers (1964)

Our next stop was at the Ancient Cliff Dwellings of the Ancestral Pueblo people in Mesa Verde. In caves carved under outcroppings of rock, the ancient Pueblos made their homes.

It was afternoon when we arrived there, and a group of young boys performed a traditional dance for us. This ended up being the highlight of the whole trip for Anna, as she finally shook off her shyness and danced along with the the beat of the drums.

We visited Denver, the capital of the state of Colorado, then continued on through several other states until we reached the mighty and magnificent Mississippi river in Hannibal, Missouri. To me, the wide river looked like the Adriatic Sea, immense with what seemed like no visible river bank on the other side. It was another moment when I felt the vastness of the United States before me.

Then, at last, we arrived home in Steger, Illinois. Before our trip to the West, we had moved from our small apartment above Mr. and Mrs. Mazzoco, to a small guest house in the back-yard of Osvaldo and Franca Boccagni.

I was so happy to live close to Franca. She was like a mother to me and taught me many things I needed to know to start a family. I particularly cherished her advise on being careful, slowing down and taking care of myself. I had always done all the heavy work around the house when I was a young girl in *Appiano*, but I was no longer that girl. I was a young woman, in a new situation…because I was now carrying a new baby in me.

Things were going well for me and my new pregnancy until February 6, 1966. That day, Joe had an accident. He was working in the machine shop of Osvaldo Boccagni when a machine press that he had repaired the day before was recalibrated by another worker. When the machine froze again, Joe went to see why, and in a moment that would change the direction of our lives, the machine suddenly unfroze and slammed down, smashing his middle finger on his right hand down to his first knuckle.

I rushed to the hospital to see him. He was pale… and angry. If the other worker had left his repair alone, he wouldn't have lost his finger. He had made clear a few times that the press they were using was worn out and had to be replaced, but that hadn't been done. Joe decided, right then, that he would not go back to work in Osvaldo's shop.

Though I was due to give birth on February 12, the scare of Joe's accident shocked my system, and I was once again afraid that I might lose my baby. I went into labor early, but on February 8, 1966, at 2pm, I gave birth to a beautiful and healthy baby boy.

Paolo Vigilio weighed eight pounds, measured 21 inches, and had hazel eyes with a touch of blue in them. I was overjoyed…and relieved. After my two miscarriages, I had hidden the fear that I would not be able to have another child deep inside me, but here I was, cuddling a new baby in my arms again.

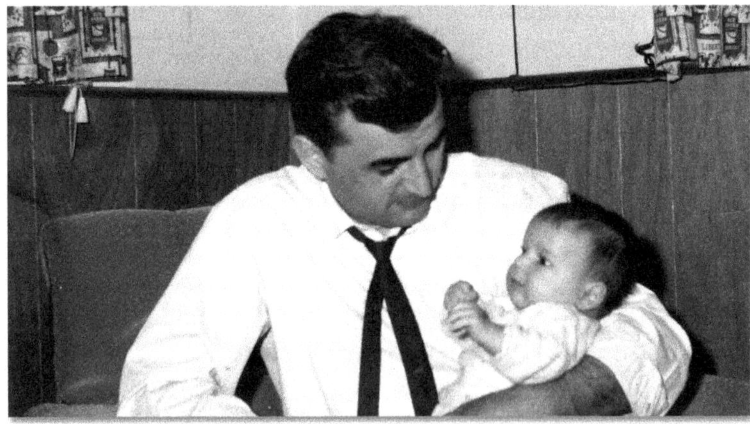

Giuseppe and Paolo (1966)

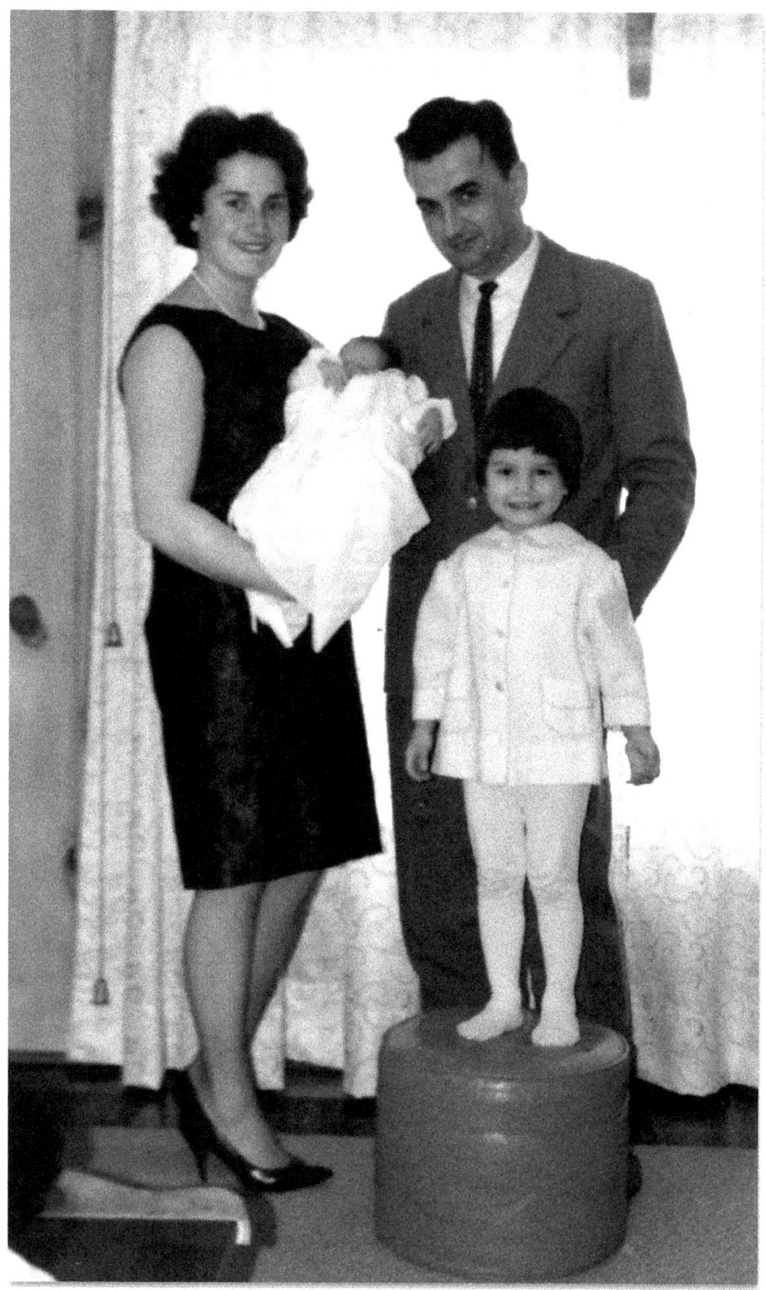

Carla, Paolo, Giuseppe and Anna Mazzucato (Feb. 1966)

Life in Michigan

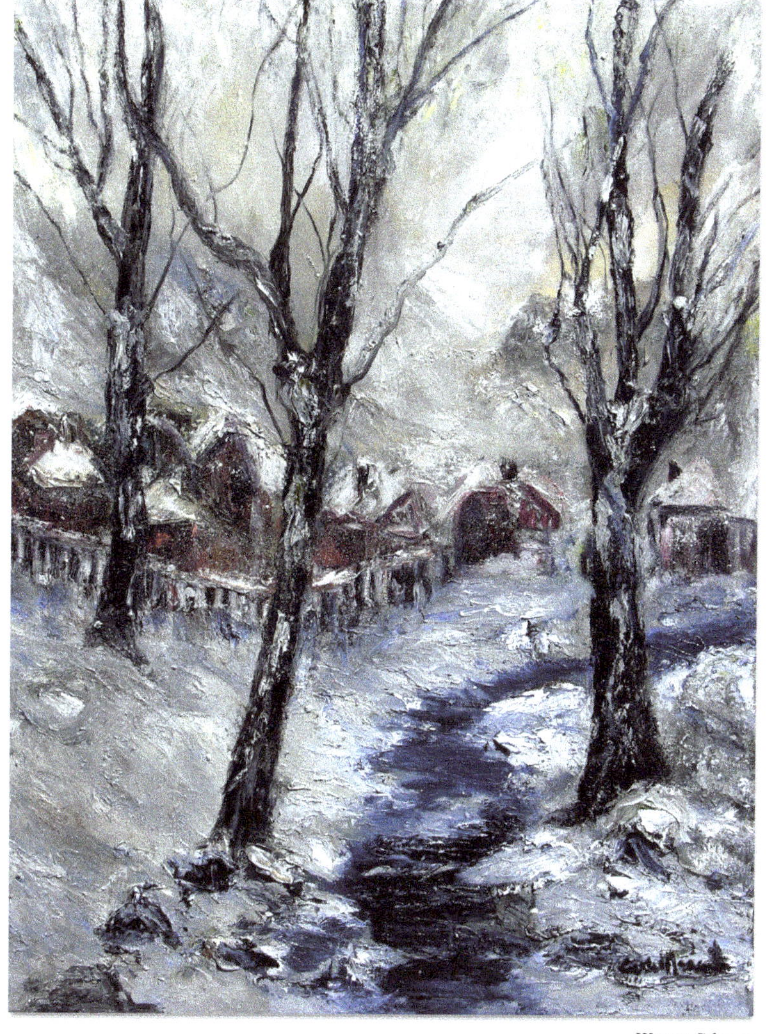

Winter Silence

Joe stayed home for the whole month of February while he recovered from his accident. Then in March, his friend Luigi Fiorelli called with an opportunity for Joe to join him at the new Ford Motor Company stamping plant in Woodhaven, Michigan, just south of Detroit. Joe went to explore the possibility, met with the people at the plant, and accepted the job offer. So, from Illinois we would have to make the 250 mile trip to a new home in Michigan.

The trip would be quite complicated, since we would travel by car with all our belongings loaded in a trailer, attached behind. Fernando, the seventeen-year-old son of Joe's friend Mario Sauro who had also moved to Michigan to work for Ford, helped with the loading and the drive, but I had to take care of both Anna, not yet three, and Paolo.

The stress affected me and by consequence, nursing Paolo became impossible. I had to try feeding him different kinds of formula, but he had a problem digesting them and broke out into a terrible body rash. Eventually, the doctor convinced me to let Paolo stay in the hospital for one day and night until his rash was under control.

When Paolo returned home, though, his sleep cycle was turned around so he slept during the day and stayed awake all night. Joe began his job at Ford, but was working on the night shift, so his schedule was turned upside down too. Trying to manage everything from our small, rented apartment in Riverview, Michigan, far away from family and friends, I felt helpless again and exhausted.

Boxes from our move to Michigan remained unpacked, just lying around the living room; I never seemed to find time or will to organize the apartment. In truth, I felt that we were not going to live there for long. We had decided to look for a house to buy, and every day that it was possible, Joe and I drove together searching in the beautiful Bretton Wood neighborhood of the city of Trenton. The tree-lined streets curved about in a welcoming way, and it was not far from West Road, the main street of town.

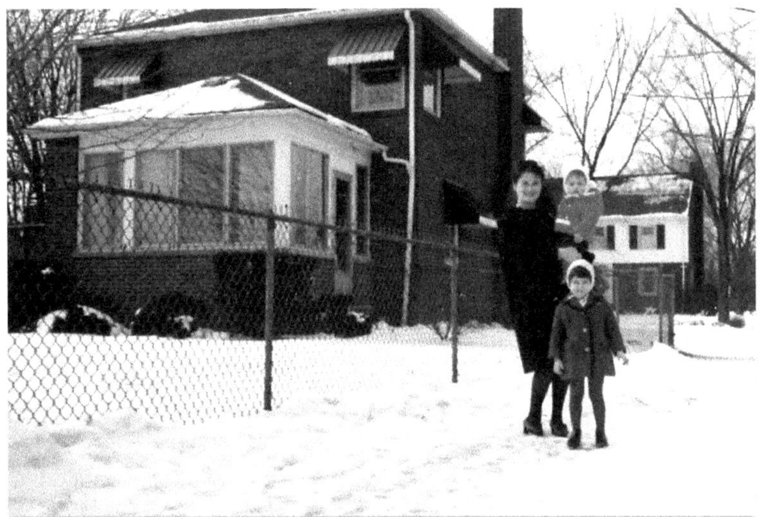

Carla, Paolo and Anna - 2605 Lenox Road (1966)

I fell in love with a Tudor-style house on a quiet corner that was selling for thirty-two thousand dollars. It was charming and would have been perfect for our small family, but it sold to a Mr. Gelina for thirty-five thousand.

Mr. Gelina, however, in moving into his new home, had to sell his old house, also situated on a cozy corner but on the next block over. So, though we would have to wait for another three months, the adorable house at 2605 Lenox Road, would become our first home in Trenton, Michigan, for the very affordable price of twenty-seven thousand dollars.

CHAPTER FOURTEEN

Returning

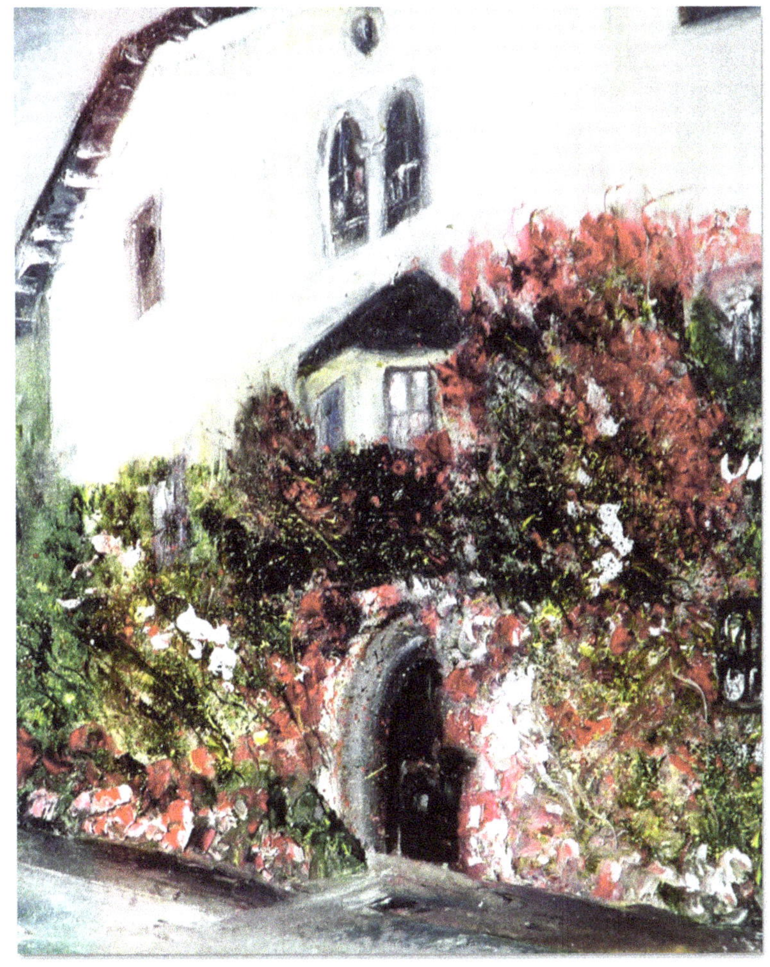

In Bloom

In June, the summer of 1966, I returned to Italy for the first time since I had departed. I had left alone four years ago; now I arrived at the *Fiumicino* airport in Rome with a husband and two children.

Joe's eldest sister, Maria, who, along with his second sister, Ida, had joined the convent of St. Paul in Rome, met us at the airport with transportation to the convent. There, all the nuns had prepared a room for us and a welcoming, Italian supper.

The arrival of our whole family was quite an event at the convent, and Anna, who seemed to have suddenly shed her shyness as soon as we touched Italian soil, found herself at ease among all the old nuns dressed in white habits from head to toe.

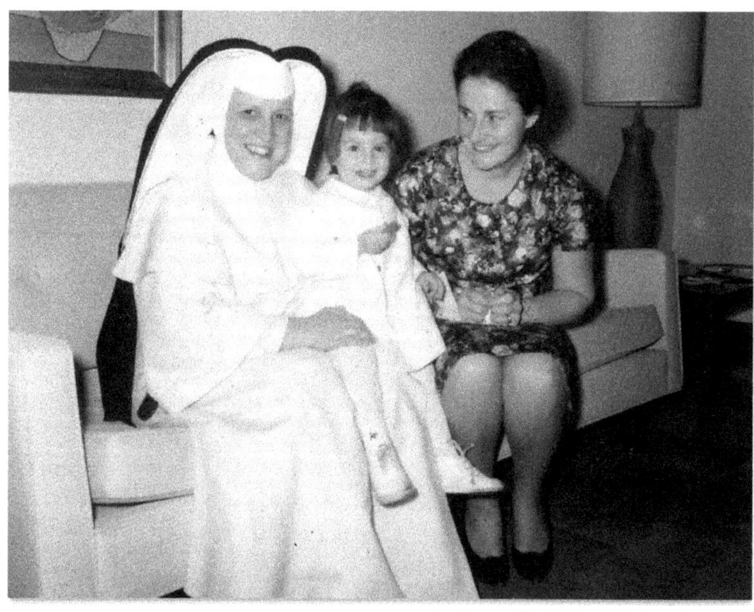

Anna... Virginia... Mazzucaaaaaaato

Joe's sister, Maria, who also went by the name Sister Virginia (in honor of her mother), proudly presented

Anna to the entire convent and to every nun they passed in each corridor. Anna, whose pronunciation was tinged with a bit of an American accent, made all the nuns smile as she repeatedly pronounced her name slowly: "Anna… Virginia…Mazzucaaaaaaato."

The next morning, after a wonderful breakfast that included a bottle of fresh cow's milk from the local farmer for Paolo, we continued our trip, heading north by train.

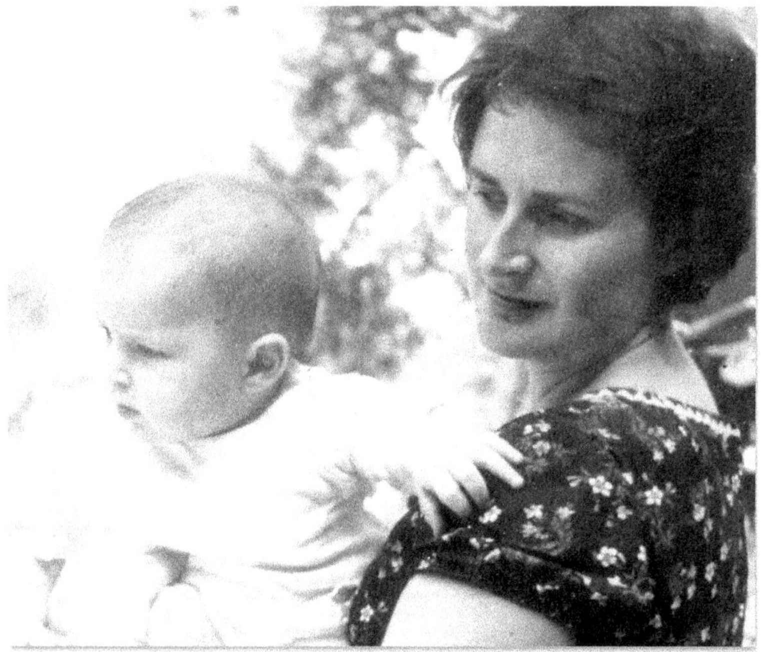

Paolo and Carla (1966)

As we approached Verona, and the first hint of the Alpine mountain peaks appeared off in the distance, my heart started to pound. It was an unbelievable feeling of joy and some anxiety at seeing the land of my youth again. I was not the same girl as when I had left, and when I saw the hills, mountains and houses along the Adige Valley, I was swept with emotion.

As the train slowed in the train station that I knew so well, I looked from the window and saw my brother, Bruno, and my sister, Lidia, with her husband, Sergio, waiting for us on the platform. Bruno was so excited for our visit that as soon as the train stopped, he reached up to take Paolo out through the train window. Joe and I then stepped down from the train with Anna and our luggage.

It had been a very long trip, and yet, I was not tired. I was anxious to see my father's house again. Strangely, every room seemed so much smaller than how I had remembered them.

That evening, we all gathered at the kitchen table, just as I had done so many years ago with Bruno, Lidia, my father and mother, and before we ate, I asked Anna to recite the short prayer I had taught her:

"Benedite Signore per il cibo
che stiamo per prendere,
Onde mantenerci in vita,
E potervi santamente servire."

(translation)
Bless us o Lord, and the food
we are about to receive,
That it may nourish us in life,
And allow us to serve you.

As Anna finished, I looked to my brother. Tears flowed as memories of the past flooded back for both of us. Then, Anna went on to recite a poem that I had taught her, a poem that my mother had written for Lidia, Bruno and me when we were young:

Volete sapere di chi sono io?
Io sono di babbo e di mamma mia.
Vedete questa manina?
È proprio tutta della mammina.
e quest'altra, eccola qua…
è proprio tutta del mio papà.
Così le mani, così gli occhietti,
le paroline e i sorrisetti,
sono divisi tutti a metà,
tra la mia mamma e il mio papà.
Non può nessuno portarmi via,
io son di babbo e di mamma mia.

Anna Carli

(translation)

Would you like to know from where I come?
I'm from my daddy and my mum.
You see this little hand right here?
It surely is from mommy dear.
And this other one, here it is,
It's daddy's hand, this one is his.
And like my hands and twinkling eyes,
my words, my smiles, my little sighs,
They all came divvied up, you see,
Half dad, half mom, and all for me.
So no one can take me away,
With mom and dad I will always stay.

Anna Carli

The next day was Sunday, and all the friends and people to whom I had said goodbye four years ago were all there in church waiting to hear of my adventures in America. It was wonderful to see them after the morning service, and since that day, every first Sunday back in

Appiano became a tradition of greeting old friends and catching up with everyone in town before beginning to visit Joe's family.

CHAPTER FIFTEEN

The Mazzucato Family

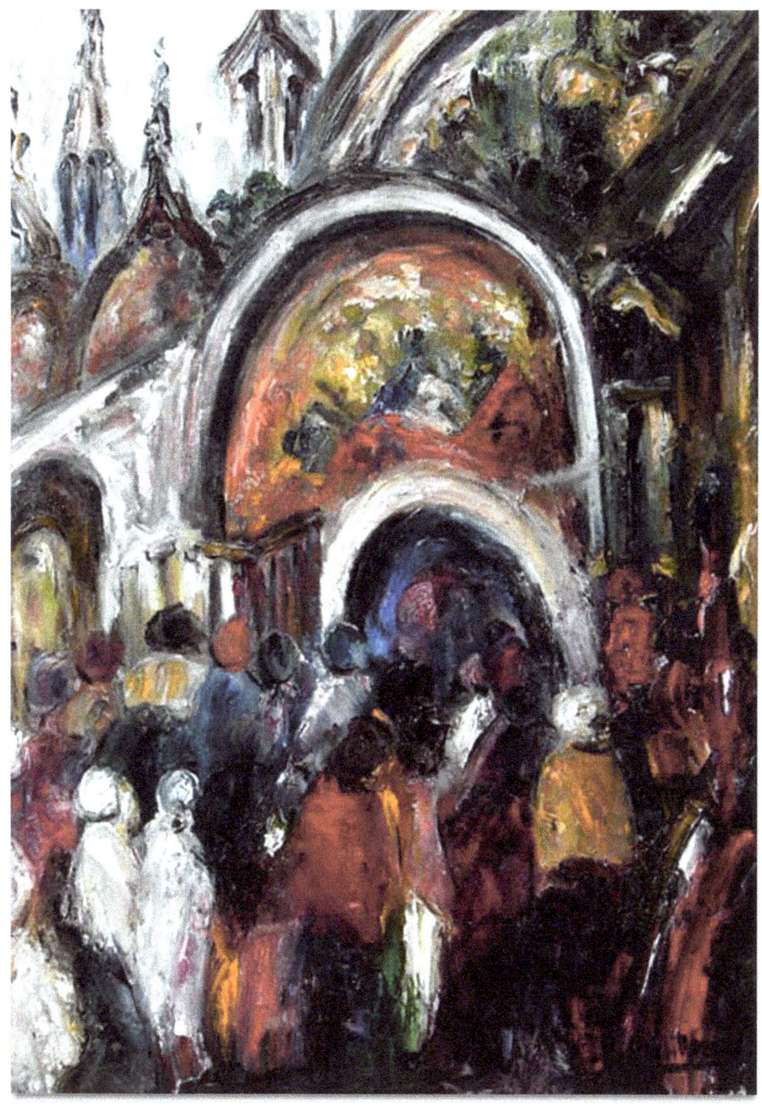

Sundown in Venice

Giuseppe was born in *Pontelongo*, near Venice, in 1925, the second son of Romano Mazzucato and Virginia Rocca. By 1938, they were a family of nine children: Tarcisio, Giuseppe, Luigi, Maria, Ida, Ottelma, Vito, Benito and Antonio.

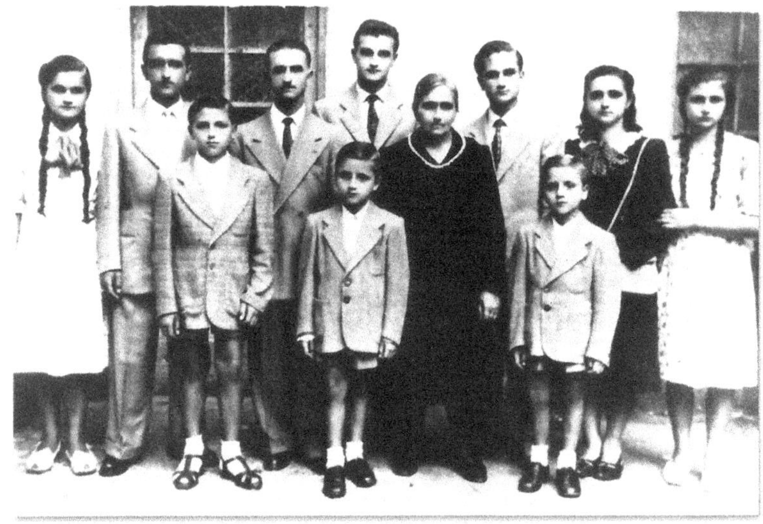

(Back) Ottelma, Tarcisio, Romano, Giuseppe, Virginia, Luigi, Maria, Ida,
(Front) Vito, Benito, Antonio

They lived on land which they farmed for a local landowner in exchange for a portion of the harvest, as was common then. At fourteen, Giuseppe had to work alongside his father in the field to help provide for his large family.

Even so, Giuseppe always found ways to divert himself from the hard work during his free time. Luigi, who was three years younger, loved to tell me all the stories of things his brother "Bepi," as he called him, had done to worry their mother, Virginia, when they had been young. Luigi was always tagging along warning Giuseppe to be careful whenever his adventures seemed too risky or dangerous.

Once, they had gone fishing in a swift flowing stream and Giuseppe had almost been swept away when he grabbed onto a bridge and flung his legs into the current to rescue a friend who had fallen in. Neither of them knew how to swim.

Other times, Giuseppe had gotten into trouble by carving out and eating the insides of melons in the field and leaving the rinds to rot, or trapping the neighbor's chickens when they wandered onto the land his father worked. After a few chickens went missing, the neighbor learned to keep them on his own property.

Virgina, was always worried that Giuseppe would get caught, if not by a neighbor, then by her husband. Romano was a strict disciplinarian and Giuseppe became a fast runner to avoid getting punished.

Giuseppe knew the fields he worked very well, and at dusk he could duck under the nearly invisible wires strung between posts along the planted rows while his father, chasing him close behind, would run into them.

Another time, Giuseppe escaped his father by leaping from a second story window and hiding in a drainage ditch until after dark. He was always considerate of his mother's concerns, though, and would whistle a signal to her in the night to let her know that he was safe and uninjured after his harrowing escapes.

For all the times Giuseppe had spent fleeing from his father, Romano was nevertheless the first person we always visited when we arrived in Italy. And it was quite clear that Romano, despite all the past mischief, was very proud of his son, Giuseppe. "Bepi" had been a troublemaker, but he had also been hardworking and responsible.

After the family had moved from the farm to the city of *Bolzano*, Romano and Giuseppe had both gotten work in the machine shop of the automaker, *Lancia*, where Giuseppe learned his trade and became one of the best and most respected tool and die makers in the company. It was what had led to his being recruited to go work in Canada and eventually in the United States.

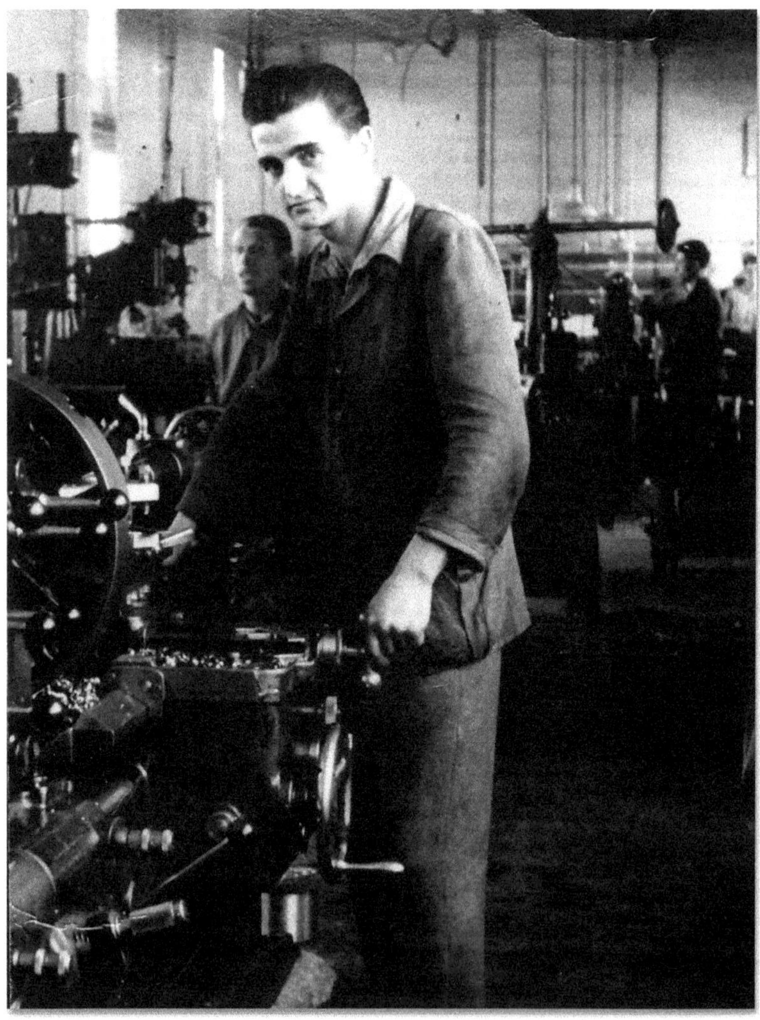

Giuseppe at Lancia (c. 1941)

During the time of Benito Mussolini, Giuseppe was already working full time at *Lancia,* but just as I had been required to participate in the singing and marching exercises of *"sabato fascista,"* Giuseppe too was ordered to attend with his age group every Saturday morning. Giuseppe begrudgingly showed up for the first few times, but decided that after a long week of working, he deserved a break, so he stopped going entirely.

On the week that his absence was noted, Giuseppe had decided to go fishing. That didn't sit well with the Fascists in charge. Under a dictatorship you obey, or face the consequences. So Giuseppe was arrested and brought up on charges of desertion. This was in July of 1943, however, and by the end of the month, Mussolini had been deposed and arrested. Mischievous "Bepi" had escaped punishment once again.

Having avoided serving under Mussolini, however, didn't protect Giuseppe once Italy surrendered and Alto Adige was annexed under Hitler. Because he was a skilled tool and die worker, however, his military service was deferred; otherwise, he would have had to report for duty in the division for which he had been selected—the second reserve regiment of Hitler's Waffen-SS.

Tarcisio, who had not escaped combat duty under Mussolini, had been sent to fight with the Italian army in Ethiopia where he remained a prisoner of war until after the war had ended. He then left for Argentina and spent many years there with his wife Elena and daughter Bianca Rosa.

Giuseppe continued working at Lancia until he left for Canada in 1959, while Luigi went abroad to look for work in Australia where he stayed for five years. Maria and Ida entered the convent of the *Paolini* sisters, and Ottelma married and moved to Bologna. Vito became a skilled tailor for a top Italian garment manufacturer until he started his own design and tailoring business, and the two youngest brothers Antonio and Benito were sent for instruction at the seminary of St. Paul in the city of *Alba*, in *Piemonte*.

When we arrived in 1966, Giuseppe's large family was still a bit spread out. Giuseppe's mother, Virginia, had passed away in 1950, and his father, Romano, now stayed with Vito and his wife Guidana and their son, Romano, named after him. They all lived in an apartment near *piazza Matteotti* in *Bolzano*.

Tarcisio, the eldest, and Luigi also lived in *Bolzano*, but Maria and Ida were at the convent in Rome, and Ottelma lived in *Bologna* with her husband, Remo. Benito was finishing his studies at the *Università Cattolica* in *Milano*, and his twin brother, Antonio, was completing his years in the seminary.

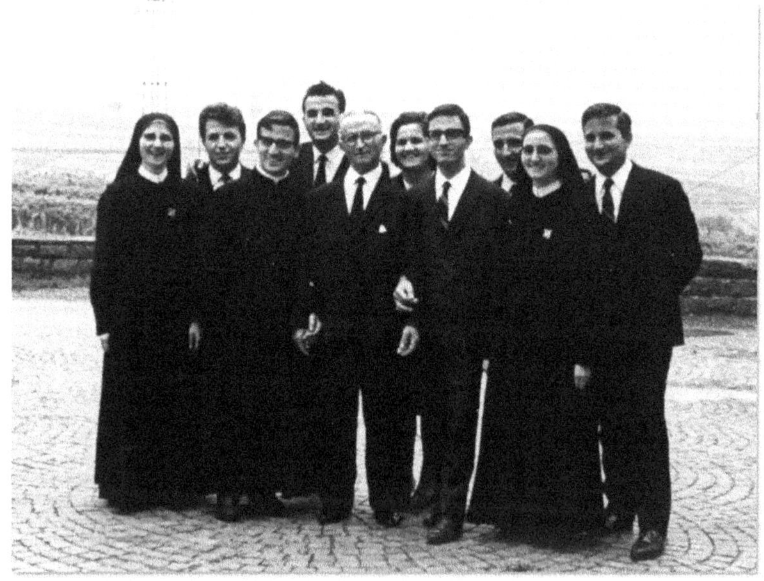

Ida, Vito, Antonio, Giuseppe, Romano, Ottelma, Benito, Tarcisio, Maria, Luigi

We spent most of that vacation at various events with the Mazzucato family—celebrating Benito's university graduation and Antonio's consecration to the priesthood, but in *Appiano*, it was Anna and Paolo who became the center of attention.

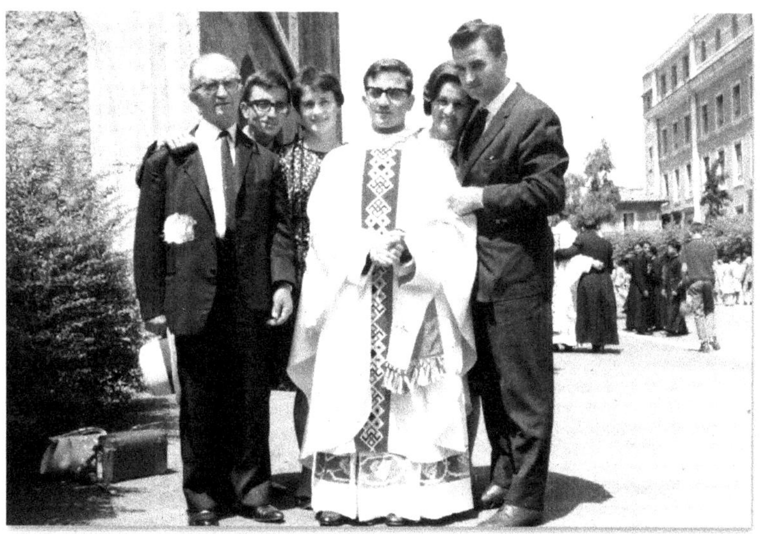

Romano, Benito, Carla, Antonio, Ottelma, Giuseppe (1966)

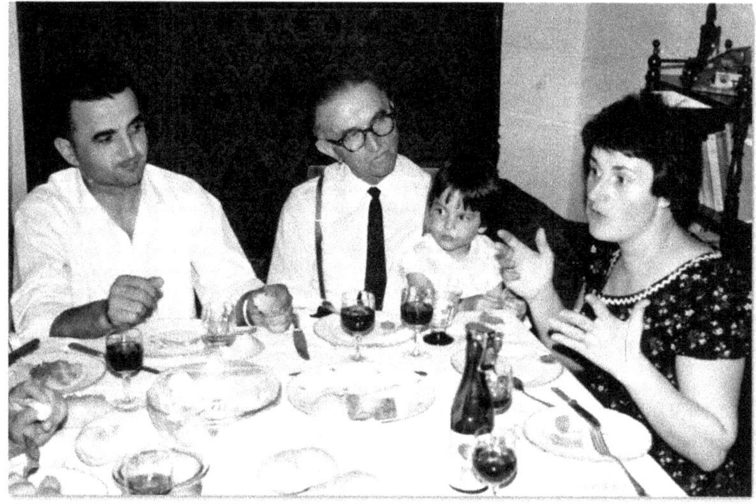

Giuseppe, Romano, Anna and Carla (1966)

Almost every day, my brother, Bruno, would ask me to "lend" him my children for the day so he could show them off to his friends all around town. It was as if they were his own children, and he wanted to spend as much time every hour with them. Even during the night, when Paolo wouldn't sleep and was keeping me up, Bruno would stay and play with him till morning so I could rest.

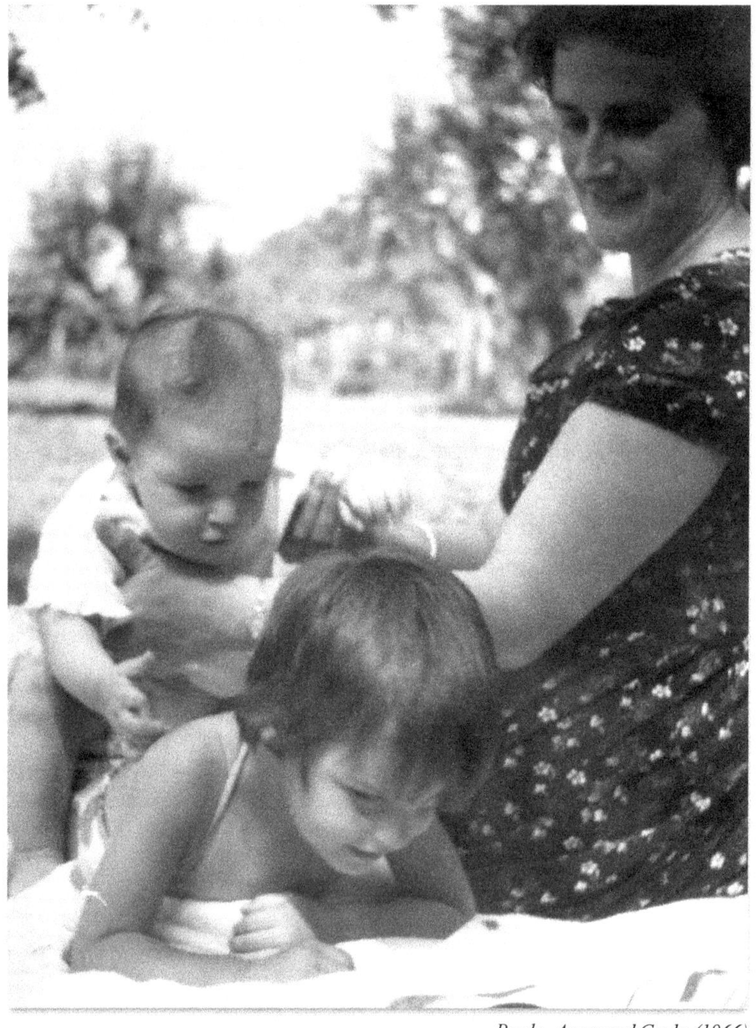

Paolo, Anna and Carla (1966)

Having so much family and so many friends around made me realize how much I truly missed them. I could go on outings with *Zia* Idotta, my mother's sister, and her husband, Ugo, and their children, Paolo and Anna Rizzi with whom I had played when I was young; I could spend time with my sister, Lidia, and her new husband, Sergio Corrà. I could walk, as I had years ago, through the orchards and vineyards around my father's house and up over the green hills and wooded trails into the mountains surrounding *Appiano*.

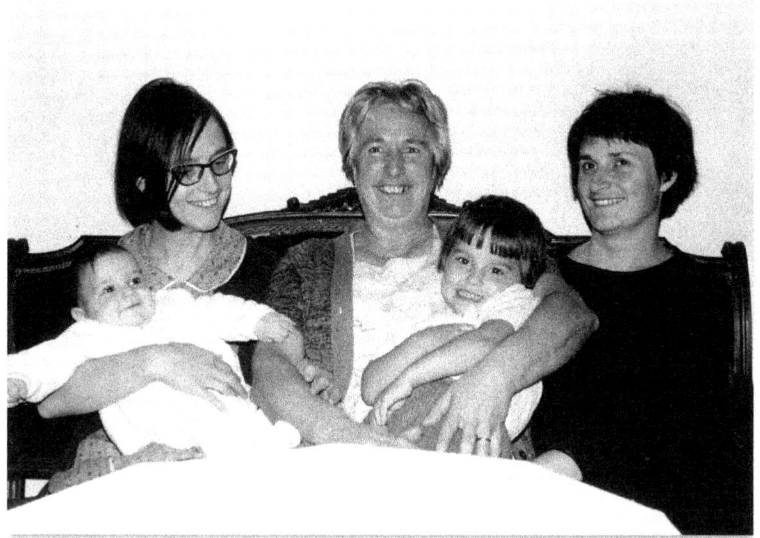

Paolo, Lidia, Peiga Pingerra, Anna and Carla (1966)

But while the people and places of my 'past' filled me with nostalgia, I was happy and proud to embrace my 'present'—my children and my new life with Joe. With them, my spirit was raised from the memories of what I had lost…to a new springtime, a season of rebirth and new hope for my future.

With September, came the time for me to return to America. Joe had left earlier to return to work, so I was accompanied to the airport by Antonio, Maria, Ida and Bruno.

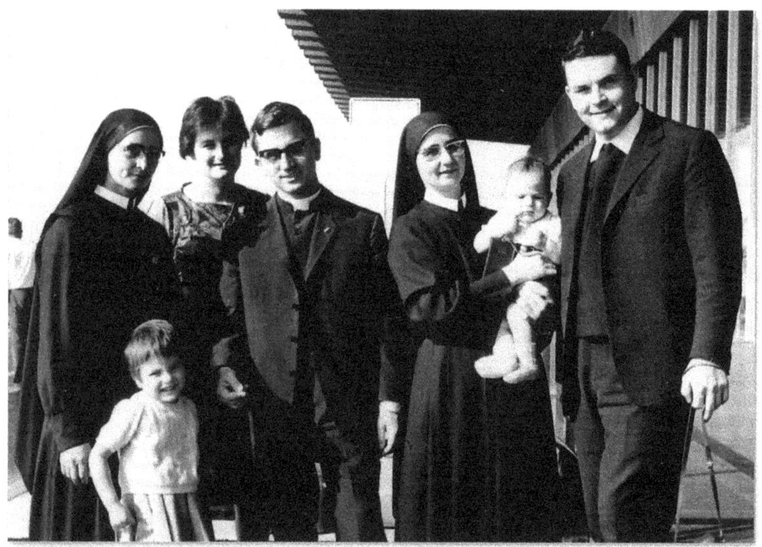

Maria, Anna, Carla, Antonio, Ida with Paolo, and Bruno

Our flight was to land first in Toronto, Canada, then continue on to Windsor, just across the border from Detroit, but because of a heavy storm, we were diverted to New York. We stayed there in the airport for hours before we could fly to Toronto. By the time we arrived, we had missed our flight to Windsor, so we had to stay the night.

Traveling alone with my two small children turned into a stressful night, but the next morning, when we arrived in Windsor, and I finally saw Joe anxiously waiting for us to arrive, the difficult journey faded and only the memory of our wonderful vacation together remained.

New Home, New Baby

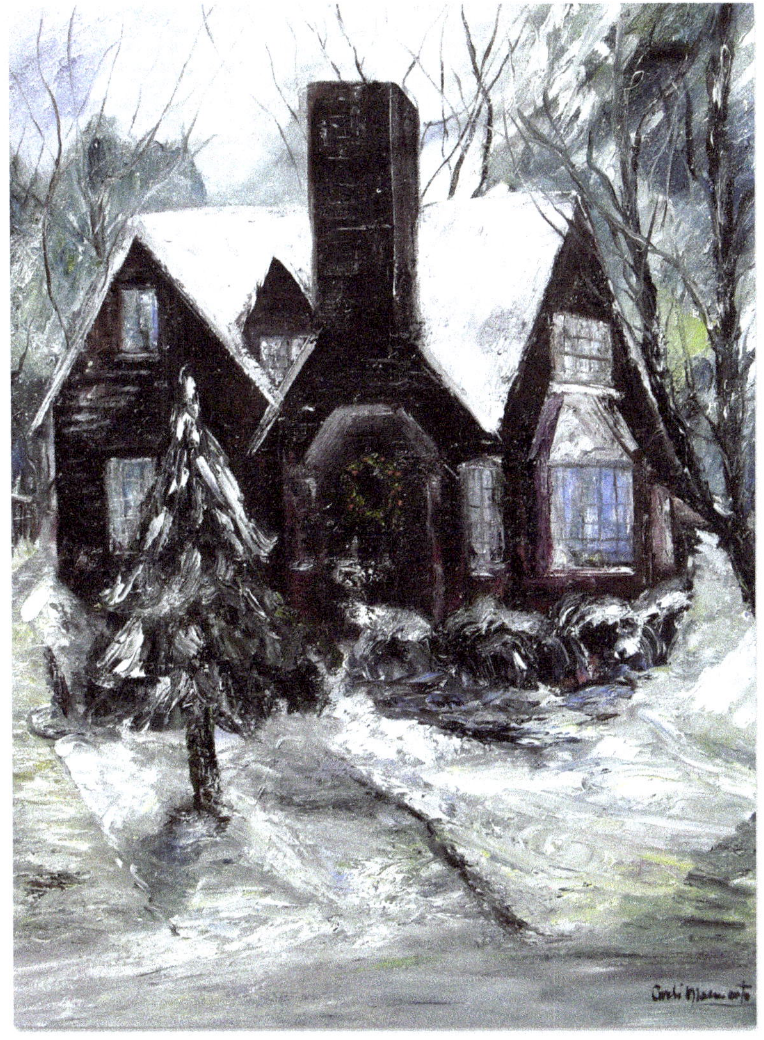

Home for Christmas

My first return to Italy, to spend time once again in my homeland, had marked a fitting close to another season of my life. My childhood and adolescence had turned, and I was now a young wife and mother with two children of my own. I was ready to begin the next part of my life in my new home in Michigan, or…almost ready. One more bit of news for our little family would complete us and send us onward with joy.

Daniela Maria Mazzucato was born on August 30, 1968. She arrived with less of the uncertainty and concern I'd had with my previous pregnancies. I was the mother with the "knowhow" this time. Everything went smoothly, and Daniela weighed 6.8 pounds at a length of eighteen inches, and was ready to charm us all with her big, brown eyes.

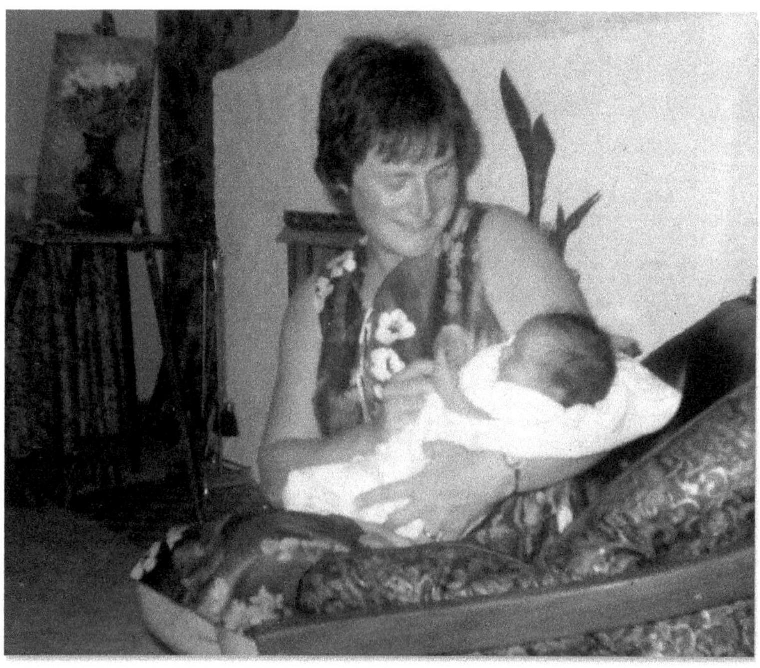

Carla and Daniela (1968)

When Joe arrived at my maternity room at Seaway Hospital, he had Anna and Paolo wait in the hallway, where they stood obediently in the outfits he had chosen for them —bright red with warm woolen stockings…on a hot, August afternoon. When they finally entered the room to see me and meet their new, baby sister, my eyes filled with tears of happiness, and I embraced them all. And now they were three.

Daniela turned out to be the "perfect baby." She followed a regular feeding schedule—every three hours— and she slept all through the night. Then, when she woke at 6 am, she always had a big smile on her face. She was so easy to please, and Anna was always happy to hold her little sister.

Paolo, on the other hand, was a bit jealous of all the attention that Daniela was receiving. When I held her and cared for her in the early hours of the day, Paolo would cry, sometimes till noon. It was exhausting, and I wasn't sure what to do to make him accept his little sister.

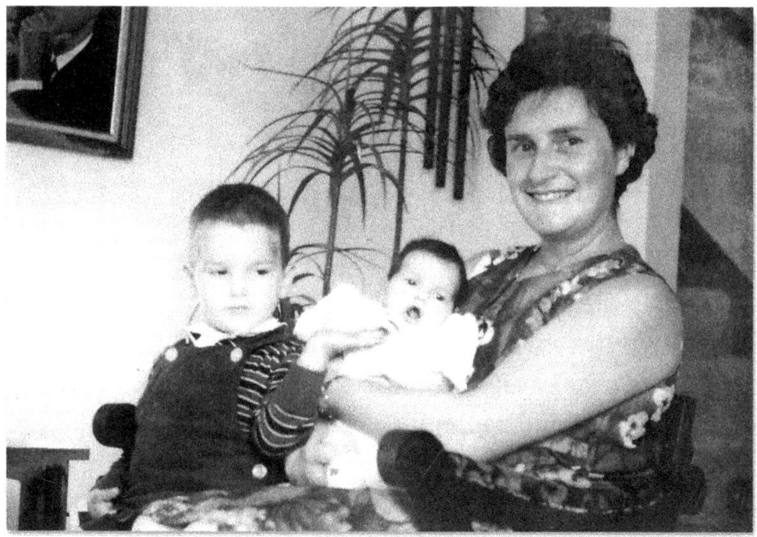

Paolo, Daniela and Carla (1968)

When my brother, Bruno, had visited us in the United States earlier that year, Paolo had stayed with my friend Jeanine Fiorelli while Bruno and I had taken Anna with us on a short trip to Washington, D.C.—a slight he hadn't forgotten. So now, when I asked him if he wanted to hold his baby sister, he would refuse and tell me to "give her to Jeanine."

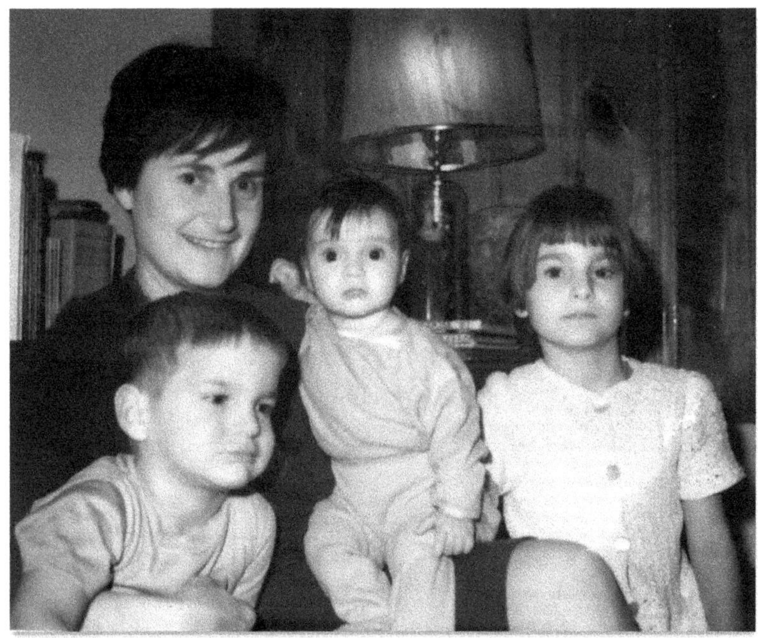

Carla, Paolo, Daniela and Anna (1969)

I didn't leave the children very often during those first years, but on occasion, a teenage girl, Karen Minnahan, from down the street was ready to baby sit. She was so happy that a new baby had arrived in the neighborhood and showed up one day with a little rattle for Daniela.

Usually, when I went out, all three of my children came too. Anna began Kindergarten class that September at Anderson School a few blocks away, so I would walk with her, pushing Daniela along in her baby buggy. Paolo walked alongside, eyes closed and sleeping as he held onto the buggy.

Anna and Daniela shared a strong, sisterly bond, and eventually Paolo embraced his little sister warmly as well. They played together, invented games together, and helped each other as they grew up together. And, needless to say, our family became the greatest source of joy for me and Giuseppe.

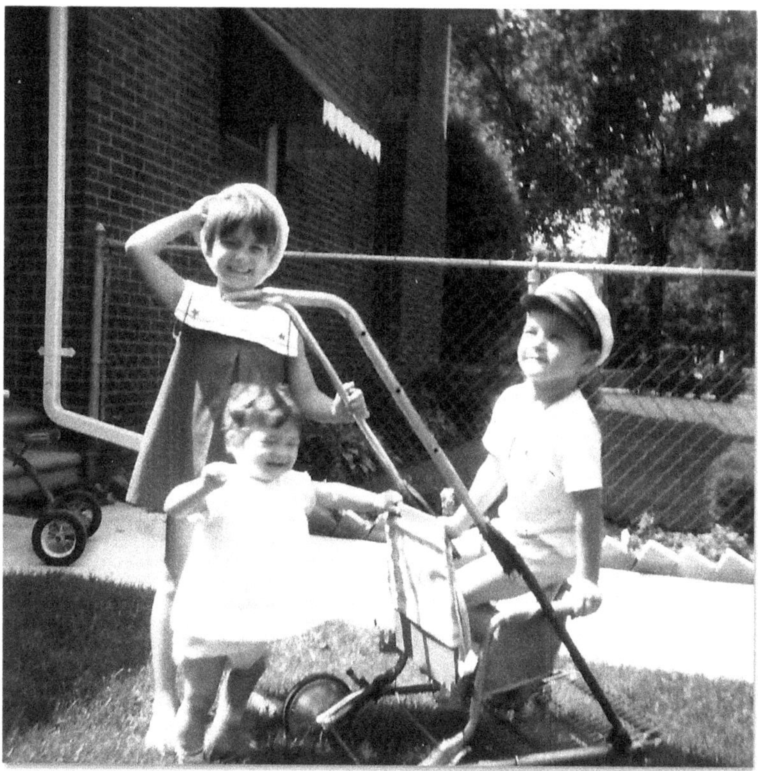

Anna, Daniela and Paolo at 2605 Lenox Road (1969)

In 1969, we moved again, but this time just across the street. 2638 Lenox Road in Trenton, was a Tudor-style, dark, brick house with a steep roof over a large living room, a dining room, kitchen, sun room, first floor bed and bathroom with two more bedrooms and another bath on the second floor. It was simply beautiful.

We already loved the street in the Bretton Wood neighborhood. It seemed like a garden to us with its tall trees and flowering shrubs, and since the house was just down the block and across the street from where we were, moving would not be difficult.

The house was owned by Mrs. Odilla DeMaire, but she needed to sell it after her husband had died. She felt alone in the big space and wanted to go to live with her daughter in California. Mrs. DeMaire had been born in Belgium, and her taste in decor was quite European. She left some of her antique furniture in the house when she left along with a large Persian rug that covered the whole living room floor.

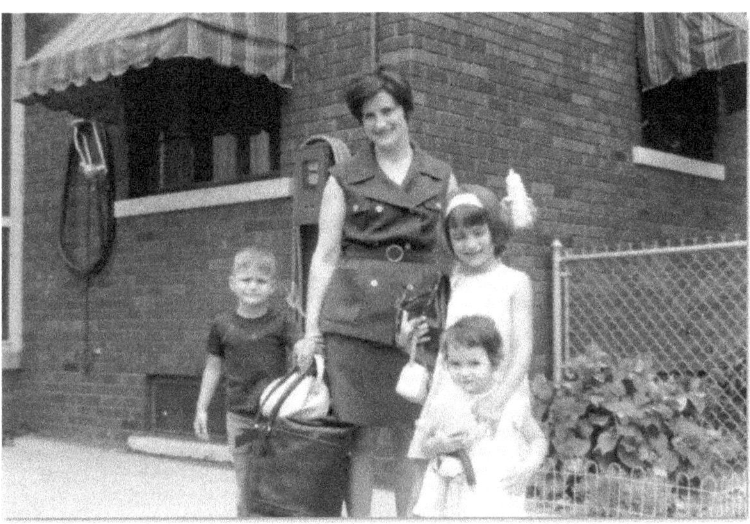

Paolo, Carla, Anna and Daniela at 2638 Lenox Road (1970)

Of course, after all the work that Joe had done to our first house, he was ready to start in on a new project.

He couldn't relax and enjoy our new home because, according to him, we needed a wider sun-room, an additional bedroom for Paolo, and...a wine cellar in the basement for when he would make wine.

He also wanted to re-landscape the entire yard of the house's double lot and plant a large vegetable garden and expand the garage to have room for his tools and a small machine shop.

His "projects" would keep him busy for many years as he worked to make our house the dream home where I would spent the best years of my life.

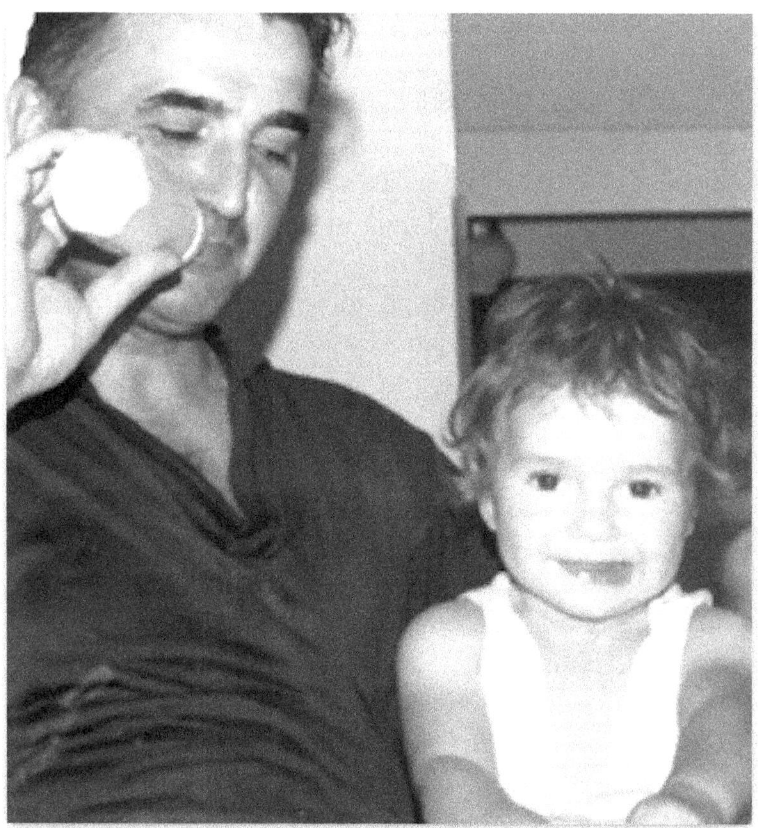

Giuseppe and Daniela (1970)

While I was so happy that my children had each other, I felt some sadness that they didn't have cousins nearby, and that they would never know my parents who had passed away so early.

One day, though, when I had gone to a paint supply store on West Road, I noticed a display of paintings by local artists on the wall. I had always loved art since my studies in Italy, and had taken up painting in Chicago, so I asked if I could display the few works I had completed too.

Days later, an older woman noticed my work in the store. There was something about the style that she liked, and she asked for my address. She then came one day for a visit.

Her name was Sophie Stamer. She was born in Austria and came to the United States when she was fourteen. Now, she was in her seventies, but I remember admiring how strong and full of life she was, tall with blondish-gray hair.

She had lived with an uncle in Connecticut before she had married an Austrian fellow by the name of Adolph. They lived on the east coast for many years, where they had lost their first child, a girl, quite young. Their second child, Bernhard was now my age and lived with his wife Dorothy near Sophie in a neighborhood on the other side of West Road.

Sophie spoke with a slight accent, which was like a melody to my ears and reminded me of my hometown. We also spoke German together, and she loved to bake—tarts and cookies and cakes. I had taught Anna, Paolo and Daniela to be polite and never take too much, but Sophie always offered a second slice of cake or another cookie, saying, "Eat. It's good for you."

Even though Joe's father, Romano, was still alive, he was in Italy, so Sophie and Adolph became like grandparents to Anna, Paolo and Daniela. It was so nice to be able to share so many happy times and holidays with them, and visiting them, which we ended up doing almost daily, became a special treat.

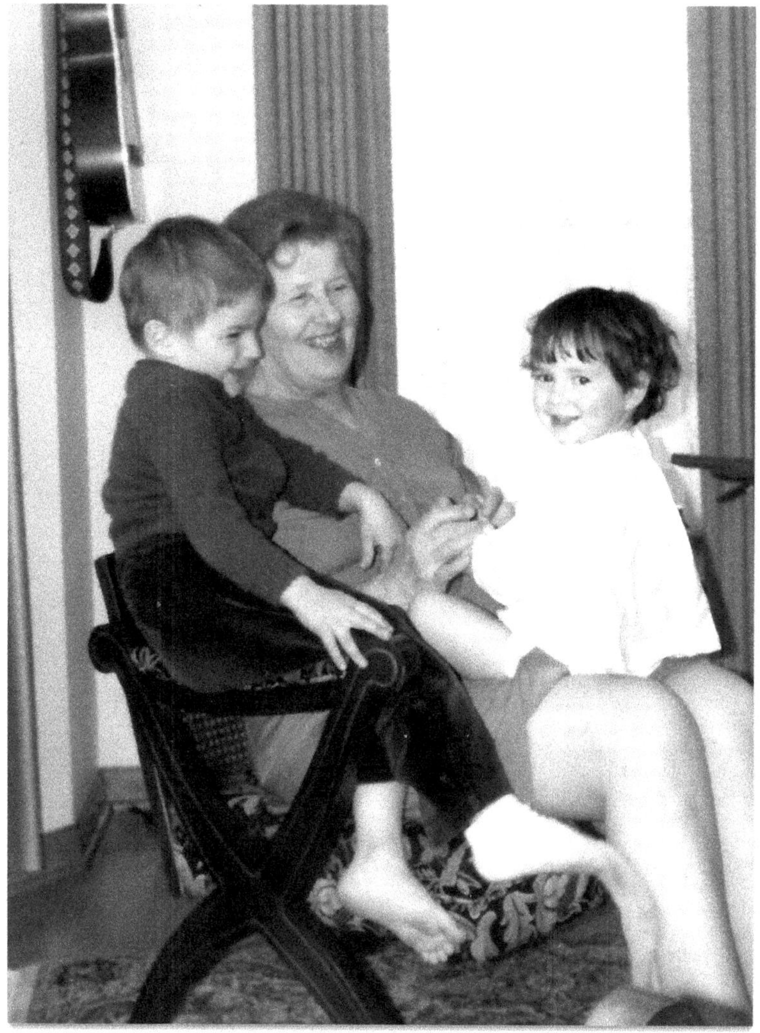

Paolo, Sophie Stammer and Daniela (1970)

CHAPTER SEVENTEEN

More Journeys

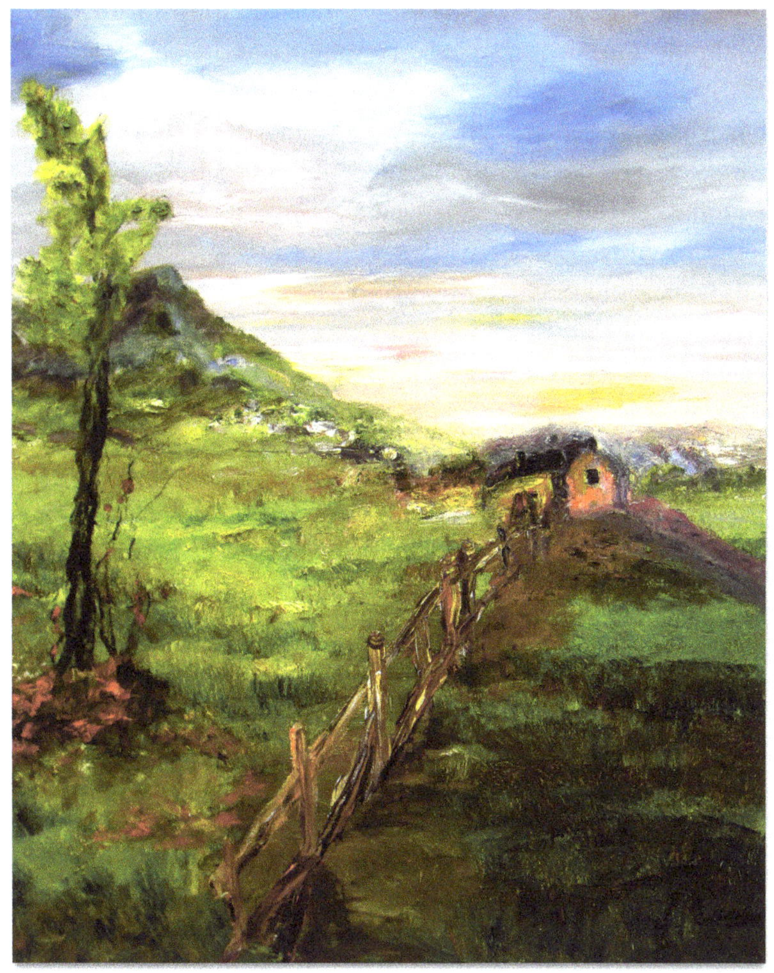

Still Meadow

Becoming a priest in the Catholic Church is quite a special event in *Tyrol* and *Trentino*. After a priest is consecrated in Rome, he returns to his hometown to celebrate his first mass.

My brother, Bruno, had become a priest in June of 1967, and for his first mass in *Appiano* there had been a big celebration in town. Because I was in America, and we had just made the trip the year before, I missed the occasion, and was very sad. As I held Anna to my heart with tears in my eyes, she looked up to me and said, "It is all good, Mamma, because you can be there in spirit." I remember being so moved to have such a little girl, only four-years-old, who could make me feel so blessed.

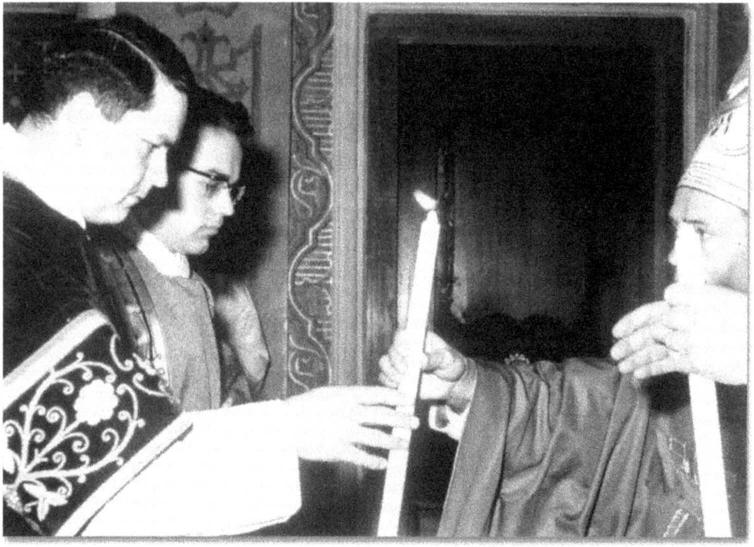

Bruno Carli, consecration (1967)

Three years later, on a sunny day in June of 1970, we would "be there" in spirit but also in person to celebrate with Bruno, when we all arrived in *Milano* for another summer vacation .

Bruno's first assignment as a priest was in the small town of *Bronzolo* in the vicinity of Bolzano. Many people knew him already, and his joyous approach to celebrating mass was particularly popular with the children of the parish.

During our vacation that summer, Bruno spent time in *Bronzolo* but came constantly to *Appiano* to play not only with Anna, Paolo and Daniela, but also with Andrea and Ivo, the two little sons of my sister Lidia.

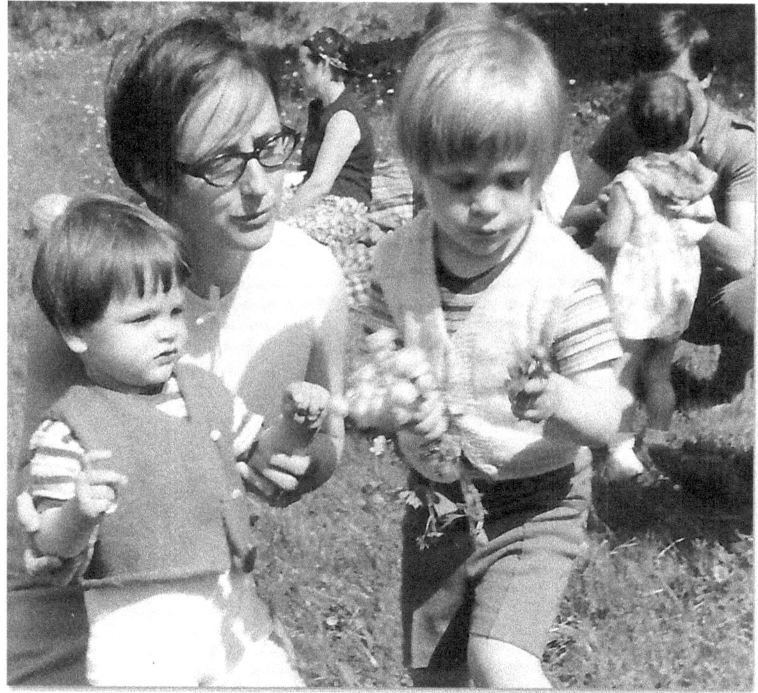

Ivo, Lidia and Andrea Corrà (1970)

I remember being amazed at how Andrea and Ivo were already speaking the German dialect of Appiano as their second language. They knew all the German fables and folklore with words and music. The courtyard of my father's house was once again a playground filled with joy and laughter, and I smiled as I looked down on the fun and games from the balcony above.

Lidia was a professor of music now and would often give us little concerts on the piano and invite us to sing the old melodies we had learned as young girls. She was an excellent teacher and had many students at the Music Conservatory in *Rovereto*. She also had students that came to her house for private lessons. I admired her patience and understanding, and her devotion to music and teaching.

That summer, we also went to spend a few weeks all together on the Adriatic Sea. We reserved three rooms at a Hotel in *Bibione* for our two families, and it turned out to be a beautiful reunion.

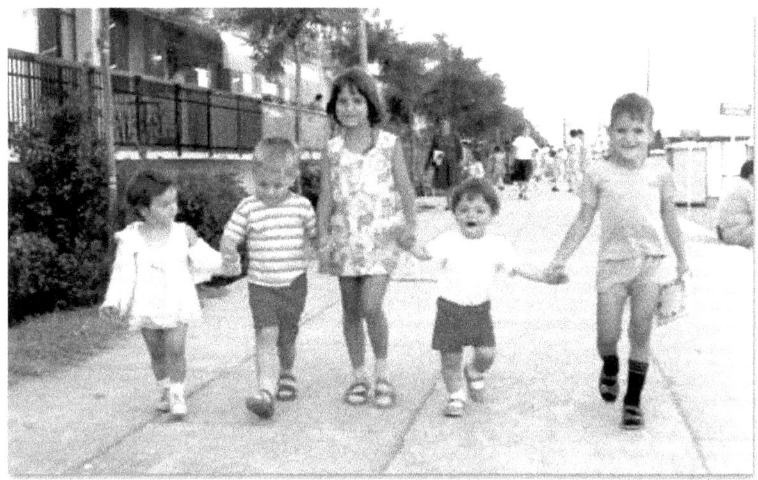

Daniela, Andrea, Anna, Ivo and Paolo, in Jesolo (1970)

Our children swam and played, building sand castles and getting to know each other. Bruno came too and taught Daniela to perform her *acrobazia*—balancing on one leg with her foot in Bruno's hand as he held her up in the air. It was a summer of fun, and we all enjoyed being together at the beach.

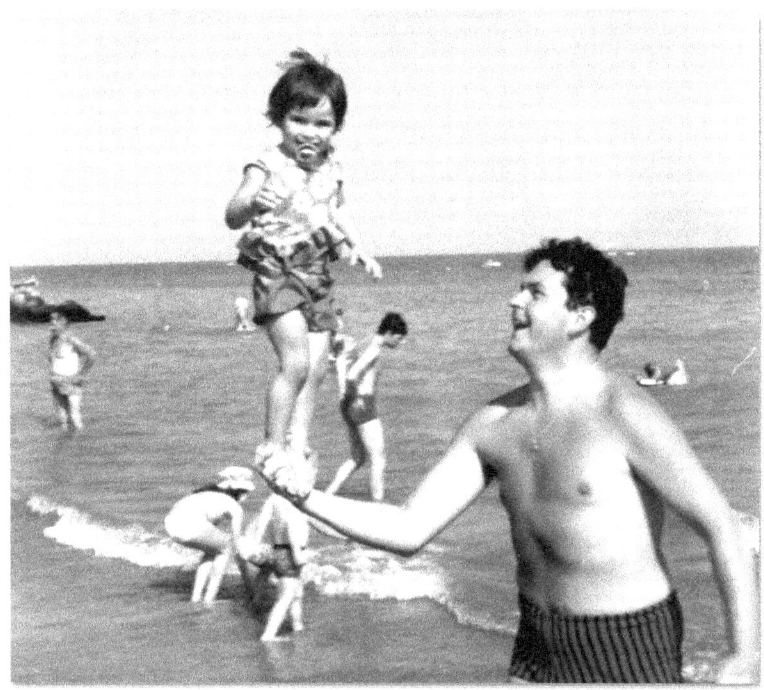

Daniela and Bruno in Jesolo (1970)

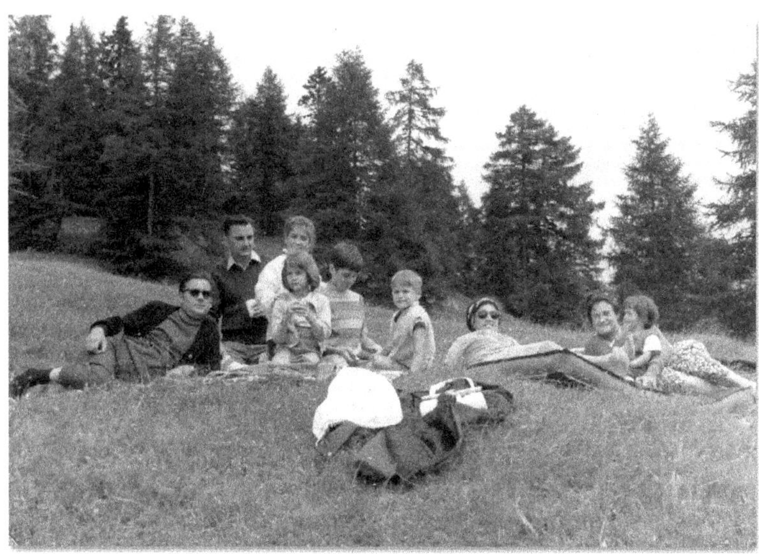

Fiorelli and Mazzucato Families: (1970)
Luigi, Giuseppe, Maria, Anna, Johnny, Paolo, Jeanine, Carla, Daniela

After our time on the Adriatic, we spent some time up in the mountains with the family of Jeanine and Luigi Fiorelli. I liked to share the beauty of the Alps and the *Adige Valley* with friends visiting from America, and they enjoyed taking long walks around the hills of *Appiano*. Further up, we would drive, then take hikes onto the tall white peaks of the Alps, up where the air was thin, our spirits high, and the view vast and beautiful .

Bruno stayed most of the summer with us, and the children grew very attached to him, particularly Daniela. So much so, that when we returned home to America at the end of summer, Daniela went through a period of sadness. She began using a pacifier which she had never used before, and spent hours looking through the album of photos we had taken in Italy.

The picture of her performing her *acrobazia* with Bruno at the beach was her favorite, and she kissed the photo and left bite marks on the corner. She missed him so. It took a while before she was back to her usual cheerful self.

In September, it was time for Anna to begin the first grade at St Joseph Elementary School. Joe and I had decided that the children would go to the Catholic School close to our home. I always felt so unsure about raising my children in a country so new to me.

My own experience—being brought up in Italy with a different language, customs and family traditions was different from anything they would experience here. Sending my children to a Catholic School gave me a sense of familiarity, tranquility and assurance.

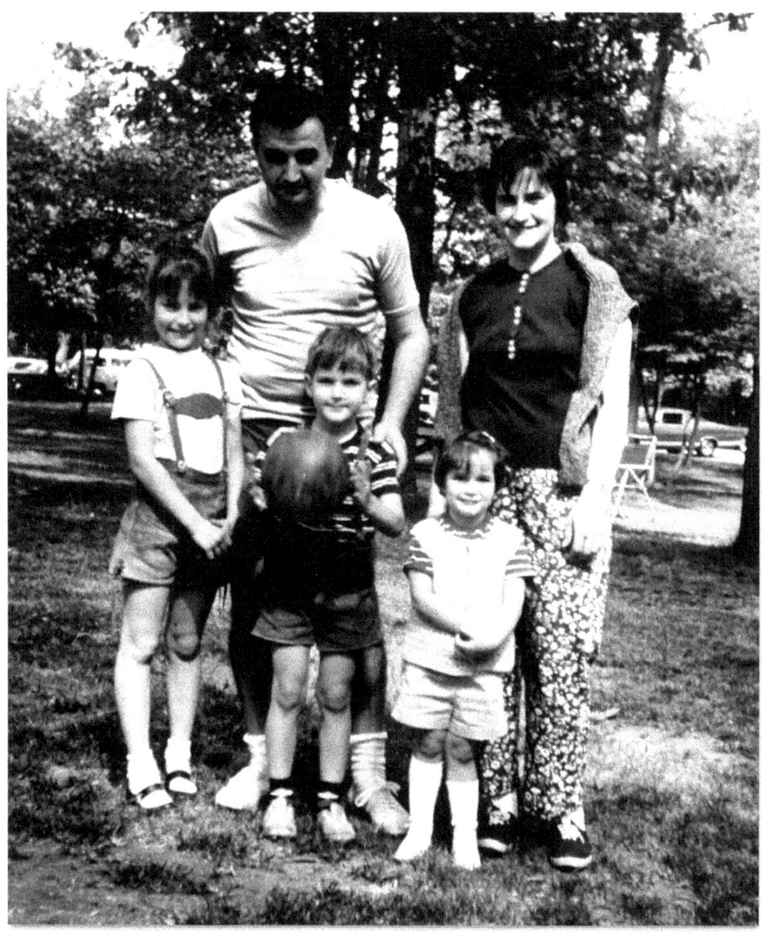

Anna, Giuseppe, Paolo, Daniela and Carla at Elizabeth Park (c.1971)

My friend Maria Louisa Beatrici, who by that time already had five children, had majored in 'Education' during her university studies and enjoyed sharing her views and offering me good advice. She was well-read in psychology and when we got together, we spent half the day discussing educational issues. It was always a nice conversation because we trusted each other and were both interested in the education and the upbringing of our children.

Since I had left Chicago and moved to Michigan, we couldn't see each other as often, but it was nice to when she and her family could visit from Downers Grove, Illinois, or when we made the drive from Trenton, Michigan, to spend a few days with them.

One summer, we went on a longer vacation together for ten days in the Upper Peninsula of Michigan. We rented two cottages in a wooded area on the shore of Lake Superior, and the children played and got to know each other, while Joe and Gino went fishing. Maria Louisa and I, of course, spent hours and hours in conversation.

Then, in the evenings, Gino would bring out his accordion, and I had learned to play some guitar, and we would sing the many mountain songs that reminded us of our home in the Alps. Eventually, all went quiet and the children drifted off to sleep in the serenity of the tranquil night.

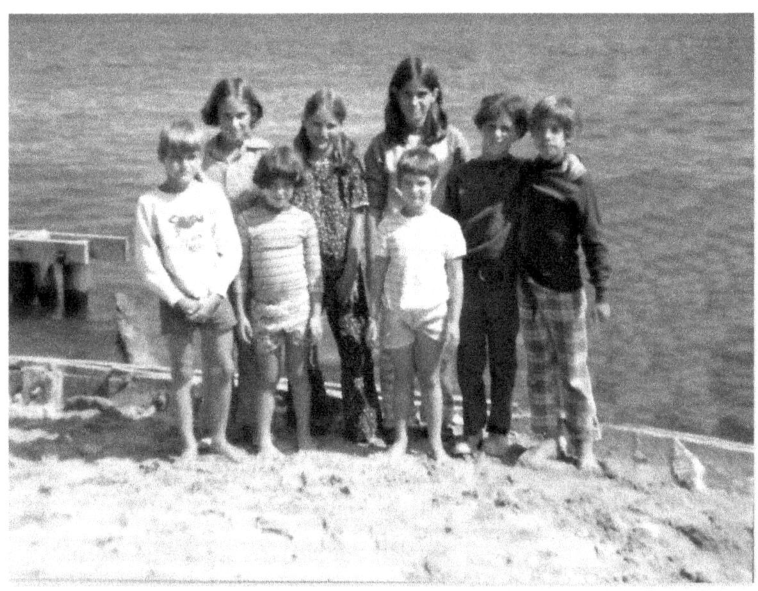

Beatrici and Mazzucato children: (1972)
Paolo, Diane, Carla, Anna, Rita, Daniela, David, Paul

Another summer, we took a vacation to Lac du Flambeau in Wisconsin, where the sister of Lidia's husband, Sergio, lived. She raised hundreds of minks on a large property out in the middle of a forest. There were three rows of pens where the animals were kept and a guest house on the lake where we could admire the sunset.

I remember that Joe was so relaxed that he decided not to shave, and he grew a bit of beard on that vacation.

On our way back, we drove up through the Upper Peninsula of Michigan, and enjoyed the beautiful, thick forests and wilderness areas that had already begun to change with approaching Autumn—bright, dazzling colors that would fade into majestic Winter white, then be reborn in Spring and the splendor of Summer.

We returned again to Italy in the summer of 1973. I was happy that we were able to spend time with friends and family and that my children would have the chance to know their uncles, aunts, cousins and Joe's father, Romano, even if Joe's mother and my parents had passed too soon for Anna, Paolo and Daniela to ever know them. We had a wonderful time that summer, visiting and hiking…spending time.

So, it was a gray and somber day, November 27, 1975, when Romano Mazzucato passed away at the age of eighty-one. Doctors performing an exploratory surgery had accidentally collapsed his lung, but he hung on, as if refusing to die, until Giuseppe was able to arrive in time to see and speak with his father. Then, he passed away.

I so wanted to be with Joe, but had to stay at home in Michigan with the children. So I wrote him a letter:

Trenton, 29 novembre 1975

Caro maritino,

Immagino che non riuscirai a scrivermi per mancanza di tempo, ma che ti farebbe piacere avere un mio scritto. I bambini hanno appreso la morte del loro nonno con profonda commozione. Il mattino seguente della tua telefonata, si sono ritirati tutti tre nella loro camera per assorbire questa notizia molto triste Spiegai loro che il nonno si era spento con calma ed era ormai contento di raggiungere la nonna in cielo; e penso che anche tu abbia questo stesso pensiero.

Sono tanto contenta che tu abbia potuto rimanere ancora alcuni giorni col tuo papà e spero che tu mi vorrai raccontare quanto è avvenuto al tuo ritorno. Gli ultimi giorni e gli ultimi momenti che ancor si vivono sulla terra conservano quel momento di verità che noi cerchiamo durante il cammino della nostra vita. La morte risolve questo problema.

Pertanto mio caro maritino, sull'esempio della sua vita e quella dei miei genitori ormai morti da tempo, cerchiamo di sentirci uniti nello sforzo costante di accettarci a vicenda nonostante gli spigoli del nostro carattere, e di lasciar perdere le irritazioni inutili e le impazienze con noi stessi e gli altri, per poter dare ai nostri "frugoli" la pace che viene dall'amore, prima che essi si avviano nel loro mondo.

Sentimi vicina, con tanto affetto, tua Carla

(translation)

My dearest husband,

I imagine that you won't have time to write, but that you might be pleased to receive a letter from me. The children have felt the loss of their nonno profoundly. The morning after your phone call, they sat quietly in their room to take in the sad news. I explained to them that Nonno passed away peacefully, and that he was happy to go and join Nonna in heaven; and you also share the same thought.

I am very happy that you were able to spend a few last days with your papà, and I hope that you will want to tell me all that happened when you return. The final days and final moments of life on Earth, provide a peaceful truth, something we seek during the long walk of our life. Death is a quiet resolution to our journey.

For now, my dear husband, as in the example of his life and that of my parents who passed away some time ago already, we should try to feel united in our acceptance of each other, our blessings and faults, and let go of useless irritations that we face together or with others, so that we can give to our "little ones" the peace that comes from love, as they begin to make their way in their world.

I am with you, with much love, your Carla

In 1976, the year after Joe's father had passed away, we all returned to Italy for our Summer vacation. The children had grown a few years now and were ready to discover all the beautiful places and trails through the Alps that I had known in my childhood.

Early in the morning, we would rise and prepare to set out to spend the day out in the fresh mountain air. Anna was always ready to go first to the bakery down the street to pick out some fresh bread so we could make and pack our sandwiches, some with *prosciutto*, some with *Nutella*, for our lunch up in the mountains. Then, away we went.

Our frequent mountain companions were our new friends Evelin Aichner with her little daughter Maike. Evelin and her husband Ulli lived in one of the apartments made when the hayloft of my father's house was renovated to create living units.

Joe's brother, Benito, who was now a teacher in Bolzano, was on vacation as well, so he could also spend time with us on our mountain trips. Together, our little group traveled all throughout Alto Adige to the many beautiful mountains and valleys within a short car ride and a pleasant hike through nature.

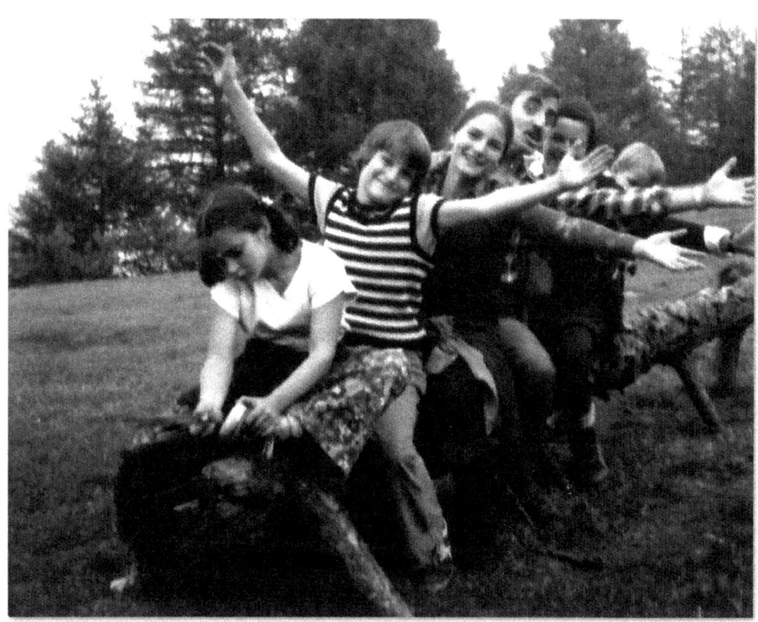

Daniela, Paolo, Anna, Zio Benito, Evelin and Maike Aichner (1976)

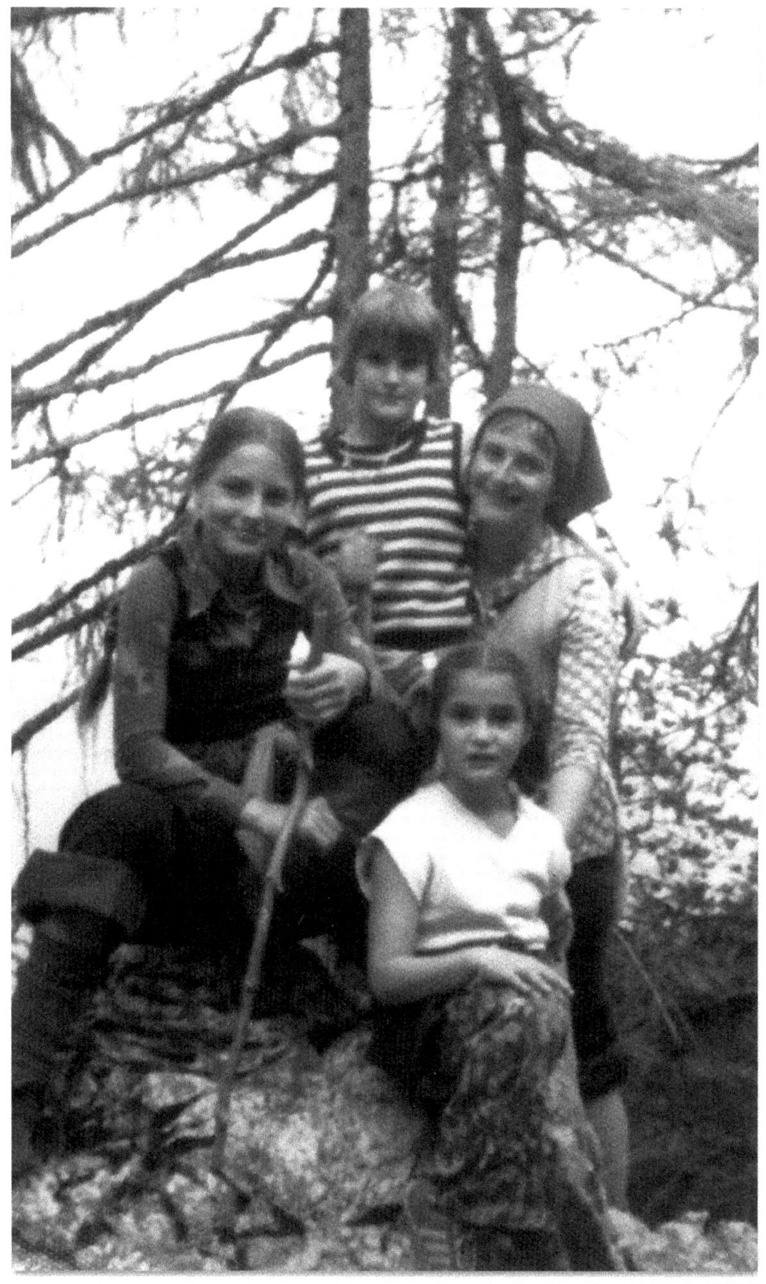

Anna, Paolo, Daniela and Carla (1976)

Because there were three languages spoken among our group—English, Italian and German—we did a lot of singing. Music was our universal language, and both Evelin and *Zio* Benito played the harmonica. A mountain hike and a lunch up in the high cow pastures always ended with a wonderful concert.

We also took a trip to *Bologna,* in the *Emilia-Romagna* region, to visit Joe's sister, Ottelma, her husband, Remo, and their two daughters Silvia and Carla. On our way down, we first stopped to visit don Luigi Borghesi, the pastor in *Val di Non* where I had spent a summer working when I was eighteen. He met us in *San Michele all'Adige* where he had just completed the installation of two beautiful, bronze doors on the church there.

Crossing into the *Veneto* region, we visited the famous *Ponte di Bassano,* the bridge over which many soldiers during World War II marched off to battle. One of the mountain songs we often sang on our mountain trips, and one of Joe's favorites, tells the story of love on the bridge where *"...noi ci darem la mano, ed un bacin d'amor."* ("we will give each other our hands and a kiss of love.")

I felt very fortunate that we were able to visit friends and family in Italy, but it was also wonderful to welcome them into our home in the United States as well.

In 1977, Joe's brother, Benito, came to visit, and we explored the shores of Lake Michigan, through Illinois and Wisconsin, then into the Upper Peninsula of Michigan before crossing the Mackinac Bridge and spending a few days in Gaylord where Mario and Anna Sauro had relocated.

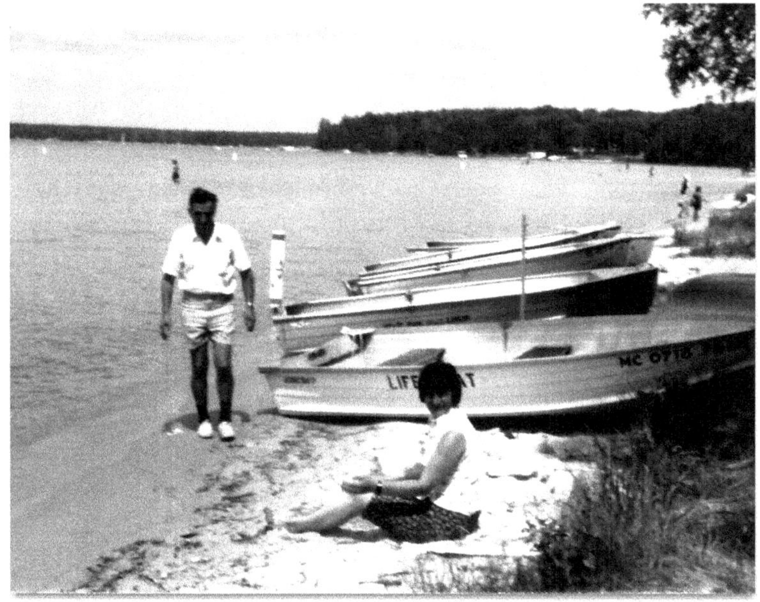

Giuseppe and Carla on Higgins Lake (1977)

Joe's sister, Ida, also came to stay with us for some time when she chose to take a long hiatus from her time in the convent. She was having some difficulty living within the restrictive lifestyle of the convent and thought she might prefer that of a lay person.

She arrived in the winter of 1977, the same year that I had purchased a building in the business district of Grosse Ile. where I planned to open an art gallery to exhibit my paintings and teach art. Ida was quiet by nature and seemed quite happy just reading and writing. I felt that she could stay with me and help in the gallery by selling books on art, but after staying with us for six months, she decided to return to her convent in Verona, Italy.

Our family vacations, for the next decade or so, were mostly spent in the United States. We enjoyed camping, and traveled east, west, north and south to explore and discover the vast land we lived in.

In the summer of 1978, we took the children on a trip to the U.S. capitol of Washington, D.C., with a stop in Harrisburg, Pennsylvania, to visit Othmar Carli, a distant cousin of mine, and his family. Othmar was an artist and had done much art restoration work in churches and public buildings including, in his younger years, at the Opera-House in Vienna, Austria. While there, he had met an American soprano by the name of Peggy. They had married and settled in York, Pennsylvania, where he continued his work, and pursued his own art as well.

Othmar spoke English with a thick Austrian accent, and preferred to express himself in his native tongue, so we spent much of the time conversing in German. He told of how, during World War II, he had received many threats from the ruling Nazis under Hitler, and how he had to hide in the woods of Vienna to survive. He ate fruits and plants that grew wild out in the remote places where he stayed safe. He later escaped to the southern border of Austria and crossed into South Tyrol, the land where I grew up, where he encountered his many Carli relatives.

I found the story of his life in Austria and later in America fascinating, and his knowledge of art and chemistry—the mixing of colors used in painting—was extensive. He also enjoyed talking about aerospace and astronomy. He loved music and would often attend concerts and musical events in nearby Gettysburg with Peggy who also enjoyed them and continued her love of music as a voice teacher with many students.

After touring the historic Civil War battlefields of Gettysburg and the vacation cottage of president Eisenhower, we continued on toward Washington, D.C., and arrived at the majestic Washington National Cathedral. As we toured the city, I was impressed by the stunning architecture, not just of the church, but all the government buildings surrounded by wide, open spaces, green parks and large avenues along the Potomac River flowing calmly like a silvery ribbon.

We then, traveled up to Boston, an inspiring city that made me feel like part of the historic past of the United States. The web of narrow streets, with few large avenues, made the city seem warm and more intimate, and I thought that it was the kind of city where I might like to live.

Up along the eastern coast, we reached the state of New Hampshire, where the infinite space of the Atlantic ocean stretched out over the water, refreshing the long and silent shore. Inland, we journeyed into the White Mountains of New Hampshire where the sparkling, silvery grey rocks reminded me of the Dolomites in my beloved Alps. Unlike the rugged peaks of the Rocky Mountains out west, these mountains, covered in green, felt more like the mountains in my memories.

In Vermont, I was drawn by the colorful vegetation and winding roads dotted with lovely covered bridges that cross the many running brooks. The stillness in the valleys and the fresh air and soft sound of flowing water, made our vacation in the East a peaceful paradise.

In 1984, we traveled in the other direction and drove into the West. Joe had bought a new Dodge Caravan, and we set out on the long, wide highway heading for California.

While we had driven to Colorado in 1964 when Anna was just one, this time, we had a full car—Anna was in college, Paolo would be starting his university studies in autumn, and Daniela would be in her third year of high school. On top of that, our friend Evelin from *Appiano* had joined us for the trip too. I never thought we could travel that far, that full, on the long road, across the flat plains of the Midwest, up over the Rocky Mountains through the busy city of Los Angeles, and finally reach the west coast to see the Pacific Ocean before us. But we did it.

We arrived on the evening of the 4th of July in time to watch the fireworks from a cliff overlooking the ocean at our Malibu Beach camping ground.

The trip back was so very interesting to me as well, because of the various stops we took. The city of San Francisco was beautiful, but I remember the many places where we camped, away from the crowds, that were also just as breathtaking.

Outside of San Francisco, we were greeted one morning by the 'mooing' of the cows that were grazing in a field near the campground. In the state of Utah, the salt flats stretched out like a sea of white, while the Old Faithful geyser in Yellowstone National Park in Wyoming amazed us with its impressive force. From the Rocky Mountain National Park and the Grand Canyon of Arizona back across the prairies to the Midwest, I marveled at the beauty of the vast country that I now called home.

Years later, when I published a book of my art, America—Celebration, I wrote of my journey as a visual diary that began in 1962 when I immigrated to the United States. I saw it as "a land steeped in history, where the lives of those who came before me were etched into the land forever." I was happy that I was able to see so much of the country while living "many seasons of time and of my life in Michigan, land of lakes and changing colors."

Thinking back on the country I had left years ago, I wrote an article for the Italian magazine "Filo Diretto," a reflection on my twenty-five years in the United States:

In these years away from my birthplace of Appiano, I have visited many states of North America and some provinces of Canada. The diversity of this country is remarkable. The panoramic view of the land is so vast; on the east side of the country the Atlantic ocean is separated from the central states by the Appalachian mountains. The humid and pastoral land is very green with luscious vegetation.

This is also the historic part of America, and its cities are different from the industrial cities of the Midwest, like Chicago and Detroit.

To reach the Rocky Mountains of Colorado, you have to cross six or seven states with infinite flat plains. The colors are mostly yellow because of the dry climate and nature's bright palette. The West is also sparsely populated compared to the East, and when you pass the mountains of Wyoming and Utah you can find the lonesome silence of nature.

It is impossible to describe the vastness of the American panorama. One has to visit it in order to truly understand and appreciate it.

Carla Carli Mazzucato

PART IV

A NEW SEASON

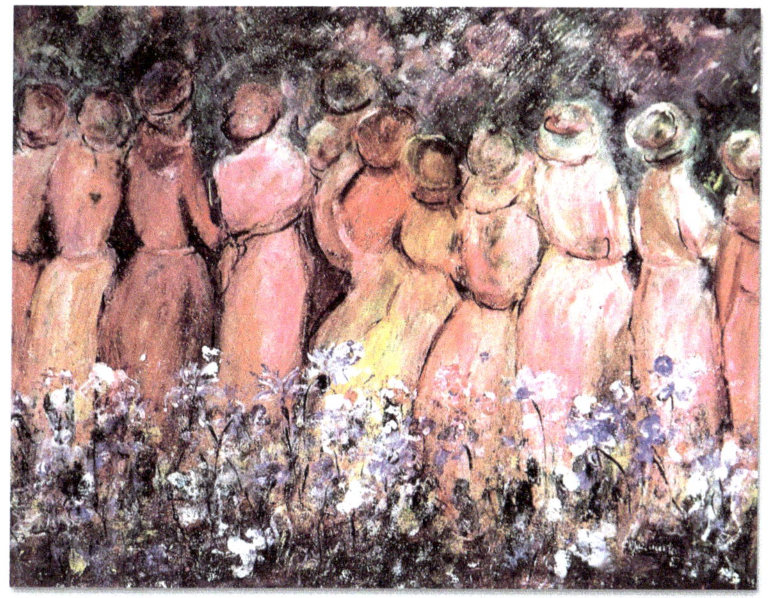

Primavera

Oh why is heaven built so far,
Oh why is earth set so remote?
I cannot reach the nearest star,
That hangs afloat.

For I am bound with fleshly bands,
Joy, beauty, lie beyond my scope;
I strain my heart, I stretch my hand
And catch at hope.

Christina Rossetti

175

Crossroads

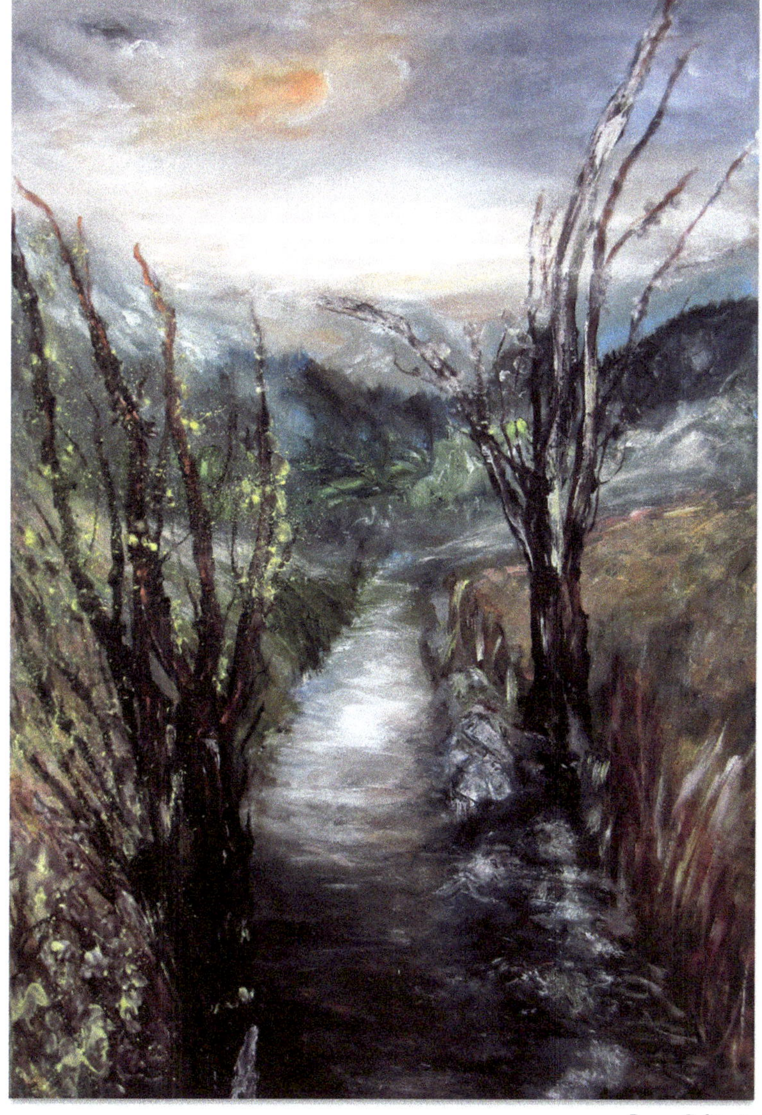

Passo Solitario

I had a friend named Lora Paciotti who had come back from Italy where she had gone for a few years to teach English, and I enjoyed listening to her talk of her experiences abroad. She had worked in New York, studied music and loved literature. Years ago she used to take Anna to a place, close to where we lived, where children could ride horses. She had a daughter named Claudia and a son, Marco, and it was always nice to spend time with her whenever we had a family event.

After she married and moved to a home north of Detroit with her husband, Adelchi Valsi, who she called Ed, I did not see her much anymore. Daniela was still little at that time, as were her children, and we became busy with our own lives.

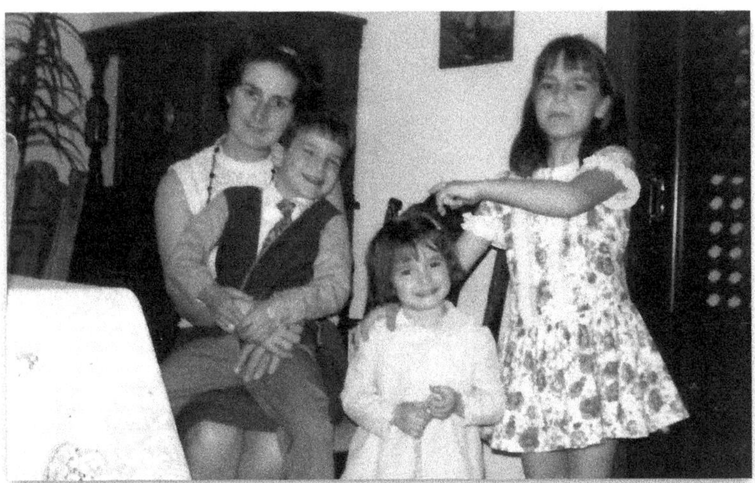

Carla, Paolo, Daniela and Anna (1971)

Many years later, in 2016, the same year we both became widows, we got in touch again and carried on a heartfelt correspondence about our friendship and our shared past. Unfortunately, I never got to see Lora again.

Before she passed away, she sent me poems that she enjoyed and gave meaning to her final days. I read them still, touched by the loneliness they convey. And yet, they create a sense of peace and tranquility too.

Autumn Day
Lord: it is time. The summer was grand.
But the sundials darken as your shadows grow,
And your wind blows free over the meadows.
Command the final fruits to swell in full;
Grant them two more temperate days,
To push them to perfection and yield
Their greatest sweetness into strong wine.
Whoever has no home now, will build no more.
Whoever is alone now will remain alone,
they will watch, read and write tedious letters
and wander restlessly here and there
along the avenues, the leaves swirling about them.

R.M.Rilke

(original text, German)

Herbsttag
Herr: es ist Zeit. Der Sommer war sehr groß.
Leg deinen Schatten auf die Sonnenuhren,
und auf den Fluren laß die Winde los.
Befiehl den letzten Früchten voll zu sein;
gib ihnen noch zwei südlichere Tage,
dränge sie zur Vollendung hin und jage
die letzte Süße in den schweren Wein.
Wer jetzt kein Haus hat, baut sich keines mehr.
Wer jetzt allein ist, wird es lange bleiben,
wird wachen, lesen, lange Briefe schreiben
und wird in den Alleen hin und her
unruhig wandern, wenn die Blätter treiben.

R.M.Rilke

There comes a time, for everyone, of life re-evaluation. For me, it came when I was in my forties. I began to feel that I needed a new direction. I did not understand my own self. I loved my husband, my children, my family, my house...and yet I felt a void. I had too many hours of free time, and I drifted without commitment. I fulfilled my responsibilities, but the moments of my day felt undefined.

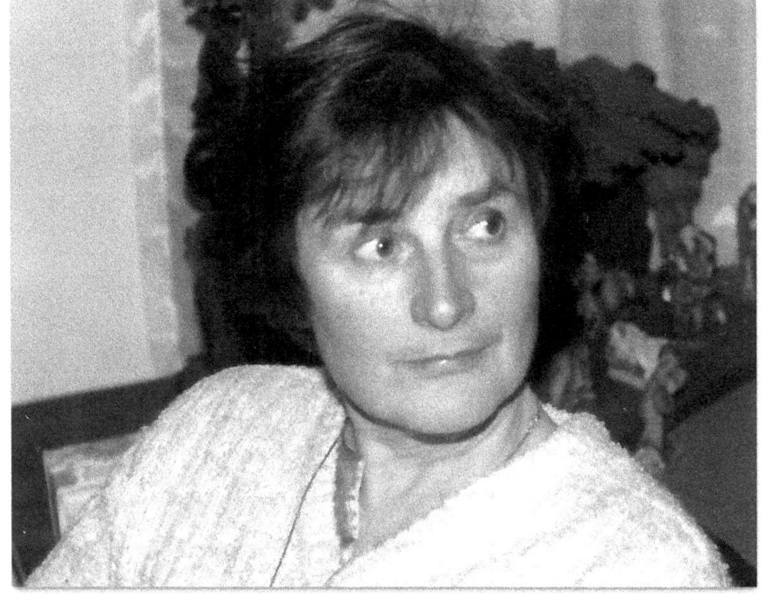

Carla (1975)

It was an internal struggle that I had that I tried to hide without understanding the reasons why I felt that way. I repeated to myself that I was happy, and yet I had no sense of fulfillment or accomplishment.

I compared myself with my brother and sister, who both had reached their professional goals. Bruno had finished his studies in theology in Rome and was now a priest, Lidia had a diploma in music and was teaching piano at the Conservatory in *Rovereto*.

I felt I was just dreaming my days away while considering indefinite possibilities. I thought that just finding a job to fill my time was not sensible…and Joe might feel offended. He was proud to be the provider of the family and I didn't think he would consider a change to the "status quo."

But truthfully, the uncertainty was mainly mine. I was not ready to step out and work in an English speaking society. I had no confidence. I lacked the language skills needed, and I didn't want anything to change, really. I loved my home and the hours I spent with my family and the people I loved. It was the life I had always dreamed of. Why then did I feel I was squandering my life with senseless dreaming? I didn't understand. I was confused and had no answer.

One answer came to me, though, when my neighbor, who was a science teacher at Trenton High School, asked me if I would be interested in teaching the Italian language for evening adult classes. Yes!

Twice a week and for five years, I taught Italian evening classes at the Trenton High School. Almost all the teachers there, who thought they might travel to Italy someday, enrolled in my class. It was the perfect thing for me—teaching an enthusiastic group of people that loved to learn, loved to travel…and loved my style.

At the end of the course, after having translated the famous arias of Puccini's <u>La Bohème</u> into English, I took them all to see the opera. I was not only gaining confidence, but also friends. It was only a first, small commitment, but it gave me the courage to try more things, and embrace the many opportunities that I would soon discover.

Finding My Way

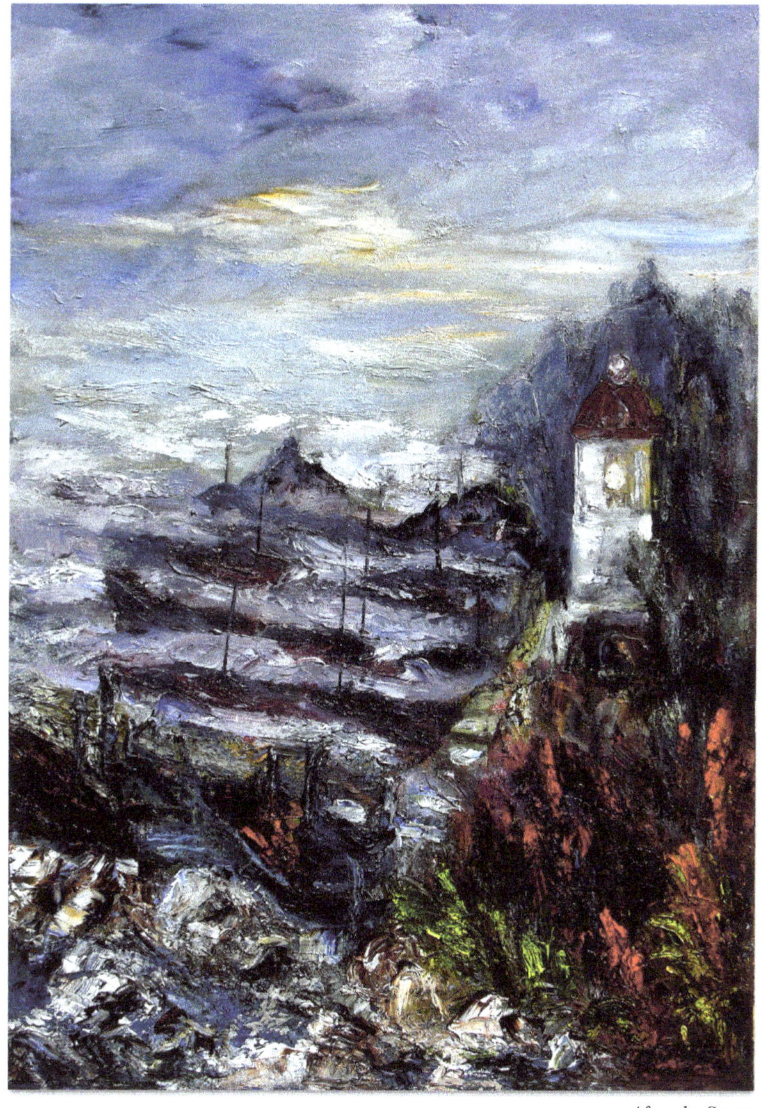

After the Storm

I became an American Citizen in Detroit on August 25, 1975. I was already familiar with the ceremony because I accompanied Joe when he received his citizenship ten years before in Chicago. Back then, however, most immigrants had come from Russia; at my ceremony ten years later in Detroit, the largest group of immigrants came from Middle Eastern countries.

On both occasions, though, I was ready to sing the patriotic hymns while the authorities distributed the Certificates of Naturalization. I enjoyed the many songs that spoke of the vast beauty of the country that I now called home, and I happily joined in singing my favorite hymn, "America the Beautiful"...from sea to shining sea.

As a new citizen, I was ready to start off in a new direction and to make a contribution to my community. I felt, though, that no matter how much I studied in private, a degree from a learning institution would provide value in reaffirming my knowledge and helping me to obtain wider acceptance in the academic world and in my field.

My grandfather had taught me the joy of learning—that knowledge nurtures creativity and provides opportunities. And though I had acquired my formal education in Italy, first at the Academy *Ca' Foscari* in Venice and then at the *Università Cattolica* in *Milano*, I had not gotten my diploma.

I had fallen in love and happily begun a new adventure. But now, years later, here in America, I wanted to go back to school. The formal education and completion of my degree would give me the confidence I needed to create opportunities in my art profession.

So, I returned to my formal studies and enrolled in the many classes that I would need in order to earn a

Bachelors, and eventually a Master of Fine Arts degree, from Wayne State University in Detroit.

Despite the challenge of learning in a new system, and new language, I found studying in America so much easier than what I had been used to in Italy. Here, the courses were more specialized on a particular subject instead of teaching a general, broader, or more global perspective.

Through this 'more focused' method, I learned quickly to express myself in writing. I had wonderful professors in my English classes, and I enjoyed studying subjects that I had never approached before, especially those that gave me the opportunity to form and express my own ideas—like American Government.

I must admit that since I had arrived in America, I had only been concerned with my family life and with family matters. I had arrived in Chicago in 1962, the golden years of American politics, when John F. Kennedy was President.

After his assassination on November 22, 1963, I had hardly followed any political news, until, once again two more assassinations shook the world—the murder of Martin Luther King Jr. and that of Robert Kennedy, both in 1968. This was the year I was pregnant with Daniela, and the terrible news agitated me so much that I had to visit Father Bracken, the pastor of St. Joseph's Church in Trenton, who was so kind and comforting that I was finally able to calm myself.

Now, as a college student, I decided I needed to learn more about how the United States, my adoptive country, really worked. I had just become a citizen, and the next year, 1976, would be the first time that I would be able to vote in a presidential election. So I registered for a class in American Government.

That year Michigan had its primary, and the instructor of my class gave me the task of studying the platform of the Democratic Party; another student would research that of the Republican Party. Then, we would present the two positions in a debate. It was a splendid occasion for me to delve into politics for the first time, and learn the difference between the two parties. After the debate I said to my instructor, "What a surprise, I am a certain and true Democrat!"

While I continued my love of learning, I decided to pursue my other passion as well. In Italy I had studied art; in Chicago I had begun to paint; and now, from my home in Trenton, Michigan, I had displayed my paintings and even sold a few. I was ready for a next step. So in the Spring of 1977, I decided to open a gallery where I would show and sell my work and teach art—oil painting, drawing and watercolor.

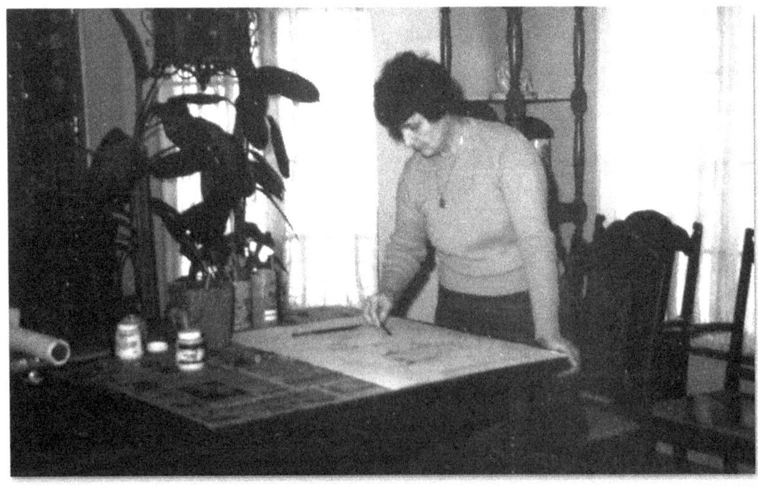

Carla Carli Mazzucato, home studio (1977)

The Alpha Art Gallery kept me busy for eight years, and I became an art curator, businesswoman and professional picture framer. The building was on Macomb Street in the central business district of Grosse Ile, a mostly residential island in the Detroit River, just over the bridge from Trenton where I lived.

I used the two upstairs rooms of the house for teaching, and the first floor to display and sell my paintings along with imported art and sculptures from Italy. The framing shop was in the basement. I taught almost every day and had about fifty students per week.

My whole family was involved at the gallery—Daniela took art classes, Paolo played violin during show openings, and Anna became a salesperson...the very best I had. She was informed and gracious, without being pushy, and she knew how to engage a client in conversation and close an art deal.

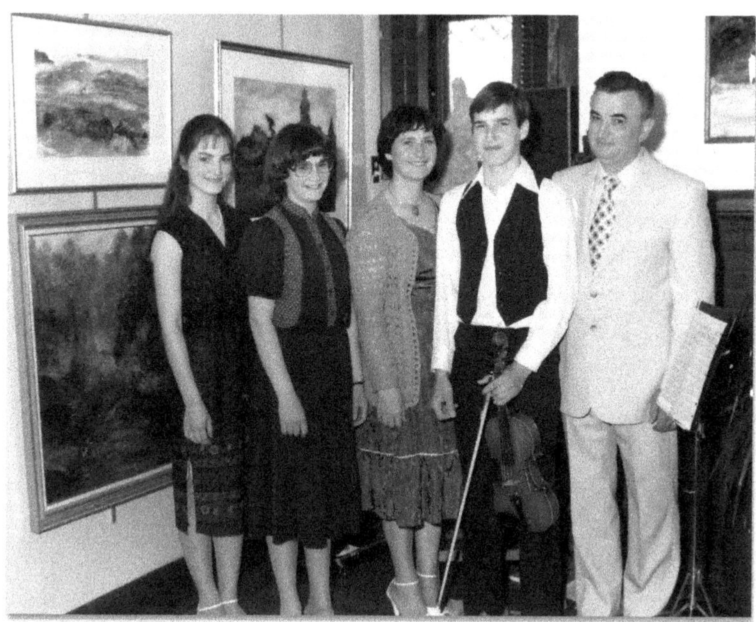

Anna, Daniela, Carla, Paolo, Giuseppe - Gallery Opening (1977)

Through the gallery, I came into contact with more and more people, and as my circle of friends expanded, I came to cherish the help and inspiration I received from so many. Alice Boughner, a dear old woman who became one of my art students but was like a second mother to me, shared her bright optimism and wisdom, while Patty Barnes and Pat Mastropaolo, who came to work at the gallery, gave me their constant friendship.

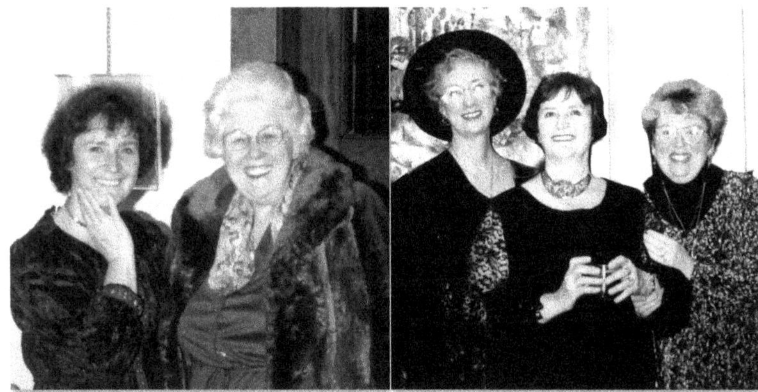

Carla and Alice Boughner (1980)

Patty Barnes, Carla and Pat Mastropaolo (1996)

The Alpha Art Gallery quickly became a center of cultural activity, and it gave me recognition and importance as an artist in the Downriver area where I lived.

As a teacher, I had become a respected authority, and I was well-regarded as a local businesswoman and event organizer who promoted the arts as the soul of the community.

I soon began to present special exhibits and show openings for other artists as well. I founded the Downriver Artists' Guild to promote local artists and provide the gallery space for an annual exhibit of their work.

Then, after a one-man show that I hosted in 1981 for Othmar Carli, he invited me to join him at the International Art Exposition in New York City to introduce my own art to a wider audience. I had worked hard to establish myself through my gallery, but now I began to consider the art world outside of my local Downriver/ Grosse Ile community.

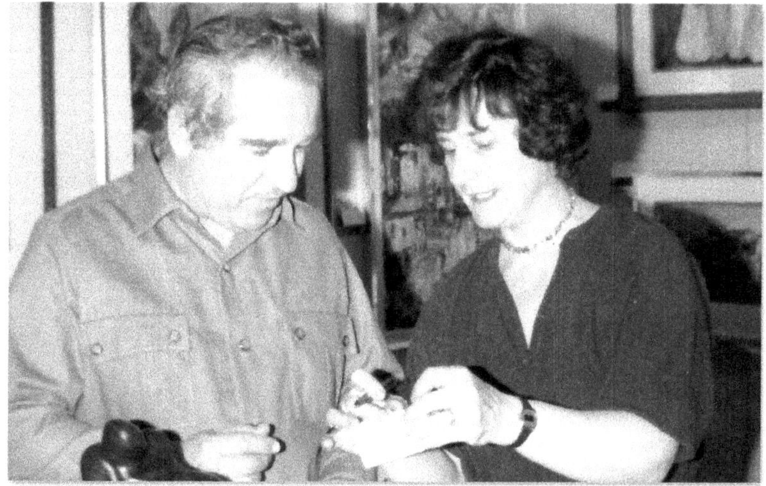

Othmar Carli and Carla, New York Art Expo (1982)

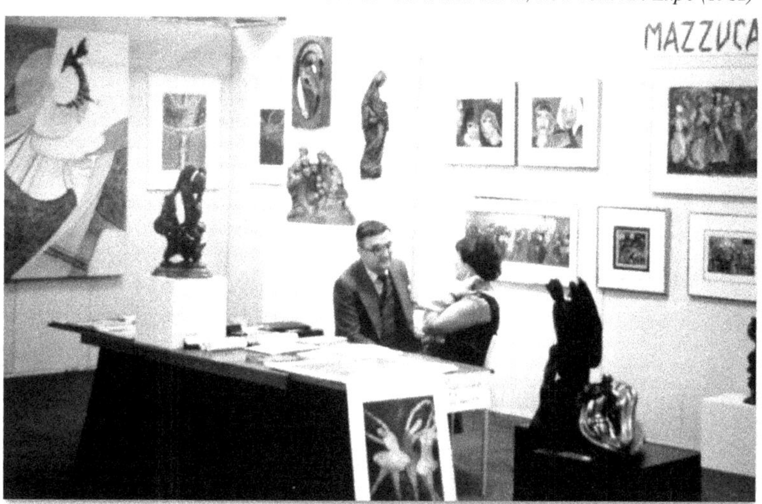

Giuseppe and Carla, New York Art Expo (1982)

I went to New York in 1982 and returned yearly through 1992. It was the beginning of a new period for me, and I traveled and presented my paintings in various galleries around the United States from New York City to Chicago, and Dallas to Palm Springs. I also returned to exhibit my work in Italy, and I received some international attention in the world of art with critiques from England and France in addition to my shows in Italy and the U.S.

In 1990, I was one of four honorees at the Downriver Council for the Arts Salute to Excellence Awards. At a festive, black-tie dinner and ceremony, I was recognized for my cultural contributions along with Vincent Porreca, George Gorno, and John Colina, and we each received a special glass sculpture designed by artist Karnig Dabanian.

I was honored to attend the event held in the beautiful Rivera Court of the Detroit Institute of Arts, a place where I would later become a gallery docent, and share my love and knowledge about the various, wonderful art collections housed at the DIA by conducting gallery tours for international visitors.

Another gala event in downtown Detroit took place on June 18,1999, when my large four foot by six foot oil painting, titled "Evening at the Opera" was unveiled in the ornate lobby of the Detroit Opera House. Commissioned by the Dante Alighieri Society for the Michigan Opera Theater, the painting was the inaugural work of art for the permanent collection now on display at the opera house.

The event, "Italian Interlude," was attended by more than four hundred guests including then Michigan Governor John Engler and Detroit Mayor Dennis W. Archer. I had been introduced, by Maestro Dr. David DiChiera, general director of the Michigan Opera Theatre, as the artist from the birthplace of opera who "translated the emotion of our common experience into a visual celebration of life."

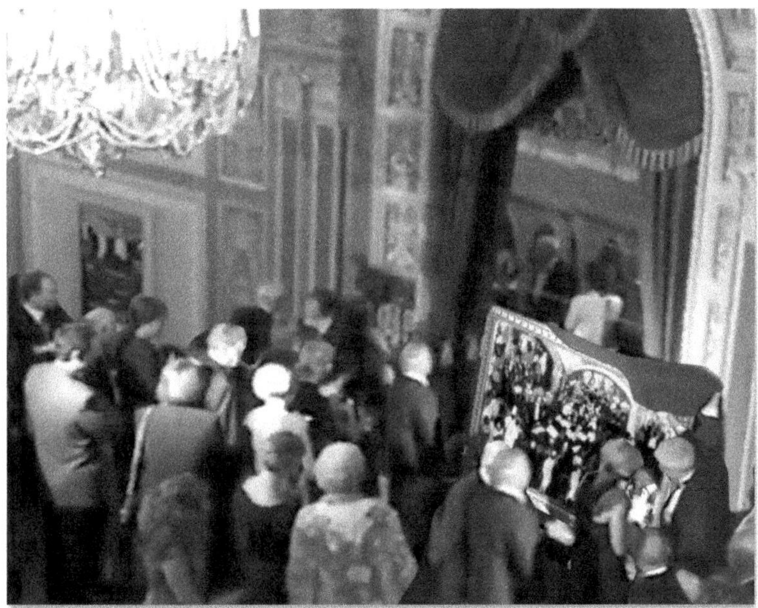

Unveiling of "Evening at the Opera" Detroit Opera House (1999)

They were kind words that recalled various reviews and critiques that my work had received over the years including those of Samuel Sachs II, the Director of the Detroit Institute of Arts from 1985 through 1997. In the foreword of the 1994 book on my art titled, <u>Mazzucato— New Horizons,</u> he had described my "modern expressionist" work as a "spiritual art" with "rhythmic compositions [that] communicate a celebration of life in the joy of the spirit."

I was so honored to receive such warm praise, and I finally felt a sense of certainty that all I had worked to achieve had not simply been "senseless dreaming." Confidence, no matter what success may come, is always an internal struggle to face, but through the embrace of community and friends, I had redefined myself and was stepping into a new season of my life.

Art in My Life

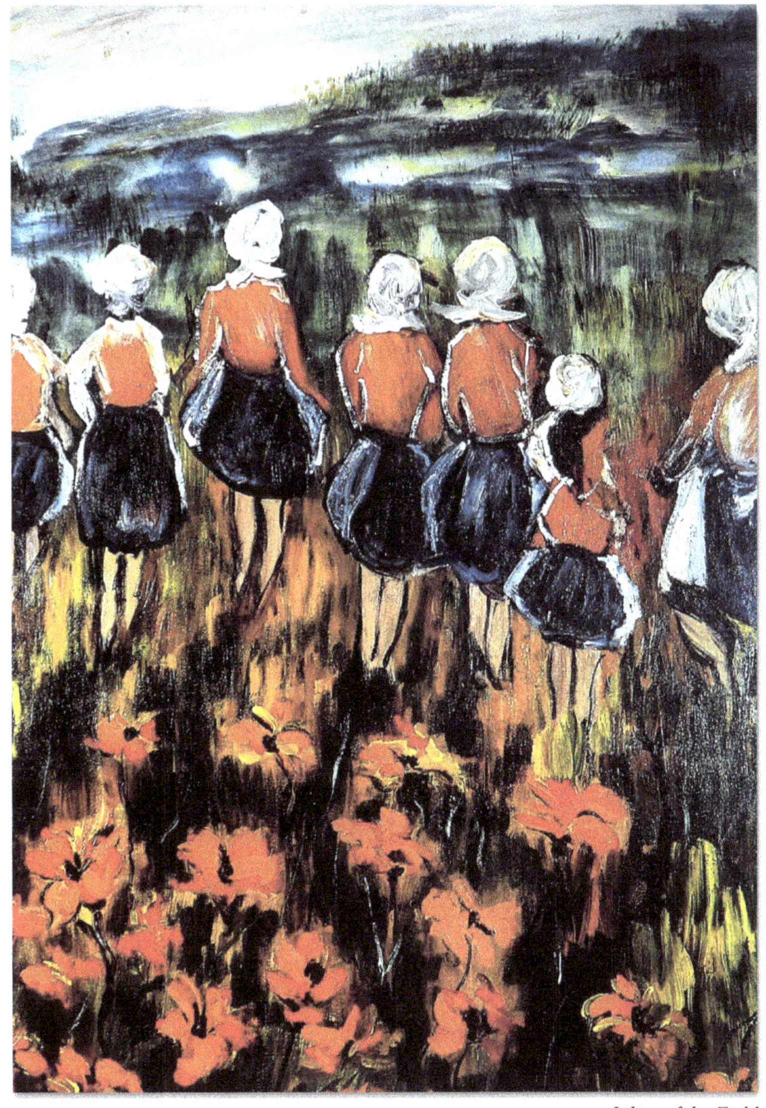

Lilies of the Field

Art became part of my life when I was quite young. My mother was wonderfully artistic, and I remember the drawings and painted watercolors she made for the many sick people she visited in their homes when helping Doctor Nicolussi.

I also loved to listen to her voice when she presented the poems she wrote for various occasions in town, or when she recited by heart written works to us at home, like the first three chapters of Dante's <u>Inferno</u>. It was like music to me.

Actual music, however, was my father's gift. My mother couldn't hold a tune, but my father played his guitar and had a beautiful singing voice. He used to sing the many German songs he knew, starting with lullabies then romantic ballades and *"Wiener Lieder"* (Songs from Vienna).

He even played funny songs to make us laugh and sing-along with him. While playing his music, he also taught us to dance the waltz, leading us around the kitchen table, while my mother cooked *canederli*, a Tyrolean bread dumpling dish, or some other wonderful meal. Those were wonderful nights.

Then, after I had transferred to the *Liceo Classico,* I studied art history for three years and had the opportunity to visit the many Italian churches and museums that housed artistic masterpieces that I had only before seen in books.

Many years later, after arriving in America, I continued my studies and graduated with a Master of Fine Arts degree from Wayne State University in Detroit. I started to teach, I opened my art gallery, and I became a docent at the Detroit Institute of Arts.

As a docent, I learned how to convey the meaning and importance of the centuries of art in the various gallery collections to the many visitors and tour groups that passed through. I presented an "Introduction to the Museum," and every year added an additional tour, specializing in a new area. I presented the gallery's *Art of the Middle Ages, Italian Renaissance, North European Renaissance, America Art* and *Modern Art,* and with every tour I gave, I gained confidence and came to enjoy my time at the museum more and more.

Even Joe came to some of my special tours, and when my cousin Catherina Carli was visiting from Munich one summer, and I led a large international tour through the museum, I could see how pleased Joe was. That gave me great joy.

I was also 'joyful' in 1997, when the Detroit Red Wings hockey team won the Stanley Cup. Hockey was Joe's favorite sport, so I created a painting—a vibrant scene of figures on the ice, celebrating a winning goal. The original painting was auctioned off at a victory event attended by the entire team, and Joe and I were invited as well.

Darren McCarty, who scored the winning goal for Detroit, won the auction and Joe, who was usually quite reserved, actually approached him to ask if he wanted to meet the artist. Joe proudly brought Darren McCarty, and a few other players including goalie Mike Vernon and defenseman Vladimir Konstantinov, back to our table to introduce me, and as pleased as I was to meet them, I was most happy because I saw how Joe, who had worked hard his entire life and supported my artistic dream, was able to participate in that dream on that day.

I had watched all the games with Joe and sketched the players and the action, and now he had gotten the opportunity to meet his favorite players, captain Steve

Yzerman, Brendan Shanahan and Sergei Fedorov. Their win had become a victory for me and Joe too.

All throughout this time, I continued to paint and exhibit both in the United States and abroad. I prepared and presented shows in *Bologna, Prato/Firenze, Appiano* and *Bolzano* in Italy, and Detroit, New York, Chicago, Palm Springs and Dallas in the United States. It was a full and fulfilling schedule, but also demanding.

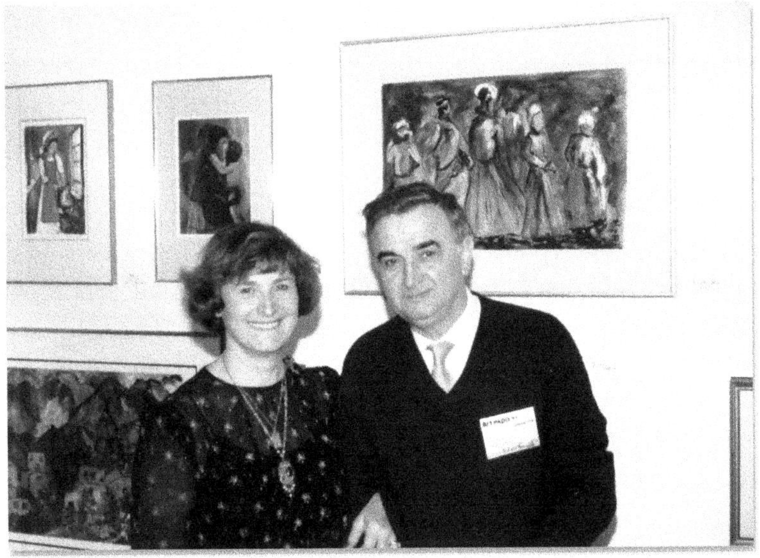

Carla and Giuseppe, on the road at ArtExpo (1985)

When Joe and I had left Italy, we always thought that we would one day return, though we didn't know when. We had made a home together in Michigan, but the memories of the people and places we had left behind were imprinted in our hearts.

Did I miss Italy? I surely felt some nostalgia for the past. Beyond the friends and family still there, the natural landscape covered in vineyards and crowned with mountaintops was scenery that gave us both a sense of serenity that we didn't have in the States.

I missed our outings to *Stroblhof*, the hikes along the trails in and around *Appiano* and the orchards that I knew so well from when I walked with my father. I missed the narrow cobblestone streets and the life in the *piazza,* the lively cafés, and even the intimacy of greeting friends at Sunday Mass.

While I was happy with what I had accomplished so far, I had to recognize that sustaining all my goals had been an enormous commitment of time, and not just for me.

Joe was involved with the framing shop and attended all the courses we took together, in various cities, to learn the framing business. He enjoyed it, but after working a full eight-hour shift at the Ford stamping plant, he now spent his afternoons and weekends cutting and assembling frames. It was all work, and I knew that continuing it all would keep us from enjoying any of it.

I wanted to advance in my profession, but to focus on that, I would have to do other things beside the work at my gallery.

After an exhibit of my art in Dallas, Texas, on the flight back to Detroit, I looked at Joe. He had fallen asleep in his seat. I could see he was tired. He had been so loving and supportive with his time for so many years, and as I watched him, I thought it was time for him to relax a bit.

When he woke up I told him that I had decided to sell the gallery, give up framing and teaching, to devote myself only to becoming the best artist I could be. He seemed surprised, but said nothing. Only a smile let me know that he appreciated the choice. So, I did it. I sold the art gallery, took a new path and turned into another season.

Even without the gallery, painting continued to be a great source of joy and fulfillment for me.

When a blank canvas takes on the emotion and fantasy in my mind, sometimes with impromptu results, the completed work can express unlimited space, the infinite distance, the eternal sky. I blend people with the world around them, and create movement toward a new horizon of harmony and peace.

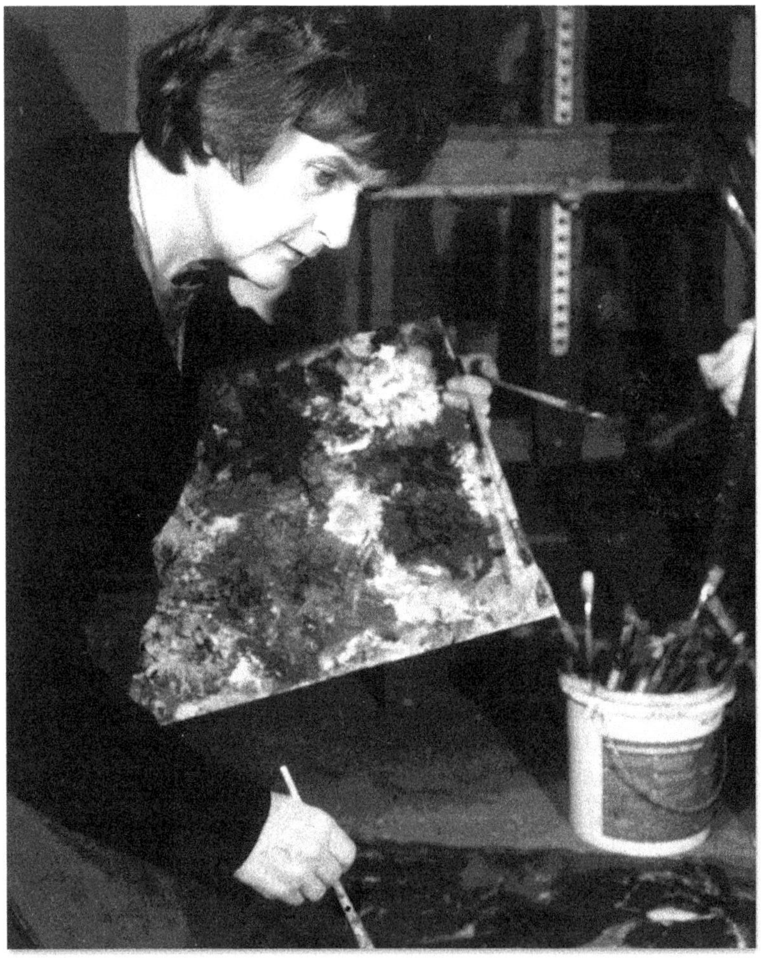

Carla Carli Mazzucato (c. 1987)

It is perhaps the optimism instilled in me by my father so many years ago, optimism that survived through war and hardship, uncertainty and fear. I traveled through many years, buoyed by memories of what had passed and urged on by the wonderful moments in my present and the hope for what will come tomorrow.

In 2001, I was able to pay tribute to the guiding influence of my father, when I was invited to exhibit my art in the *Castle San Valentin*, in *Appiano*, town of my birth. It was a "homecoming" exhibit, and I was quite happy to revisit the nostalgic places and moments from my past on canvas. I imagined looking from the window of my father's house, and painted the landscapes that I remembered—the castles and homes that rose among the vineyards.

I walked again with my father, in memory, along the path by the brook that leads to the little church of *Maria Rast*; the narrow streets that wind their way up to *Stroblhof* and on to *Thurnbach* and its therapeutic baths of chestnut leaves. Finally, I walked through the woods around the lake of Monticolo, and I painted my green valley of *Appiano* with all the variety of color that my palette could hold to describe the beauty of the place.

The book <u>Heimkehr</u> (Return to My Homeland) was published for the show, and the paintings contained within the pages express my feelings in every shade and hue of the changing seasons.

Seasons have always represented the passage of time, from our beginning to our growth and transformation. Nature's pattern mingles in our soul like the symbolic cycle of our life, as winter shadows give way to the brightness of summer sun that fades into the colors of autumn.

These are the thoughts that paint my imagination with the vivid fall colors I remember from *Appiano* and Michigan, and the golden tones of the hillsides in the West.

In 2005, an exhibit of my work entitled "A Glimpse of Tuscany" was presented by the co-director of the *Guggenheim Gallery* at Chapman University in California. Here too, I was able to paint and relive the serenity I had felt when I had roamed the hills of Tuscany and enjoyed the magnificent art and monuments in the city of Florence.

The following year, marked the first of three exhibits at the *Bowers Museum* in Santa Ana, where works from my "America" and "Venice" series were displayed.

That autumn, I returned to Italy for an exhibit at the *Prisma Gallery* in *Bolzano*, and over the next few years, had shows in Florida, Connecticut, and Las Vegas, Nevada.

Laguna Beach, California—a charming art colony with over 100 art galleries and artist studios—became a favorite spot for me, and the gallery *La Bottega d'Arte* presented my paintings to fine art patrons on the west coast at numerous showings, art walks and gallery events.

For each of these shows, the paintings selected represented various moments in my life, seasons past, the places I have been and the people I have encountered and come to know through time. All have influenced my perception of life and profoundly shaped my artistic expression.

Through my Spring, Summer, Autumn and Winter in art, I paint my life as I want it to be remembered, with joyous light and color. My art is my life, a sentiment that my son captured in a poem he wrote to me when he was a young boy.

The Artist

A dab of white
To cool my mind,
So full of thoughts
Of what I'd find,

> *If I were free to roam and paint,*
> *and show the world my works of art.*

A dab of blue
to soothe the pain,
I get when pond'ing
What I'd gain,

> *If I were free to leave and paint,*
> *and show the world my works of art.*

A dab of red
to spur me on,
In thinking when
The day will come,

> *When I'll be free to run and paint,*
> *and show the world my works of art*

And now some brown
for thankless days,
Some purple fear
And lonely grays,
Some envious green
for that I lack,
Some hopeful gold
Frustration black—

> *But Stop!*

I've painted much
a brush can't tell—
My life a portrait
painted well.

> *And I am free to love and paint,*
> *and show the world my works of art.*

pvm

CHAPTER TWENTY-ONE

Special Moments

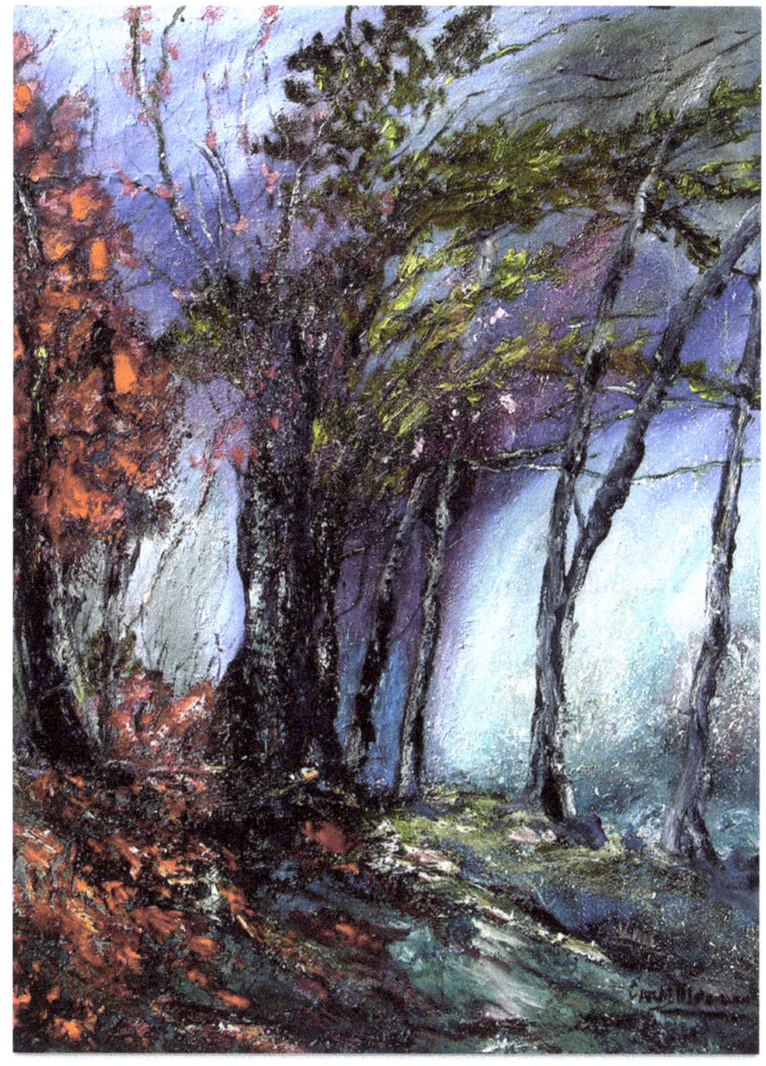

Colors of the Wind

Each of us preserves deep within our memory, an intimate collection of special moments from our past that mark the different seasons of our life. We can recall affectionate voices from our infancy, the excitement of youthful dreams and feelings of first love, and relive both happy days spent with friends as well as dreadful times spent in the darkness of war. We each have a connection to an inner voice that tells our story through time.

Sitting here, remembering my distant past, I am drawn to recall the past more recent—the memories that tell the story of my children, the best part of my life and love with Giuseppe. Our children are ours but briefly, in that time when they are unable to care for themselves and before they depart to fulfill their own lives and destiny with the blessings of their own families.

For them we have tried to shine as a beacon of light during cloudy days, to help them smile when they were sad or to share their pain and tears as we sought to protect them with our hope and love. And through our time with them, they have begun their own stories as they set off on their journeys through their seasons of life.

They too will listen to the voices within and learn to create and collect their special moments as they discover the potential for great fulfillment in themselves. They each have different gifts and their voices will rise as mine becomes quiet and I pause to listen.

Now I feel their story in the continuation of mine, their ideas and dreams—like individual Autumn leaves that matured into a glorious canopy and now color the ground all around me. So many moments opened my mind to a new world, their world, and enriched the tapestry of my life.

I remember how proud Giuseppe was when he watched his young children race at a picnic hosted by the Caboto Club in Windsor, Canada. It made me think of Giuseppe, as a boy, running like the wind through the fields of *Pontelongo* after having caused some mischief of some kind. Anna and Paolo both won the races for the children their age, and Daniela who was still too young, raced with the older children, not wanting to be left out. Many years later, Paolo became a distance runner in high school, and Daniela a sprinter, and in each race and each victory, Giuseppe relived his own youth again.

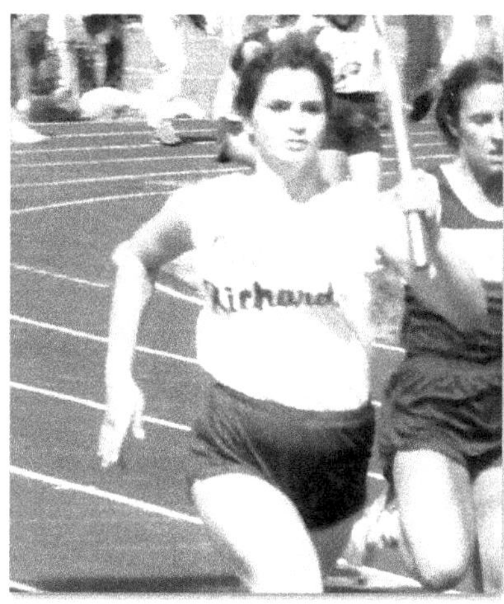

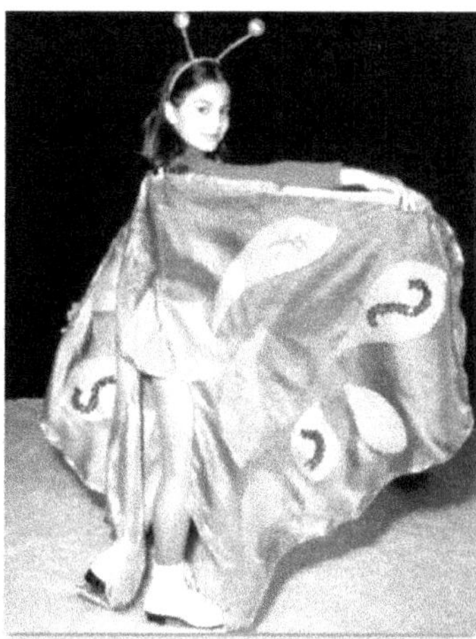

Daniela (1986)   *Anna (1971)*

Just as special, was the time I spent at the local ice rink, where my children each took skating lessons. I waited on the hard benches beside the rink while they practiced, wanting them to experience as many different possibilities in life till they discovered their dreams as I had tried to do in mine. And as Giuseppe and I watched the figure-skating ice show at the end of the season, when Anna performed, dressed as a lavender butterfly, I hoped that those dreams would transform them so they could take flight.

Anna enrolled at Wayne State University to study theater, and there too I enjoyed watching her explore possibilities. In the two beautiful university theaters, the Hillberry and Bonstelle, I watched Anna perform the plays of Shakespeare and other playwrights, thinking back on the joy that my mother, also Anna, always found from performing theater. When Anna played Juliet in <u>Romeo and Juliet</u>, I was so impressed with her ability; then, in <u>Agnes of God</u>, I was more than proud. I was astounded by her dramatic capacity in presenting such intense scenes. It was as if my daughter had disappeared, and only the character, the profoundly troubled, young Agnes, remained on stage.

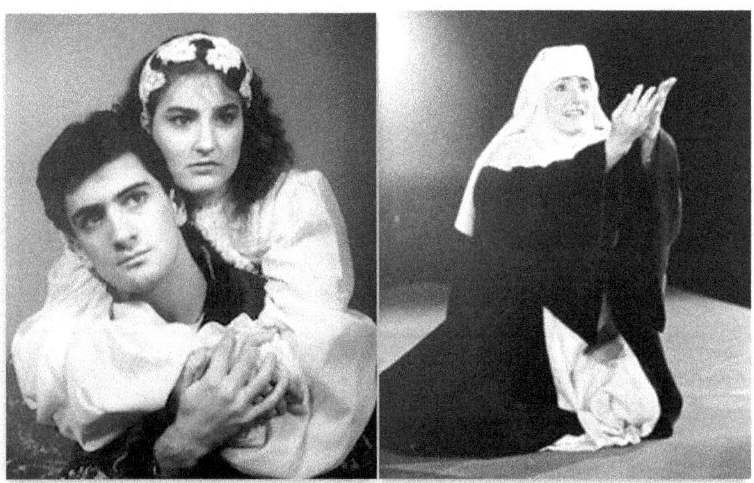

Anna in <u>Romeo and Juliet</u> and <u>Agnes of God</u>

After my children all left home, Anna for Los Angeles, Paolo and Daniela for college, I was left alone. As consolation, I would drive by myself up to Detroit and park outside the apartment where Anna had lived when she was a student. I imagined that she was still there in Detroit, and I stayed for a while, tearful and nostalgic for the days that had passed into memory, like a faded dream.

As Paolo finished his studies at Northwestern University in Evanston, Illinois, he got some notice when his stage-play, <u>Politicos</u>, was produced at the Organic Theater in Chicago.

He then prepared for a trip to Moscow, in what was then the U.S.S.R., where he and one of his classmates proposed to film a coproduction with Russian students at the Gerasimov Institute of Cinematography (V.G.I.K.). <u>The Bridge Project</u> would be the first-ever collaboration between American and Soviet students.

In July of 1988, Paolo and fellow filmmaker, Robert Kath, made the first trip to Moscow to meet the Soviet students that would join the project. They selected a song to tell the story of a young Russian boy and American girl who hoped to bridge the gap between their two countries and cultures, and wrote the story they would film together. They then returned in September, with a crew of students from both Northwestern and V.G.I.K., to film in Moscow, Leningrad (now St. Petersburg), and then in Chicago.

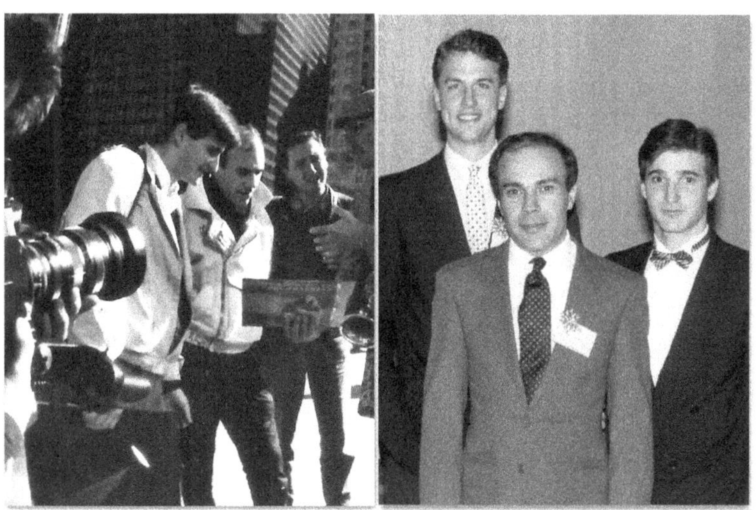

Filming in Chicago— Robert Kath, Boris Airapetyan, Paolo Mazzucato

It was a hopeful project, made during a hopeful time when Mikhail Gorbachev's *Glasnost* and *Perestroika* gave us all hope for a more open relationship between Russia and the United States. The Bridge Project, went on to win several awards and was screened in American embassies during the 1990 summit between Presidents George Bush Sr. and Mikhail Gorbachev. Paolo then moved to Los Angeles to study motion picture producing at the University of Southern California.

Daniela chose International and Public Relations in the James Madison College at Michigan State University in Lansing, for her career path. The field of study created many possibilities for professional growth and opportunities to form lasting friendships.

She studied in Tours, France, in 1984, through a university foreign exchange program, and was already speaking fluent French by the time that I went to visit her with my brother, Bruno, and nephew Paolo. We also got to spend time with Bruno's good friend, Pierre-Marie Beaude, and explore the many beautiful areas of France.

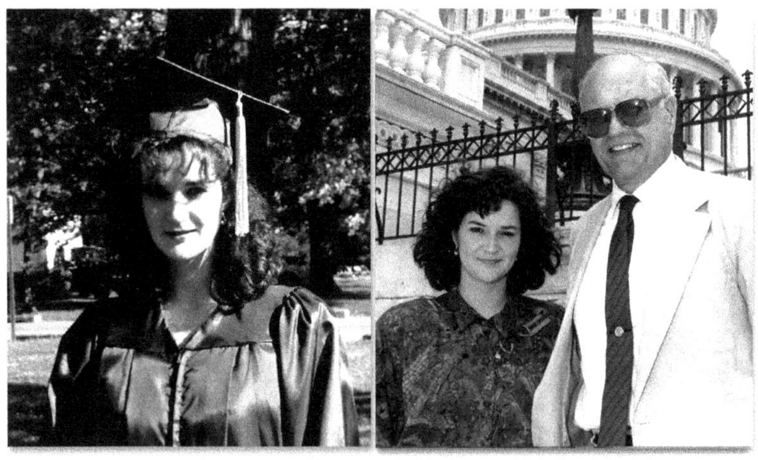

Daniela with Congressman John Dingell (1991)

Daniela also needed to complete an internship to fulfill the requirements for her diploma, so she accepted a staff position in the state office of U.S. Congressman John Dingell in Michigan. After completing her internship and graduating, she was asked to continue working for him in the House of Representatives' offices in Washington, D.C. She went on to work on Capitol Hill for many years before eventually moving to Los Angeles to work in film animation at the Walt Disney Company, then later DreamWorks and Netflix.

Now that the children were all in California, Joe and I anxiously awaited the arrival of Christmas each year.

The magic of Christmas always makes it the best time of the year. Not only is it a time of spiritual significance, but it is also when families come together beneath the lights in the sky and the streets. Lighted doorways welcome us home to cozy rooms where green Christmas trees and red flowers greet us. We may cuddle together by the fireplace and sing Christmas carols or listen to the soft music of the season that enters our soul and makes us feel part of a wider world of peace and abundant love.

And for us, it was our time of reunion.

Anna, Paolo and Daniela would return to Michigan for the holidays and we could celebrate once again as we had during the years of their youth.

They would remember the simple Christmas plays they had performed for me and Joe—nativity puppet shows with characters made from decorated lunch bags or cut from cardboard that would appear over the back of the couch to enact the story of Jesus' birth.

Daniela, with her angelic voice, and Paolo and Anna would each narrate a passage from the Gospel, until the puppet shepherds and angels concluded with a chorus of *It Came Upon a Midnight Clear.* Then we all joined in singing from our books of Christmas carols while Anna accompanied on the piano and Paolo on his violin.

With the ringing of a small bell, Daniela then carried out the baby Jesus to his place between Mary and Joseph in our nativity scene. And after we all offered a special prayer to the baby Jesus, we would gather around the Christmas tree, our *Tannenbaum,* to open gifts.

I still remember when my mother would ring the bell to announce the birth of the baby Jesus to all the family gathered in our kitchen in *Appiano* years ago. "Angels" had visited our living room and left Christmas gifts for us, and we entered from the kitchen to see the pine tree that my mother had decorated with all kinds of ornaments, candles and the many good cookies she had baked the day before.

A whole corner of the room had been reserved for a nativity scene assembled on a large table covered in fresh moss, gathered from the woods of *Appiano.* A small path made with white baking flower led to the small stable, and angels floated above the manger where baby Jesus was laid between Mary and Joseph, and watched over by an ox and a donkey.

Before this nativity scene, we sang Christmas carols in German, Latin and Italian—*Stille Nacht, Adeste Fideles* and *La Notte di Natale*—before we went to open our presents under the tree.

Our Santa Claus, the *Heiliger Nikolaus,* came for us on December 6th together with the *Krampus,* a devilish figure (usually played by our cousin Richard, in costume). He came with clanking chains to scare all the children that had not behaved well during the year, and would take them away in a large basket he carried on his back.

I knew that the *Krampus* was my cousin Richard, but nevertheless, when I heard the sound of approaching chains, I would be so frightened that I would run and hide somewhere, not to be found.

The version of Christmas we celebrated in my childhood differed quite a bit from the more elaborate feast that my children would prepare for me and Joe during the many years we lived in Michigan, but the season always remained my favorite.

Michigan winters blanketed everything with snow, and it was often quite cold outside. Inside by the tree and beside the crackling fire in the fireplace, however, the evening of celebration, singing and togetherness was always quite warm.

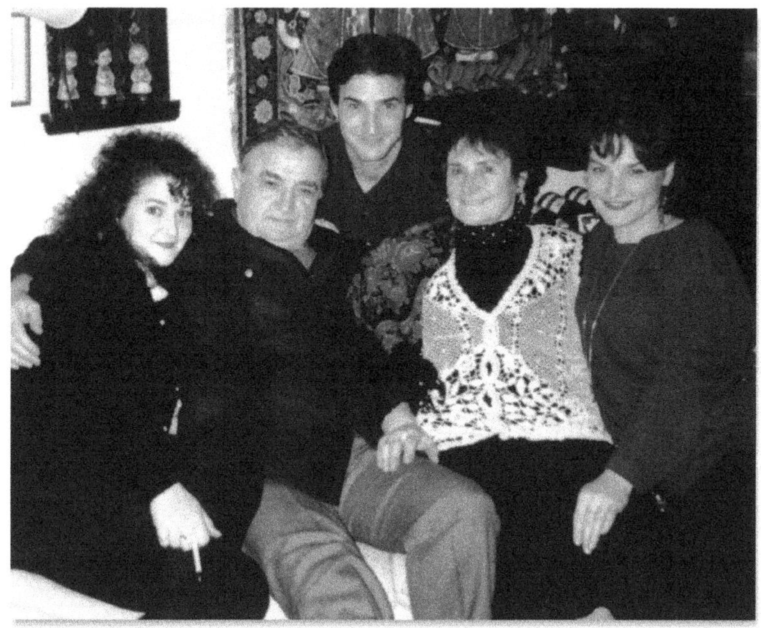

Daniela, Giuseppe, Paolo, Carla, Anna (Christmas 1994)

In 1987, Joe had decided to finally retire. He had worked his entire life, since his early teenage years, following opportunities that brought him from Italy to Canada and then the United States, where he had become a most skilled and respected tool and die maker at the Ford Motor Company.

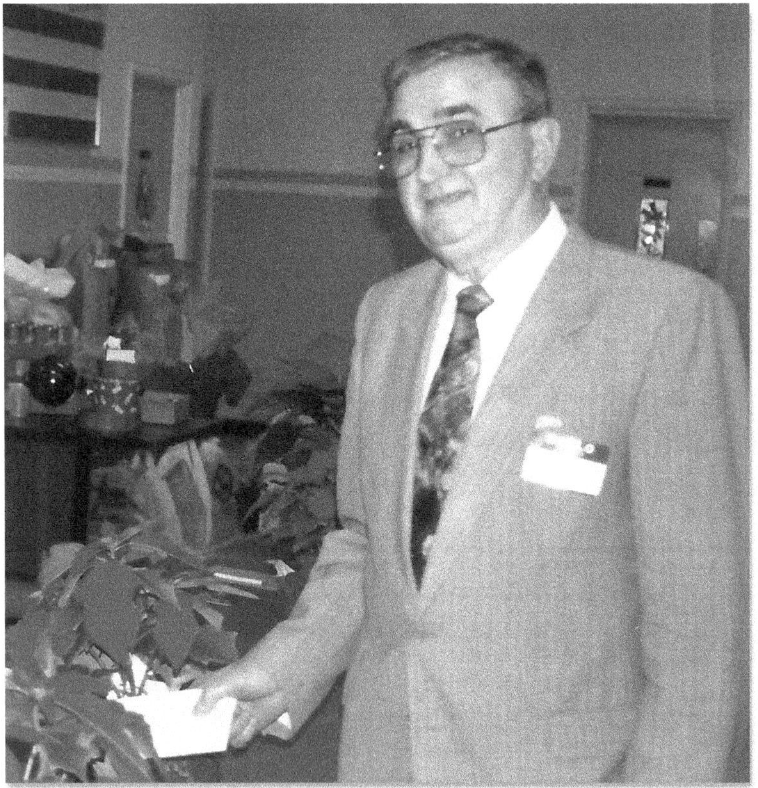

Giuseppe, Ford Motor Company Retirement (1987)

But our children were all situated or firmly on their paths now, and I think he felt that his mission was complete. He was honored at a retirement dinner, and together we looked forward to the next stage of our lives together.

That stage began with an announcement from Anna:

This day I will marry my friend,
the one I laugh with,
the one I live for, dream with, love.

Anna had met Brian Teixeira while they were students at Wayne State University. They had both moved to Los Angeles, and now, years later, on July 9, 1988, they married at St. Cyprian's Church in Riverview, Michigan.

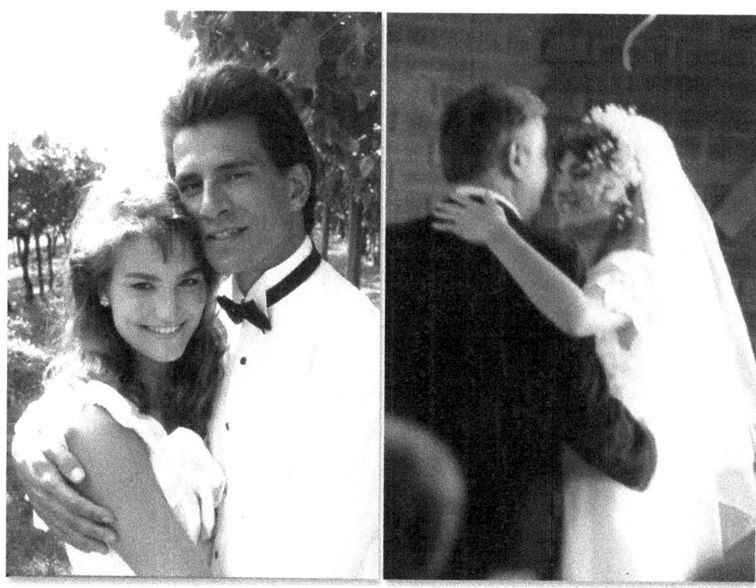

Anna and Brian Teixeira　　　*(June 9, 1988)*　　　*Giuseppe and Anna*

I felt a mixture of emotions at the news—joy, and yet somehow, disbelief. I loved Anna and Brian and thought they were a "perfect match," but realizing that my daughter was all grown and moving on brought back memories of when she had played Shprintze, one of Tevye's young daughters, in her high school production of <u>Fiddler on the Roof</u>. *"Is this the little girl I carried?"* and

"When did she get to be a beauty?" The words and pensive melody of the play's wedding song came to mind as I watched Anna on her special day and thought:

Sunrise, sunset, Sunrise, sunset, Swiftly flow the days;
Seedlings turn overnight to sunflowers,
Blossoming even as we gaze.
Sunrise, sunset, Sunrise, sunset, Swiftly fly the years;
One season following another,
Laden with happiness and tears.

Sheldon Harnick, Fiddler on the Roof

Five years later, in 1993, Paolo married too. He had met Karyn Kubo, while at Northwestern University, and after he had made his film in Russia, and completed his graduate studies in Los Angeles, we all traveled to Karyn's home in Honolulu, Hawaii, to share in their special day as well.

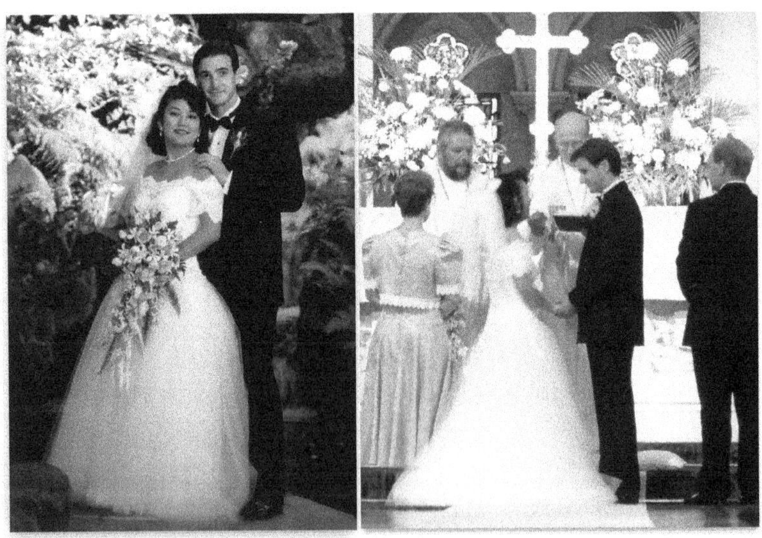

Karyn and Paolo Mazzucato   *(August 21, 1993)*   *with Bruno Carli*

My brother, Bruno, flew out to co-officiate the ceremony, and we spent a lovely week visiting with Karyn's family and touring about the island of Oahu.

The next bit of big news came five years after that when Karyn gave birth to my first beautiful granddaughter, Olivia Maria, in April.

And that same year, 1998, Anna had some similar news. She had been cast in the leading role in a Los Angeles stage production of Shakespeare's <u>The Merchant of Venice</u>, and while congratulating her for her role as Portia, Anna announced that she was going to have a baby. I was confused at first. I knew the play, and was sure that Portia did not have a baby in the story. Anna explained, "No, not Portia, me!" And so I had tears of joy, and my second wonderful granddaughter, Mikaela Maria, arrived in September.

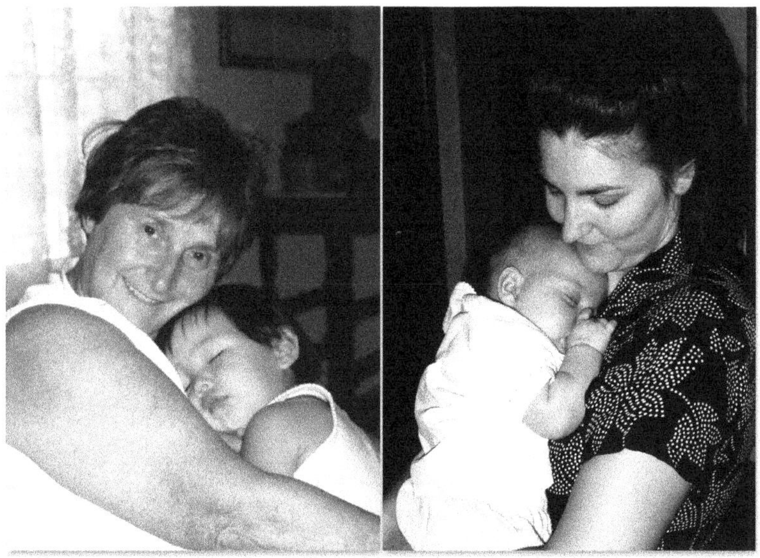

Carla and Olivia , Mikaela and Anna

While Daniela had been working in Washington, D.C., Joe and I felt that staying in Michigan—between Daniela on the East Coast and Anna and Paolo on the West—was the right place for us. But when Daniela moved to Los Angeles as well, and we received the big news of the coming arrival of two grandchildren, I decided we should trade Michigan and the green plains of the Midwest for the sunny and rolling hills of Southern California.

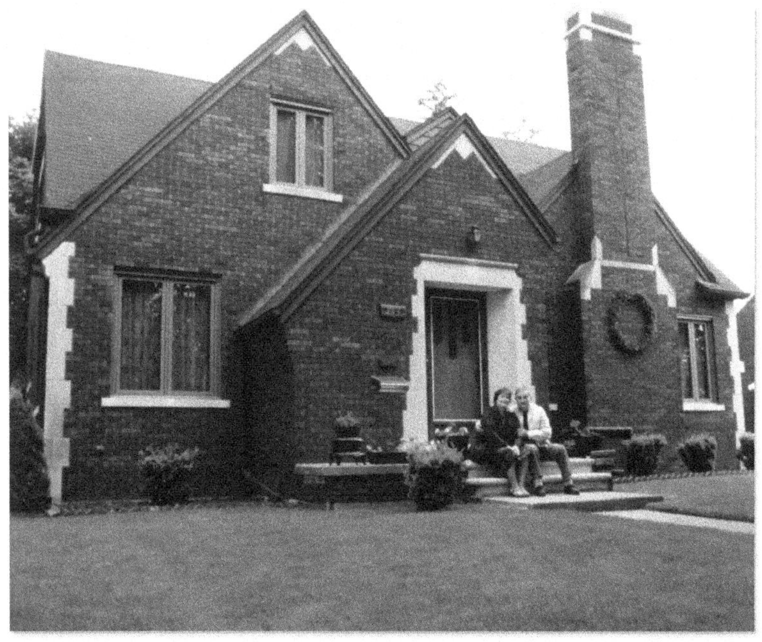

Mazzucato Home - 2638 Lenox Road - (1968-1998)

A NEW HOME

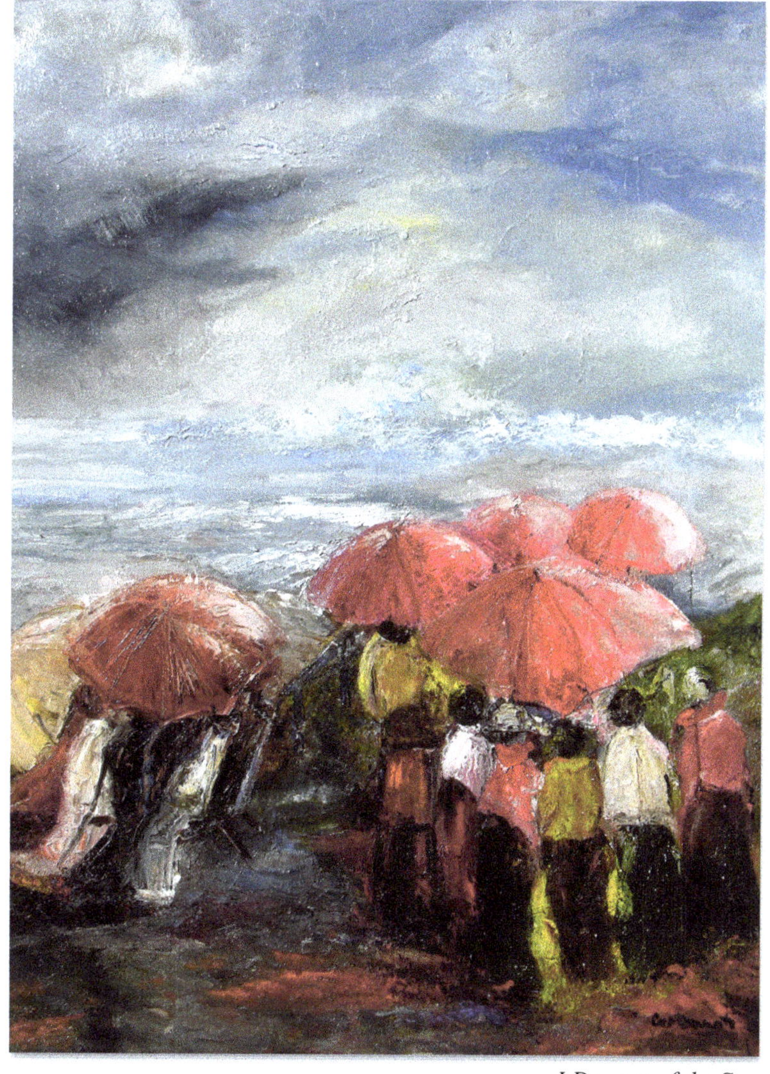

I Dreamt of the Sea

Life in California

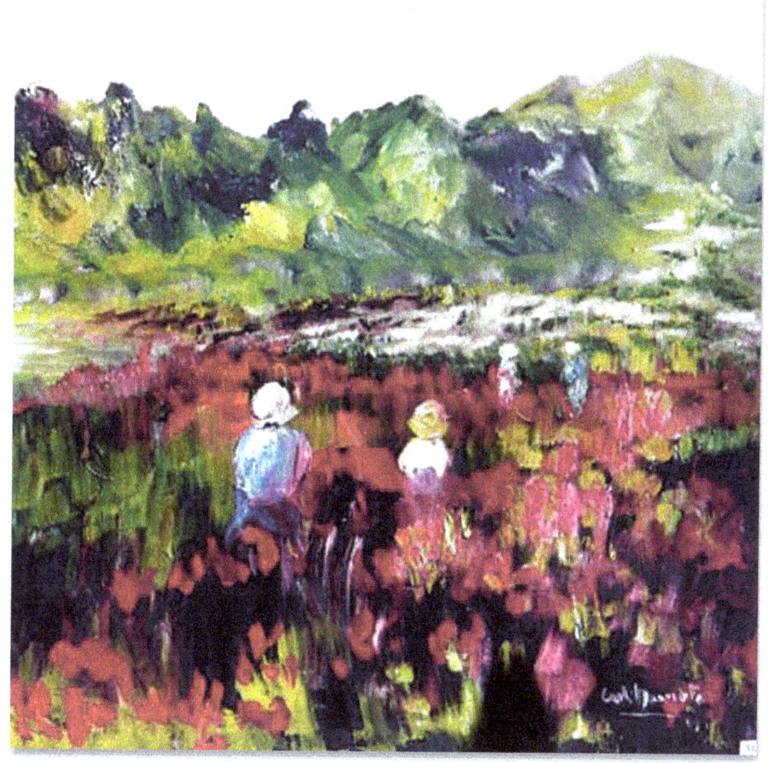

California Poppies

Is it so small a thing, to have enjoyed the sun,
to have lived light in the spring,
to have loved, to have thought, to have done?

Carla Mazzucato

The house Joe bought in Orange County, California, in 1998 lies among the pleasant hills in the city of Tustin. From where the house is situated, along the "paseo," a greenway and flowered path through the group of homes, it is a short thirty-minute walk to the top of our hill.

From there the view is fantastic. To the southwest is the ocean that brightly shines on the horizon, turning gold and bright orange at sunset; to either side are rolling hills intersected by gently curving streets and highways that form a corridor to the north and east.

On a clear day, under the blue California sky, a crown of mountains off in the distance rises as if to protect the sparse towns and cities spread over the vast landscape. The variety of cool and warm colors, blue, green, yellow and white complete the picture.

Inspiration in life and art certainly comes from the beauty that surrounds us. The California sun and vivid landscapes filled me again with the desire to express my emotions on canvas, and I began a new series of paintings, a tribute to America, my adoptive home. But I found the strongest inspiration came not from place, but from people.

By the time Joe and I came to live on the west coast, we already had two granddaughters. Two more girls arrived three years later in 2001. Olivia was joined by her sister Julia in May, and Mikaela welcomed her sister Kiara in September.

Looking into the bright eyes of my beautiful granddaughters, I saw the world again as a place of endless possibility. They are all so unique with different dreams for what their future might be, and I can only guess for now all that they will accomplish in their hopeful futures.

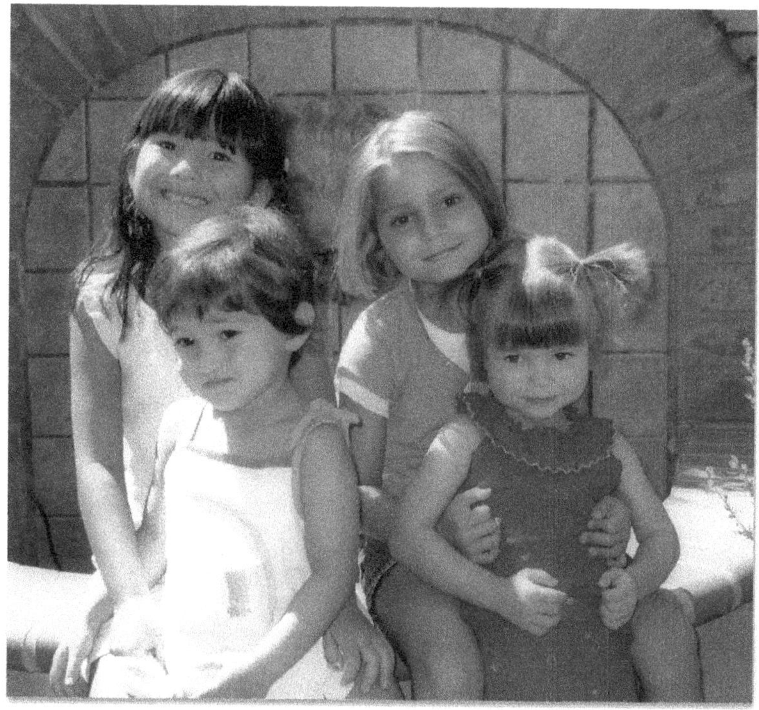

Olivia, Julia, Mikaela, Kiara (2003)

I cannot forget the worries, however, that I had to endure when Anna was expecting Kiara. Joe and I were at the Marco Polo Airport in Venice, Italy, ready to return home to the United States after our summer vacation. But on that morning in New York City, September 11, everything changed.

We heard about the terrible attack on New York, and every flight was cancelled. We had to wait three more weeks before we could fly back.

During this time Joe and I went to a restaurant to view the television and listen to the news. The fear and disbelief were pervasive, and all the newspapers reported on the horrible tragedy including the local paper of the Italian "Filodiretto" which wrote:

221

The date of September 11, 2001 can never be forgotten; it is a wound in the heart of the world... In this moment, as some have said, we are all Americans, we all are citizens of the world in mourning because of this atrocious attack on liberty... The flag of solidarity is at half-staff, a trumpet sounds with heartbreaking notes of silence. This is the hour to reflect and pray, each of us in our own creed."

Ernesto Pisani

What a relief it was when we were back again in the place we called home, where we could take our granddaughters for a peaceful walk, or just stay in our beautiful garden where a fountain, spouting water from a reassuring stone lion, refreshed our spirit and bathed the hot summer months in tranquility.

And as before, we waited with anticipation and hope for the coming Christmas season, when we could once again come together, now in a much larger group, to celebrate our family.

Of course, in Southern California, the winters are without snow, and our expanded family had brought together new traditions from Guyana in South America (where Anna's husband, Brian, is from), and from Hawaii (where Paolo's wife, Karyn was raised).

The Christmas trees are now much bigger, with hundreds more ornaments and lights. The carols and the music are still played occasionally by Anna and Paolo, but now also by Olivia and Karyn on piano and Mikaela, Anna and Brian on guitar, and even sometimes a tune by Julia on flute.

Together we formed a choir that was both jubilant and, quite often, funny. Joe used to join us by singing his verse of the song <u>The Twelve Days of Christmas</u> where his "Nine Ladies Dancing" was the most eagerly awaited line in each round of the song. He enjoyed it, and we all joined our singing with laughter and joy each new year we were together again. *Alleluia!*

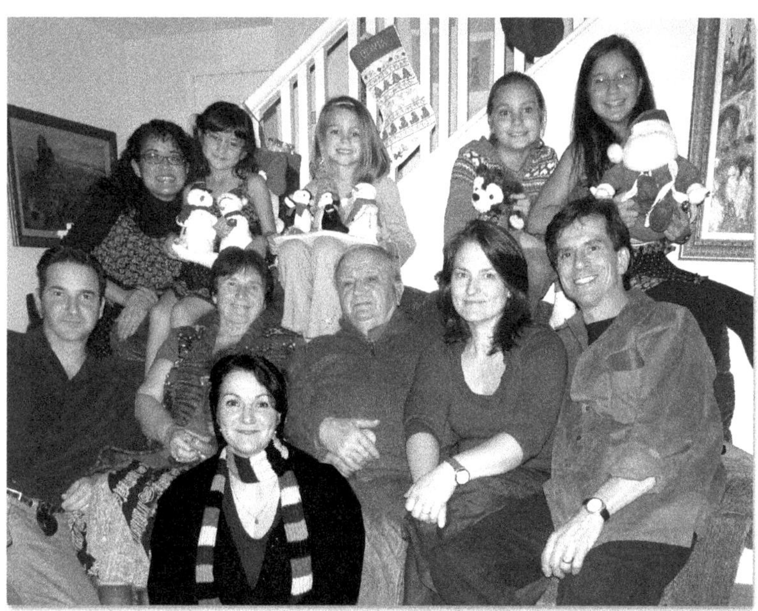

Christmas 2008 —(Top) Karyn, Julia, Kiara, Mikaela, Olivia, (Middle) Paolo, Carla, Giuseppe, Anna, Brian, (Front) Daniela

I look forward to that wonderful music every year, and we still sing the Christmas carols, but Joe's voice is now only in my heart. He passed away on December 21, 2016.

CHAPTER TWENTY-THREE

Faith

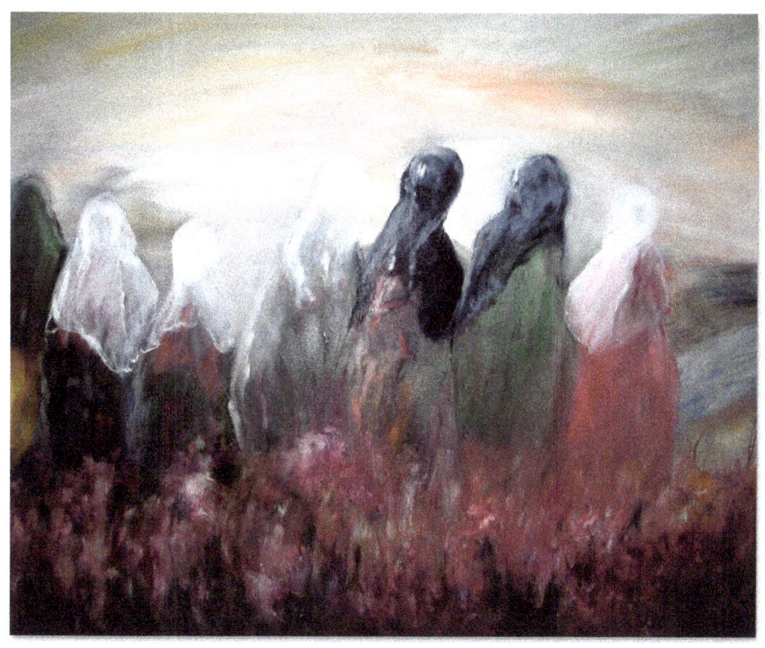

Valley of Hope

This is the new day we will embrace,
and the new world we envision,
where all are welcomed, all are cherished,
and all can be called home.

from the poem "A New Day," pvm

How can we just go on with our life when part of us is gone? I reflect on the story of my life now, and I ponder how there is beauty in my faith. It is old—yes, ancient in fact—but it still gives me meaning beyond myself. It shows me purpose.

I will face my final journey with courage, and patiently reflect on the way Jesus lived his life to enter more deeply into the mystery of God, the mystery of relationships and the mystery of life. Only He has words of eternal life.

Marriage can be the longest time you live with one person, the person you promise to love for as long as you live. My union with Joe lasted for fifty-four years. The unity you establish at the altar in your younger years may not always be smooth and simple, but with every stage of life you can assess the profound bond you have created through the years.

There may be days of crisis and there may be some days of sorrow, but it is then that you find comfort from the person who knows you best, and with whom you created many moments of happiness and joy.

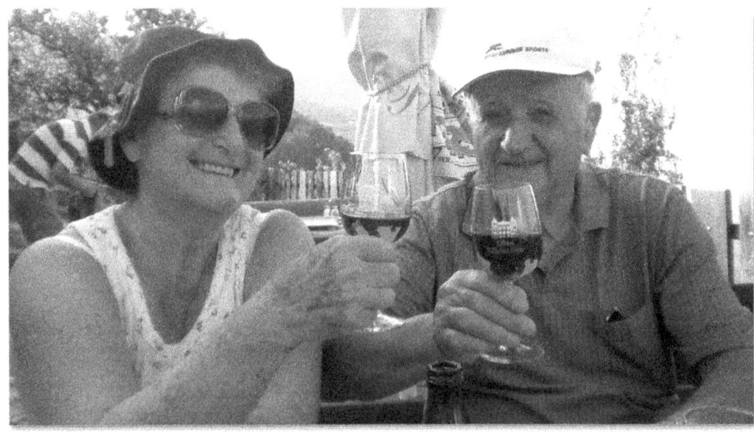

Carla and Giuseppe Mazzucato (2010)

Now I have to set aside any self-limiting ideas that may fill my mind, and proceed with courage to create more happy moments. Wherever my spiritual search leads and whatever doubts my faith may raise, I know that even science cannot comprehend the supernatural. I have to call out with hope and faith: Lord, let me hear your voice, Lord show me the way.

Throughout my life I have been confident in the faith that my parents passed on to me, and my Catholic Church gave me guidance, with rules and dogma, to be closer to God.

And yet I remember that I was only in my teens when I started to question the mystery of redemption. I asked our assistant pastor, Dr. Pavlic, "Why did God send His Son to redeem us? Why send Jesus to death? What purpose did it serve? And why death, and why not justice? There was real evil in the world. Why not stop it?"

These were the questions I posed to myself, even as I accepted the tenets of my Christian religion and felt that the truth put forth by the pope in Rome must be valid for me too. I just needed humility in my quest for answers.

I realize, though, that I had not the will to go further with my scrutiny of religion and faith back then. There was also a sense of peace in accepting the faith of my fathers which offered the stability that came from a life built on faith, hope, and love.

In later years, however, when I reached a certain maturity, I had time to ponder deeply the meaning of life and the pursuit of happiness. I turned to the great philosophers and religions of the world. I was searching for the path that would present the moment of truth due right now, in the present, and not postpone justice until some apocalyptic time.

In the past decade, I began listening to the discussions on faith by Reza Aslan, who was born in Iran but came to the United States as young student and became a biblical scholar who writes with an understanding of religion steeped in history, language and scriptural studies.

After having written <u>No god but God</u> in which he discussed the Islamic faith, he turned his focus to Jesus, seeing him as one of the many would-be messiahs who sprang up during Rome's occupation of Palestine.

His book <u>Zealot: the Life and Times of Jesus of Nazareth</u> is a vivid, persuasive portrait of the world and societies in which Jesus lived and the role he most likely played in both. Jesus of Nazareth, the dominant figure in the history of mankind, and the extraordinary man of the Christian faith, is only considered in his historical context.

It is a well-researched, readable biography of Jesus of Nazareth, and Aslan develops a convincing and coherent story of how the Christian church, and in particular Paul in his Letters, reshapes Christianity's essence.

Aslan concludes that all religions only show us the way to communicate with God, and that the "water of Truth" comes from the same well—the one and only well of the Universal One.

My focus in exploring the faith of my culture, was to rediscover the true Jesus of the Gospels, before the influences of the Christian and Catholic church established by Paul of Tarsus, and later controlled by the Roman hierarchy.

I read intently the books of Prof. Bart D. Ehrman about Christianity, and those by the many authors who wrote about the historic Jesus of Nazareth:

Jesus and His Jewish Influences,
Jesus and the Gospels,
How Jesus became God,
The History of Christianity:
   From the Disciples to the Reformation,
A History of Christianity in the Reformation Era,
Comparative Religion by. *Prof Charles Kimball,*
Philosophy, Religion, and the Meaning of Life
   by *Prof. F. Ambrosio,*

These books reinterpreted the scriptures for me and provided meaning in the context of the world today.

Pope Francis is truly the pontiff for our time, and invites us to profoundly examine our beliefs and the religion we choose to guide us to eternity. Pope Francis has often put into words simple truths that I have also felt and come to trust.

> *Having faith does not mean having no difficulties, but having the strength to face them, knowing we are not alone.*
> *Pope Francis*

I do believe in God, and I have faith in goodness even though there will never be proof of God's existence. It is a belief based on faith alone. I know that I cannot prove God's creation or divinity, but I believe in the power of the Spirit and accept the mystery of life as I follow the example of Jesus. He is *Via, Vita, Veritas.*

At the end of 2020, in the midst of the terrible coronavirus pandemic that swept over the entire world, I once again spent Christmas reflecting on the blessings of my life. In the beautiful, illuminated garden of my California home, my children and their families gathered, distanced and masked, to sing together again the beautiful Christmas carols that have always brought joy to our spirit and peace to our life in celebrating that Christ is born!

While the winter season often makes me remember those days in the past when soft, white flakes fell from the sky over my home in *Appiano* or down onto the rooftop of my home in Michigan, on this Christmas Evening, this holy and silent night, I felt grace falling from above.

It came because I opened my heart to the promise of hope and the bountiful love of all the dear people I have met along my journey.

This love is so fully expressed in a song, a gift I received from my granddaughter Mikaela, the daughter of Anna and Brian.

Windows to the Soul
by Mikaela Teixeira

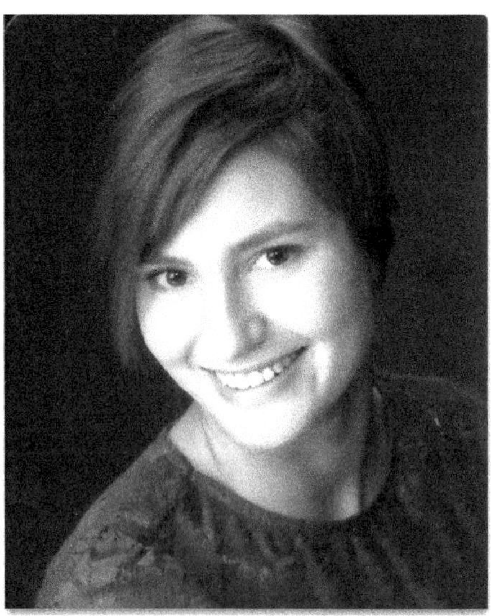

I always thought that I was wise,
till I looked into my grandmother's eyes
     As the car pulls up after the two-hour drive
     I realize a couple of hours isn't enough time.
     As you enter the wooden, grey, old garden gates,
     you enter an Italian wonderland for just the day.
I always thought that I was wise,
till I looked into my grandmother's eyes.
     The stories she narrates from long ago,
     At times leave you speechless,
     wonderstruck, and hungry for more.
I always thought that I was wise,
till I looked into my grandmother's eyes.
     The laugh she shares is infectious,
     as you learn about the lessons from her life's dreams.
     Now your past, present, and future
     are a little less terrifying than they seemed.
I always thought that I was wise,
till I looked into my grandmother's eyes.
     She sits in her chair quietly, mouselike, meek,
     with a tenderness in her gaze.
     As you confide in her about life
     And the journey that you're taking,
     you start to wonder,
     "What is in her head?
     What is this beautiful person thinking?"
I always thought that I was wise,
till I looked into my grandmother's eyes.
     As our time together comes to an end,
     I wave goodbye to a Nonna, a mother, a friend.
     Though two weeks isn't really long,
     It feels like an eternity especially with what the world has
     strung along.
     I open the door to the passenger side,
     take a deep breath and close my eyes.
     I turn my head as I begin to wave
     and just like that, everything changes.
I always thought that I was wise,
till I looked into my grandmother's eyes.
I truly hope I will be wise,
but, till then, I have my grandmother's eyes.

And so, with a song, I saw the potential for good in our youth. Despite the sometimes downward direction the world takes, I knew that through my actions I will be remembered for my part in the journey. My granddaughters Olivia, Mikaela, Julia and Kiara will change the world, and their life history will be blessed with so many moments and memories, and they will grow and rise and live out the dreams in their hearts and minds as I have in mine.

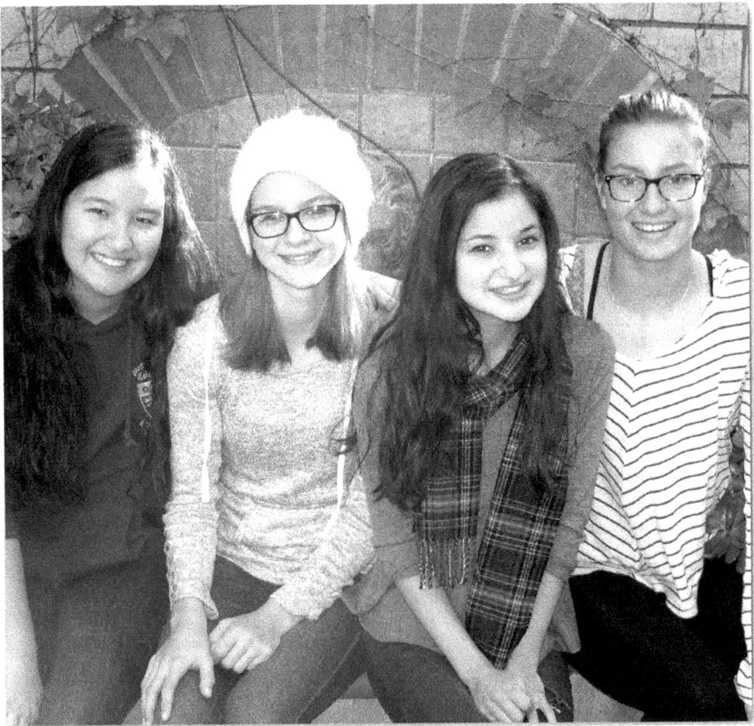

Olivia, Kiara, Julia, Mikaela (2015)

CHAPTER TWENTY-FOUR
Finding My Voice

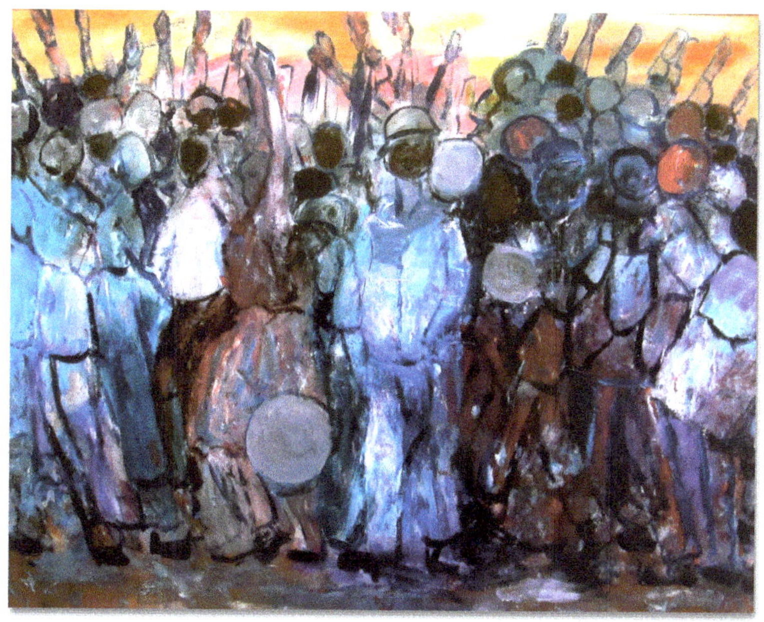

Voices

Change is only imprinted in the steps that I take, when I
move beyond the limits of what might be,
and grasp with purpose for that which, through my
effort, will be.

Then my story, my struggle, made strong by a dream and
bright with hope, Will live in that better day.

And then, I will celebrate.

from the poem "Celebration," pvm

When I was finishing up my studies at Wayne State University, I had taken a course in Black History and Culture. Just as becoming a citizen had urged me to learn more about U.S. democracy, living and studying in Detroit made me realize I knew very little about the history of race in the United States as well.

The first time I saw a person of African descent was in Venice when I had gone to the Italian Consulate Office for my papers to enter the United States. The lady I saw was simply beautiful—tall and slender with dark, black hair arranged in a dramatic style, wearing jewels and walking elegantly through the *piazza* and attracting the attention of everyone there. I thought to myself that in America I would certainly see more such beautiful people.

But when I got to Detroit in 1966, the city was already in chaos. Hundreds of black protestors took to the streets in August for three days, and the next year, the 1967 Detroit Riot that made history resulted in over one thousand injuries and 43 deaths. It was not a beautiful scene.

Back then, I was not really involved with what happened outside of my family. I lived in a suburban neighborhood with mostly white neighbors and had no contact with people of color who mostly lived in the city in areas that I heard called the ghetto. It seemed that the "law" thought of them as "second-class citizens," and the rights that we were all supposed to enjoy under the Constitution were not equal for them. I had no idea what it was to be "black" in America.

The course I took in Black Culture taught the full sweep of African-American history, from the origin of slavery, through five centuries of events that brought Africans to America where they developed a unique religious and social culture against unimaginable odds and despite continual, violent oppression. Black culture was created and defined within these brutal conditions and became extraordinarily rich and compelling in a way that I could only begin to imagine.

It was through a friendship with a student in my class, however, that I gained a clearer perspective.

Thelma was a black woman, about my age, who had encountered many instances of racism, bigotry, hatred and intolerance. She knew her history, starting with the Emancipation Proclamation signed by President Lincoln during the American Civil War. While blacks thought then, that they were finally free, their emancipation was only the first step towards true freedom.

While we were having lunch together, she wanted to tell me her story, and about how various Presidents of the United States had conflicting ideas about the rights of her race through history. She wanted to tell me about the march from Selma to Montgomery in 1965 when peaceful protestors were beaten by police simply for wanting their right to vote. She would say with passion: "The fight for Black lives remains far from done, as long as people are treated differently based on nothing more than the color of their skin."

It was an eye-opening experience for me, and I had to ask her, "Thelma, I am white. Do you hate me?" She shook her head with a smile. Of course not. I was a good friend.

She invited me to go with her to a service at her Baptist church, and I was moved by the powerful singing of Gospel music. The congregation joined in joyously, some singing solos and clapping their hands. The service elevated my spirit. Thelma wanted me to sing along, and I would have liked to, but the music was so different. I was not able to follow the rhythm, and my voice was feeble and soft in the way that nobody would hear me anyway. But I was grateful for the inspiring experience of faith, love and culture, thanks to my friend Thelma.

I saw Barack Obama for the first time on television when he gave his uplifting speech at the Democratic National Convention in 2004. I knew then that his profound words, sometimes quietly poetic, expressed the vision of a man who could inspire people to a greater future.

Three years later in the Spring of 2007, in Springfield, Illinois, then Senator Obama announced his candidacy for President of the United States. I had already read two of his books and listened to every speech he had made. I even had a calendar of all his iconic quotes. His Audacity of Hope reassured me that in a time of war, a conflict that had been dragging on in Iraq and Afghanistan since September 11, 2001, we could still find unity and peace.

According to Obama's hope, "Out of the long political darkness a brighter day will come." There were battles, though, that we needed to fight, "…battles against ignorance and intolerance; corruption and greed; poverty and despair." He firmly believed that we were standing at the crossroads of history, where we could make the right choices, and meet the challenges that faced us.

His optimism gave me hope. One of his first priorities was to bring affordable healthcare to all. He also recognized the urgency of dealing with "climate change." He believed that "…we can turn this crisis of global warming into a moment of opportunity for innovation, and job creation, and an incentive for businesses that will serve as a model for the world."

I hoped that all the obstacles standing in the way of true progress for our country would be set aside. A new majority and sense of unity and common purpose in the political arena with the power of millions of voices calling for change would certainly prevail. I even created a large painting of Obama's "Yes We Can" moment in Chicago when he accepted the Democratic Party's nomination for President—a painting that represented "Possibility."

Unfortunately, political posturing and obstruction, in place of good-faithed governance became the norm for Obama's opposition during his two terms as President.

Even so, the resonance of Obama's message created a movement that led to the breaking of an age-old racial barrier. Well into his campaign he was questioned about his race, and he gave his most eloquent speech of 2008—"A More Perfect Union." Before an audience at the National Constitution Center in Philadelphia, Pennsylvania, he spoke of racial tensions and racial inequality in the United States, and examined the Constitution of the United States as a document left unfinished and stained by the sin of slavery. The Constitution promised all Americans liberty and justice, but it fell short of that promise for many.

Obama expressed those ideas that I had discovered since I had arrived in the United States—that we have different stories, and though we do not look the same, and we come from different places, we have a common hope that with a perfect union we can heal our old racial wounds.

He hoped that together we would solve the monumental problems that confronted us all: two wars, a falling economy, a chronic health care crisis, and devastating climate change.

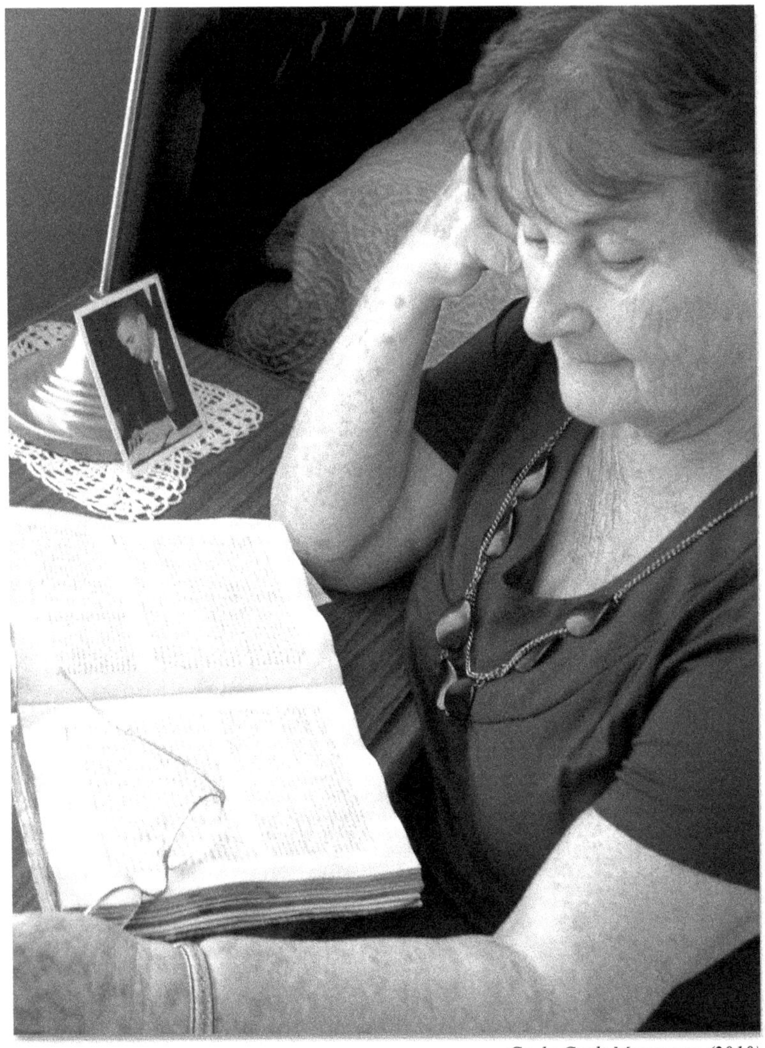

Carla Carli Mazzucato (2010)

I liked his ideas and followed all his policy positions, though I felt let down by his decision to send forty thousand more troops to Afghanistan. Even his healthcare effort fell short, in the face of defiant Republican opposition. Though the Affordable Care Act became law, not a single Republican voted for it despite the constant delay tactics and compromises that weakened the final bill.

But Obama was a man of compassion and hope. By showing respect for the political process he was proclaiming that he would restore our moral standing so that America would once again be "that last best hope for all."

His presidency was not without mistakes, but his intentions were honest. I loved to hear the speeches he gave in all the foreign countries he visited. He was respected by our allies abroad, and made the world safer and more united than before, though...not a perfect union.

In Obama's 2008 victory speech in Chicago he stated that: "Tonight we proved once more that the true strength of our nation comes not from the might of our arms or the scale of our wealth, but from the enduring power of our ideals: democracy, liberty, opportunity, and unyielding hope."

In contrast to the eight years of the Obama presidency, 2016 brought us four years of Donald Trump, who by all truthful accounts was crude, self-interested and dishonest. We have seen how fragile our democracy really is, and how by allowing lies and corruption to go unanswered, we risk being destroyed from within by greed, power-lust, a health pandemic and treason. What a shame for America.

240

My Path To Eternity

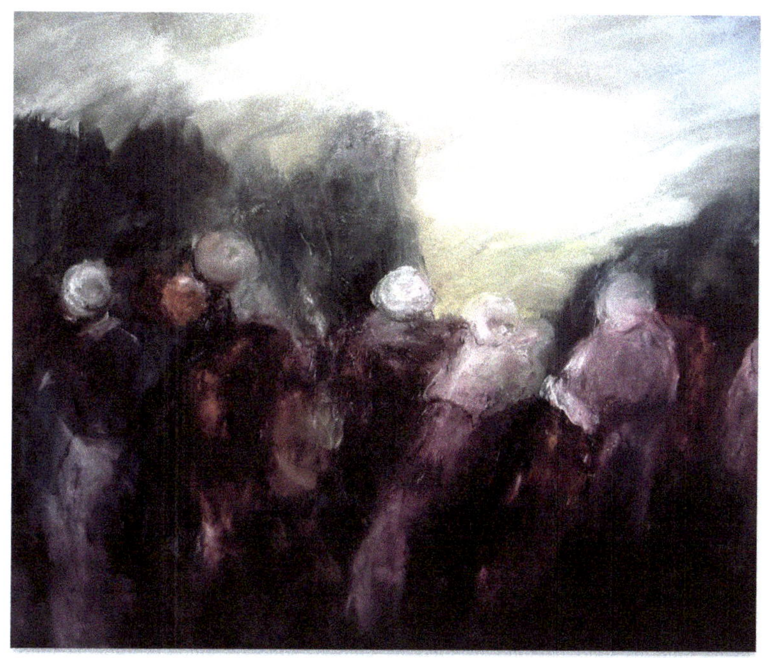

Evening Last Light

And I embrace you——
As you offer yourself, revealed now in the day's
light on a new shore, shining with the promise of
a future filled with hope.
You are possibility.

from the poem "Possibility," pvm

My question in composing my thoughts and memories of my past on paper, is to ponder the meaning of life. In the long history of humankind the reason for our existence has been a search to find the identity of the individual soul, and then ask the question, "What is my purpose? Why am I here?

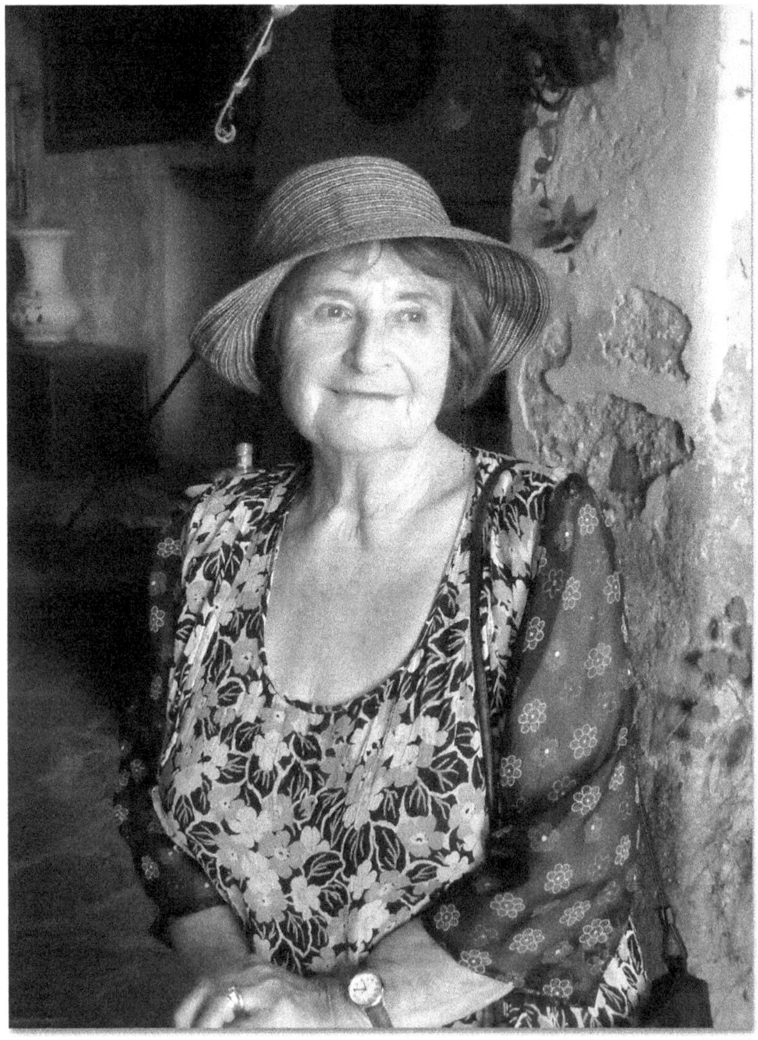

Carla Carli Mazzucato (2018)

There are natural, scientific, philosophical, and even practical reasons to the answer, but most people also believe in some form of spiritual existence, and a force with which, through their faith, they can communicate with the Infinite.

Religion is a universal and a prominent component of human society. Our different cultures let us choose the type of religion we want to follow: a path like Buddhism, a tradition like Judaism, or any other of the many religious teachings that give voice to our various faiths.

The differing beliefs in a personal deity that has ordered the chaos of the universe, whether arising from Judaism or Christianity, Zoroastrianism, Islam or African Spiritualism, are all legitimate. And whether the revelation comes from a deity or a tribal leader, or from objects connected with a deity, the mystery of our life is enshrined in one universal truth, that love can unite us all.

According to Joseph Campbell in his study <u>The Power of Myth</u>, all religions have myths or sacred stories to convey profound meaning to our existence—an answer to the question we all ask. Even so, that answer, that meaning, remains a mystery to me.

My search for truth is still connected to solving the basic questions of my existence. But all of scripture is only a collection of words in need of interpretation, and I have not found an absolute answer in reading or in learning about other religions.

My quest is ultimately for an understanding of the historical Jesus, a personal and internal quest. It is a spiritual conversation and meditation with the power of the Spirit.

My hope is that evil will be destroyed; My faith is that justice will be satisfied. I need this belief to give sense to my existence; I need this belief so that I can find joy when I, one day, will pass on to an existence beyond this world, where I will reunite with all the dear people I lost in life. "Jesus, *Via, Vita, Veritas,*" will be my path to eternity.

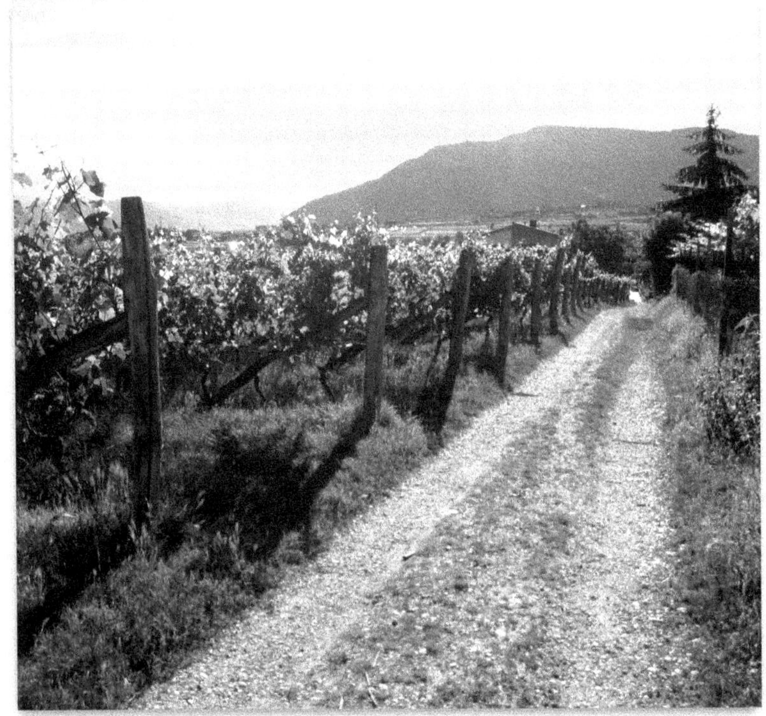

My Path Home — Appiano

I have discovered that one of the many ways God speaks to me is through my moods and emotions which I have learned to express through art. I will go on, therefore, painting my life with my hopes and dreams, as well as the joy and sadness that comes with every season.

I will roam through time and spend spring in my memories of the land of my youth; and when the fading light of day arrives, I will remember the green landscapes of my middle age and the America I love; and finally in the approaching darkness of infinite space in time, I will sense the silence of the coming season, and recall the words of my favorite Italian poet, Giacomo Leopardi:

E come il vento odo stormir tra queste piante,
io quello infinito silenzio a questa voce
Vo comparando: e mi sovvien l'eterno,
E le morte stagioni, e la presente
E viva, e il suon di lei. Cosi` tra questa
Immensità s'annega il pensier mio:
E il naufragar m'è dolce in questo mare

da "L'Infinito" di Giacomo Leopardi

I compare the unending silence beyond
with the sound of the wind rustling through trees,
and I am reminded of eternity,
of seasons past, dead and gone,
and the present, alive now with her voice.
And so, within this immensity
my thoughts are drowned,
though I find it sweet to be adrift in this gentle sea.

from "The Infinite" by Giacomo Leopardi

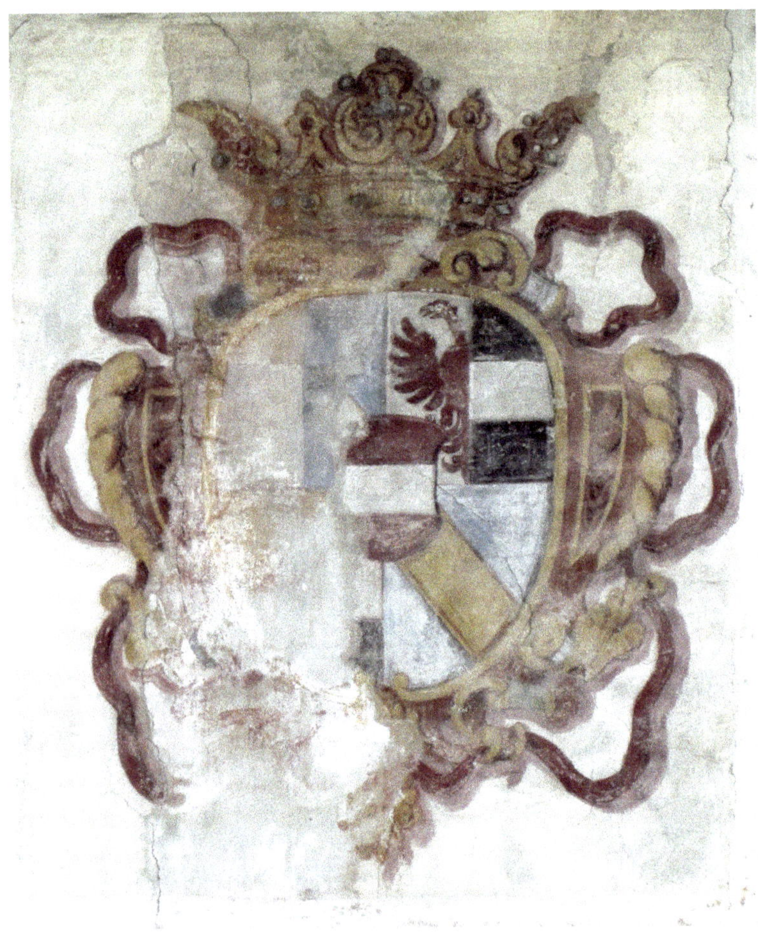

Coat of arms of the Thun family on the west-facing wall of Angerburg,
the noble residence built in 1680 and owned around 1800 by
count Emanuel Maria Thun, Prince-Bishop of Trento.

The house and property was purchased in the late 19th century by Vigil Carli
and remained the home of the Carli family and their descendants for generations.

Family Geneology

<u>underlined</u> people appear in biography

\+ denotes marriage

⌐ denotes siblings

Famiglia **BELLA**

Giovanni Bella (23 JUN 1842—12 MAR 1921)
\+ Monika Fichtner (4 MAY 1852- 7 NOV 1920)
- <u>Dorotea (Retti) Bella</u>
  - \+ Giovanni Parmesani
    - <u>Aldo Parmesani</u> + Giuseppina
      - Gianluigi Parmesani
- <u>Ida Bella</u>
- Massimiliana (Maxi) Bella
- <u>Luigi Bella</u> (8 MAR 1883 — 15 DEC 1953)
  - \+ <u>Carlotta Menapace</u> (16 SEP 1876 — 20 AUG 1919)
    - <u>Anna (Annetta) Bella</u> (9 JAN 1911 — 19 AUG 1959)
      - \+ <u>Vigilio (Gilli) Carli</u> (2 NOV 1898 — 5 OCT 1947)
        - <u>Lidia Carli</u> (3 FEB 1934 — 16 NOV 2010)
          - \+ Sergio Corrà (10 OCT 1930)
            - <u>Andrea Corrà</u> (8 NOV 1967)
              - Sergio Corrà (26 DEC 2010)
            - <u>Ivo Corrà</u> (20 APR 1969)
              - \+ Mirka Cevenini (3 MAY)
                - Zeno Corrà (6 FEB 2006)
                - Vera Corrà (25 FEB 2010)
        - **Carla Carli** (2 NOV 1935)
          - \+ <u>Giuseppe Mazzucato</u> (6 DEC 1925 — 21 DEC 2016)
            - <u>Anna Virginia Mazzucato</u> (27 APR 1963)
              - \+ <u>Brian Teixeira</u> (2 FEB 1956)
                - <u>Mikaela Teixeira</u> (9 SEP1998)
                - <u>Kiara Teixeira</u> (30 SEP 2001)
            - <u>Paolo Vigilio Mazzucato</u> (8 FEB 1966)
              - \+ <u>Karyn Kubo</u> (31 JUL 1965)
                - <u>Olivia Maria Mazzucato</u> (2 APR 1998)
                - <u>Julia Chiemi Mazzucato</u> (22 MAY 2001)
            - <u>Daniela Maria Mazzucato</u> (30 AUG 1968)
        - <u>Bruno Carli</u> (4 APR 1941)
    - <u>Ida (Idotta) Bella</u> (8 DEC 1912 — 21 AUG 1972)
      - \+ <u>Ugo Rizzi</u> (19 JAN 1908 — 28 JAN 1994)
        - Paolo Rizzi (28 JUN 1938 — 5 MAY 2012)
          - \+ Cristina Naletto
            - Silvia Rizzi (14 NOV 1986)

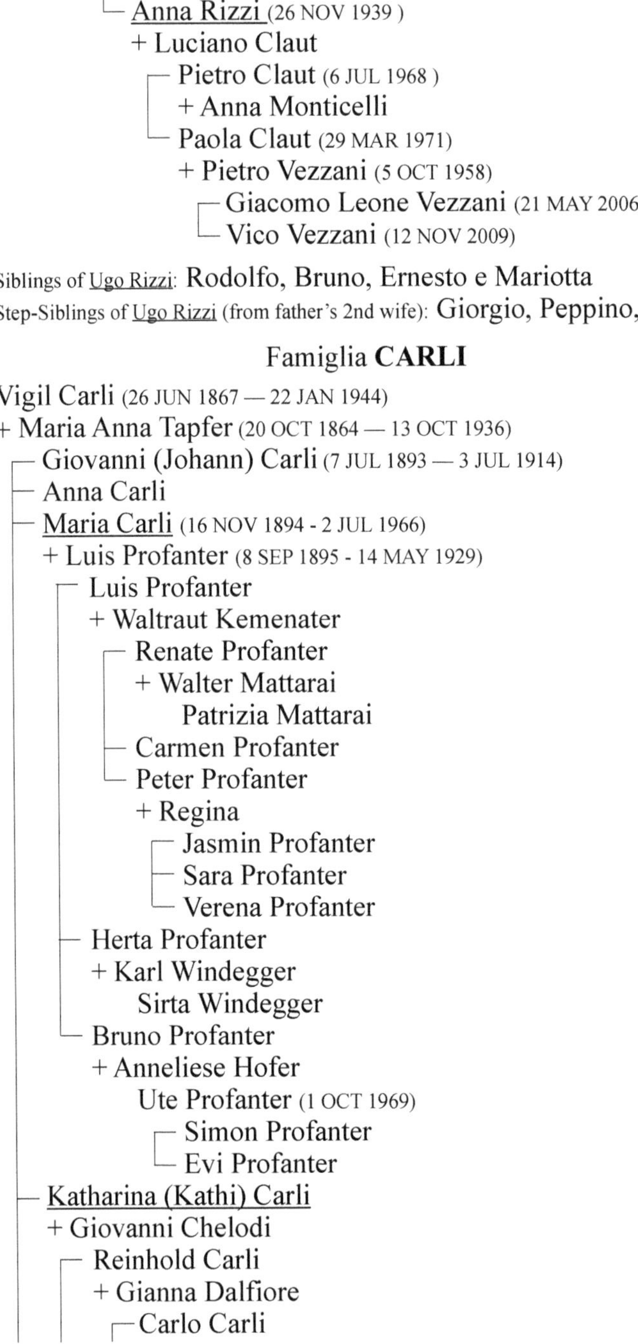

└─ <u>Anna Rizzi</u> (26 NOV 1939)
  + Luciano Claut
    ─ Pietro Claut (6 JUL 1968)
      + Anna Monticelli
    └─ Paola Claut (29 MAR 1971)
      + Pietro Vezzani (5 OCT 1958)
        ┌─ Giacomo Leone Vezzani (21 MAY 2006)
        └─ Vico Vezzani (12 NOV 2009)

Siblings of <u>Ugo Rizzi</u>: Rodolfo, Bruno, Ernesto e Mariotta
Step-Siblings of <u>Ugo Rizzi</u> (from father's 2nd wife): Giorgio, Peppino, <u>Elena</u>

Famiglia **CARLI**

Vigil Carli (26 JUN 1867 — 22 JAN 1944)
+ Maria Anna Tapfer (20 OCT 1864 — 13 OCT 1936)
  ─ Giovanni (Johann) Carli (7 JUL 1893 — 3 JUL 1914)
  ─ Anna Carli
  ─ <u>Maria Carli</u> (16 NOV 1894 - 2 JUL 1966)
    + Luis Profanter (8 SEP 1895 - 14 MAY 1929)
      ┌─ Luis Profanter
        + Waltraut Kemenater
          ┌─ Renate Profanter
            + Walter Mattarai
              Patrizia Mattarai
          ─ Carmen Profanter
          └─ Peter Profanter
            + Regina
              ┌─ Jasmin Profanter
              ─ Sara Profanter
              └─ Verena Profanter
      ─ Herta Profanter
      + Karl Windegger
        Sirta Windegger
      └─ Bruno Profanter
        + Anneliese Hofer
          Ute Profanter (1 OCT 1969)
            ┌─ Simon Profanter
            └─ Evi Profanter
  ─ <u>Katharina (Kathi) Carli</u>
    + Giovanni Chelodi
      ─ Reinhold Carli
        + Gianna Dalfiore
          ┌─ Carlo Carli

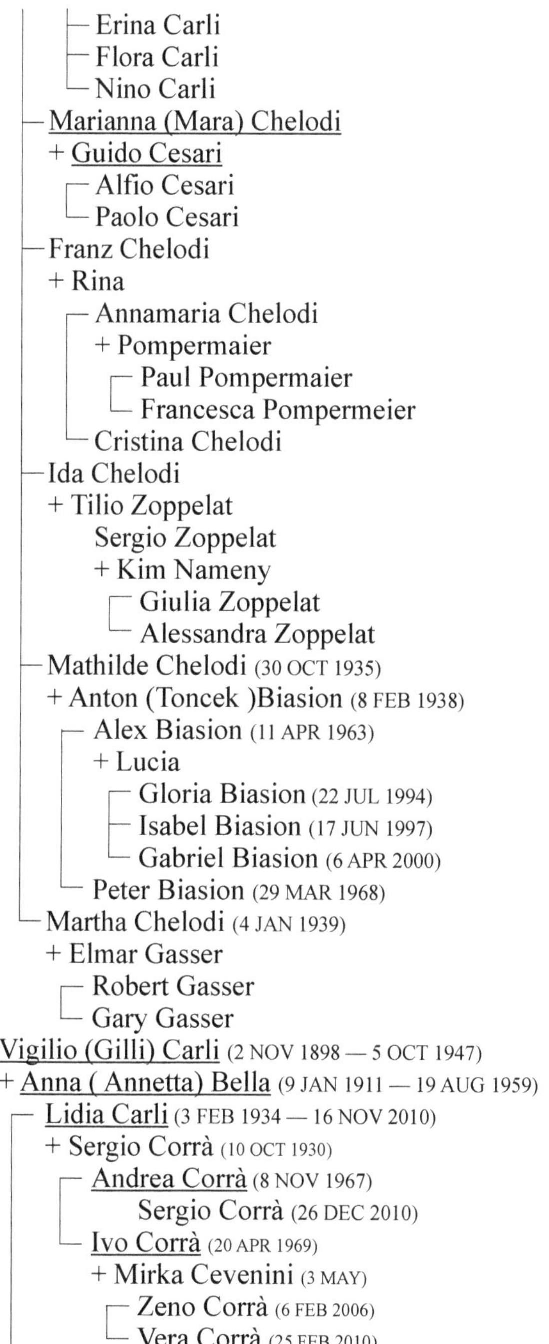

├─ Erina Carli
├─ Flora Carli
└─ Nino Carli
— Marianna (Mara) Chelodi
  + Guido Cesari
  ┌─ Alfio Cesari
  └─ Paolo Cesari
— Franz Chelodi
  + Rina
  ┌─ Annamaria Chelodi
  │   + Pompermaier
  │   ┌─ Paul Pompermaier
  │   └─ Francesca Pompermeier
  └─ Cristina Chelodi
— Ida Chelodi
  + Tilio Zoppelat
    Sergio Zoppelat
    + Kim Nameny
    ┌─ Giulia Zoppelat
    └─ Alessandra Zoppelat
— Mathilde Chelodi (30 OCT 1935)
  + Anton (Toncek)Biasion (8 FEB 1938)
  ┌─ Alex Biasion (11 APR 1963)
  │   + Lucia
  │   ┌─ Gloria Biasion (22 JUL 1994)
  │   ├─ Isabel Biasion (17 JUN 1997)
  │   └─ Gabriel Biasion (6 APR 2000)
  └─ Peter Biasion (29 MAR 1968)
— Martha Chelodi (4 JAN 1939)
  + Elmar Gasser
  ┌─ Robert Gasser
  └─ Gary Gasser
— Vigilio (Gilli) Carli (2 NOV 1898 — 5 OCT 1947)
+ Anna (Annetta) Bella (9 JAN 1911 — 19 AUG 1959)
  ┌─ Lidia Carli (3 FEB 1934 — 16 NOV 2010)
  │   + Sergio Corrà (10 OCT 1930)
  │   ┌─ Andrea Corrà (8 NOV 1967)
  │   │   Sergio Corrà (26 DEC 2010)
  │   └─ Ivo Corrà (20 APR 1969)
  │   + Mirka Cevenini (3 MAY)
  │   ┌─ Zeno Corrà (6 FEB 2006)
  │   └─ Vera Corrà (25 FEB 2010)

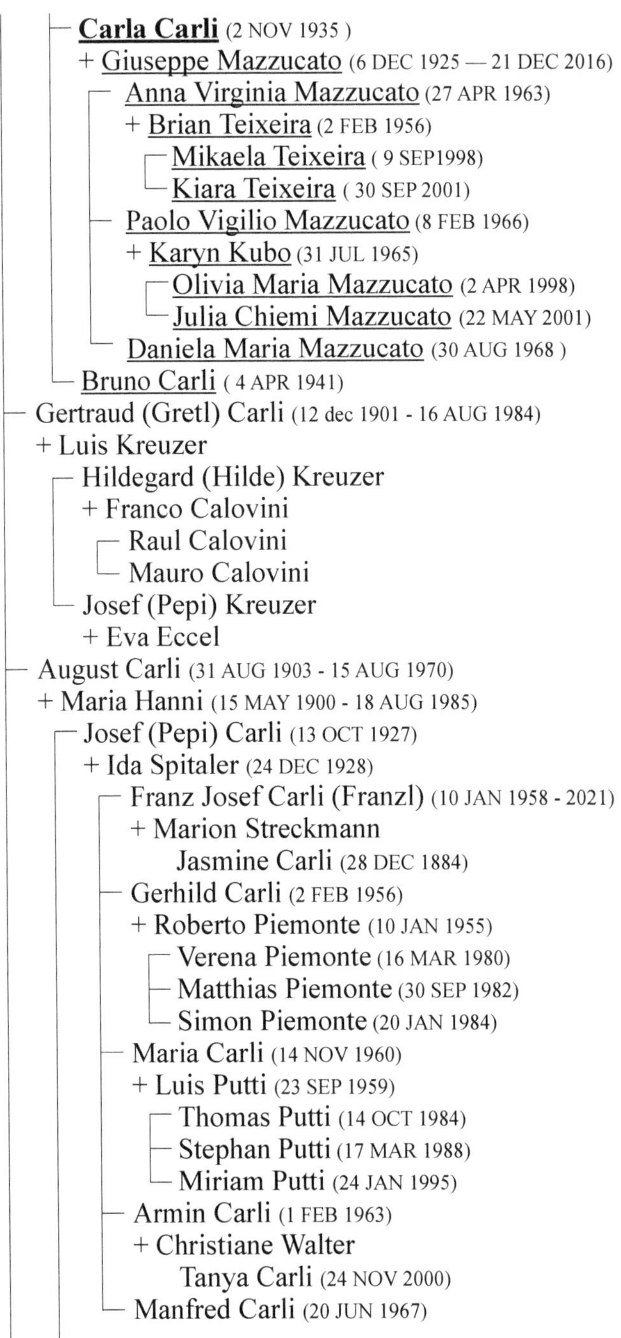

Carla Carli (2 NOV 1935)
+ Giuseppe Mazzucato (6 DEC 1925 — 21 DEC 2016)
Anna Virginia Mazzucato (27 APR 1963)
+ Brian Teixeira (2 FEB 1956)
Mikaela Teixeira (9 SEP 1998)
Kiara Teixeira (30 SEP 2001)
Paolo Vigilio Mazzucato (8 FEB 1966)
+ Karyn Kubo (31 JUL 1965)
Olivia Maria Mazzucato (2 APR 1998)
Julia Chiemi Mazzucato (22 MAY 2001)
Daniela Maria Mazzucato (30 AUG 1968)
Bruno Carli (4 APR 1941)
Gertraud (Gretl) Carli (12 dec 1901 - 16 AUG 1984)
+ Luis Kreuzer
Hildegard (Hilde) Kreuzer
+ Franco Calovini
Raul Calovini
Mauro Calovini
Josef (Pepi) Kreuzer
+ Eva Eccel
August Carli (31 AUG 1903 - 15 AUG 1970)
+ Maria Hanni (15 MAY 1900 - 18 AUG 1985)
Josef (Pepi) Carli (13 OCT 1927)
+ Ida Spitaler (24 DEC 1928)
Franz Josef Carli (Franzl) (10 JAN 1958 - 2021)
+ Marion Streckmann
Jasmine Carli (28 DEC 1884)
Gerhild Carli (2 FEB 1956)
+ Roberto Piemonte (10 JAN 1955)
Verena Piemonte (16 MAR 1980)
Matthias Piemonte (30 SEP 1982)
Simon Piemonte (20 JAN 1984)
Maria Carli (14 NOV 1960)
+ Luis Putti (23 SEP 1959)
Thomas Putti (14 OCT 1984)
Stephan Putti (17 MAR 1988)
Miriam Putti (24 JAN 1995)
Armin Carli (1 FEB 1963)
+ Christiane Walter
Tanya Carli (24 NOV 2000)
Manfred Carli (20 JUN 1967)

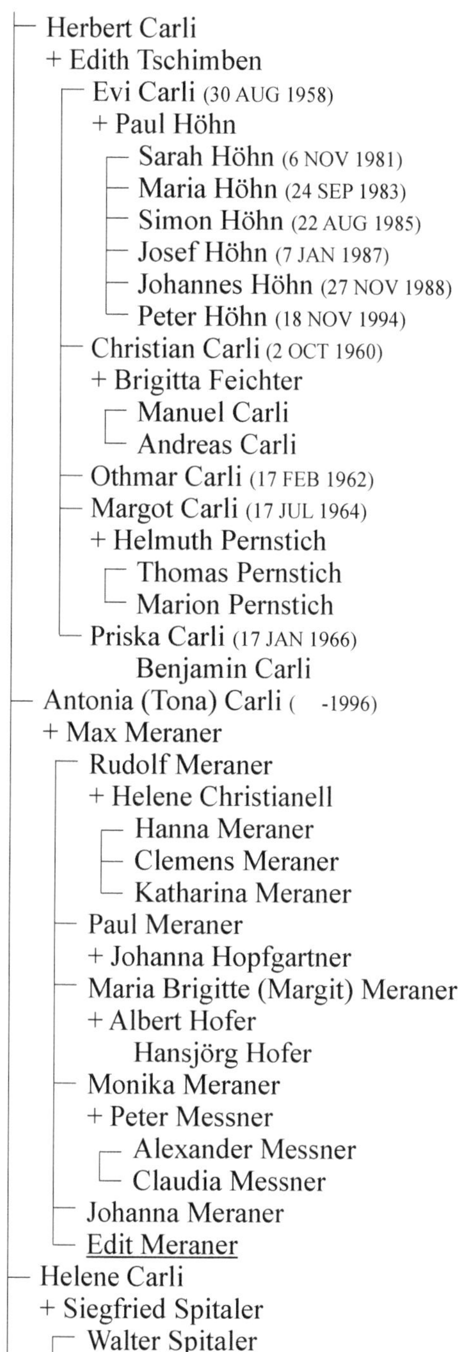

Herbert Carli
+ Edith Tschimben
  Evi Carli (30 AUG 1958)
  + Paul Höhn
    Sarah Höhn (6 NOV 1981)
    Maria Höhn (24 SEP 1983)
    Simon Höhn (22 AUG 1985)
    Josef Höhn (7 JAN 1987)
    Johannes Höhn (27 NOV 1988)
    Peter Höhn (18 NOV 1994)
  Christian Carli (2 OCT 1960)
  + Brigitta Feichter
    Manuel Carli
    Andreas Carli
  Othmar Carli (17 FEB 1962)
  Margot Carli (17 JUL 1964)
  + Helmuth Pernstich
    Thomas Pernstich
    Marion Pernstich
  Priska Carli (17 JAN 1966)
    Benjamin Carli
Antonia (Tona) Carli (-1996)
+ Max Meraner
  Rudolf Meraner
  + Helene Christianell
    Hanna Meraner
    Clemens Meraner
    Katharina Meraner
  Paul Meraner
  + Johanna Hopfgartner
  Maria Brigitte (Margit) Meraner
  + Albert Hofer
    Hansjörg Hofer
  Monika Meraner
  + Peter Messner
    Alexander Messner
    Claudia Messner
  Johanna Meraner
  Edit Meraner
Helene Carli
+ Siegfried Spitaler
  Walter Spitaler

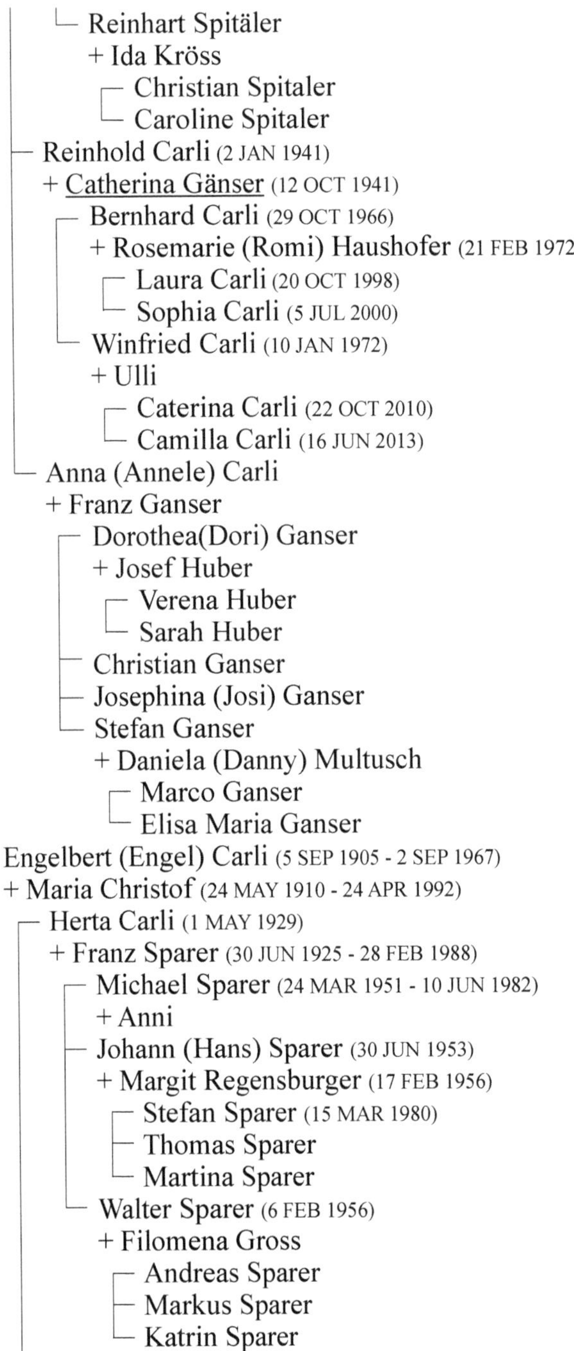

```
    └─ Reinhart Spitäler
       + Ida Kröss
          ┌─ Christian Spitaler
          └─ Caroline Spitaler
  ─ Reinhold Carli (2 JAN 1941)
    + Catherina Gänser (12 OCT 1941)
       ┌─ Bernhard Carli (29 OCT 1966)
       │  + Rosemarie (Romi) Haushofer (21 FEB 1972)
       │     ┌─ Laura Carli (20 OCT 1998)
       │     └─ Sophia Carli (5 JUL 2000)
       └─ Winfried Carli (10 JAN 1972)
          + Ulli
             ┌─ Caterina Carli (22 OCT 2010)
             └─ Camilla Carli (16 JUN 2013)
  └─ Anna (Annele) Carli
     + Franz Ganser
        ┌─ Dorothea(Dori) Ganser
        │  + Josef Huber
        │     ┌─ Verena Huber
        │     └─ Sarah Huber
        ┌─ Christian Ganser
        ┌─ Josephina (Josi) Ganser
        └─ Stefan Ganser
           + Daniela (Danny) Multusch
              ┌─ Marco Ganser
              └─ Elisa Maria Ganser
─ Engelbert (Engel) Carli (5 SEP 1905 - 2 SEP 1967)
  + Maria Christof (24 MAY 1910 - 24 APR 1992)
     ┌─ Herta Carli (1 MAY 1929)
     │  + Franz Sparer (30 JUN 1925 - 28 FEB 1988)
     │     ┌─ Michael Sparer (24 MAR 1951 - 10 JUN 1982)
     │     │  + Anni
     │     ┌─ Johann (Hans) Sparer (30 JUN 1953)
     │     │  + Margit Regensburger (17 FEB 1956)
     │     │     ┌─ Stefan Sparer (15 MAR 1980)
     │     │     ┌─ Thomas Sparer
     │     │     └─ Martina Sparer
     │     └─ Walter Sparer (6 FEB 1956)
     │        + Filomena Gross
     │           ┌─ Andreas Sparer
     │           ┌─ Markus Sparer
     │           └─ Katrin Sparer
```

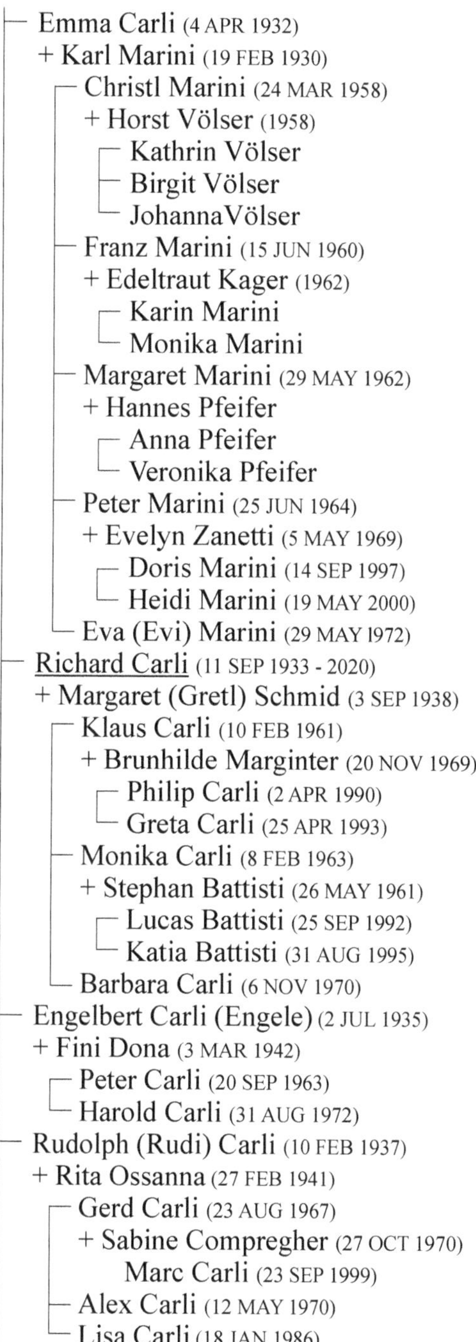

Emma Carli (4 APR 1932)
+ Karl Marini (19 FEB 1930)
    Christl Marini (24 MAR 1958)
    + Horst Völser (1958)
        Kathrin Völser
        Birgit Völser
        JohannaVölser
    Franz Marini (15 JUN 1960)
    + Edeltraut Kager (1962)
        Karin Marini
        Monika Marini
    Margaret Marini (29 MAY 1962)
    + Hannes Pfeifer
        Anna Pfeifer
        Veronika Pfeifer
    Peter Marini (25 JUN 1964)
    + Evelyn Zanetti (5 MAY 1969)
        Doris Marini (14 SEP 1997)
        Heidi Marini (19 MAY 2000)
    Eva (Evi) Marini (29 MAY 1972)
Richard Carli (11 SEP 1933 - 2020)
+ Margaret (Gretl) Schmid (3 SEP 1938)
    Klaus Carli (10 FEB 1961)
    + Brunhilde Marginter (20 NOV 1969)
        Philip Carli (2 APR 1990)
        Greta Carli (25 APR 1993)
    Monika Carli (8 FEB 1963)
    + Stephan Battisti (26 MAY 1961)
        Lucas Battisti (25 SEP 1992)
        Katia Battisti (31 AUG 1995)
    Barbara Carli (6 NOV 1970)
Engelbert Carli (Engele) (2 JUL 1935)
+ Fini Dona (3 MAR 1942)
    Peter Carli (20 SEP 1963)
    Harold Carli (31 AUG 1972)
Rudolph (Rudi) Carli (10 FEB 1937)
+ Rita Ossanna (27 FEB 1941)
    Gerd Carli (23 AUG 1967)
    + Sabine Compregher (27 OCT 1970)
        Marc Carli (23 SEP 1999)
    Alex Carli (12 MAY 1970)
    Lisa Carli (18 JAN 1986)

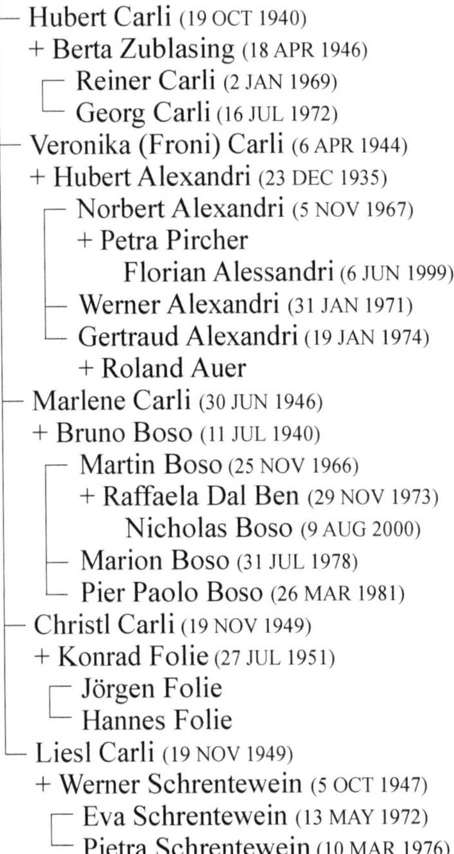

— Hubert Carli (19 OCT 1940)
  + Berta Zublasing (18 APR 1946)
    ⌐ Reiner Carli (2 JAN 1969)
    └ Georg Carli (16 JUL 1972)
— Veronika (Froni) Carli (6 APR 1944)
  + Hubert Alexandri (23 DEC 1935)
    ⌐ Norbert Alexandri (5 NOV 1967)
    │ + Petra Pircher
    │   Florian Alessandri (6 JUN 1999)
    ├ Werner Alexandri (31 JAN 1971)
    └ Gertraud Alexandri (19 JAN 1974)
      + Roland Auer
— Marlene Carli (30 JUN 1946)
  + Bruno Boso (11 JUL 1940)
    ⌐ Martin Boso (25 NOV 1966)
    │ + Raffaela Dal Ben (29 NOV 1973)
    │   Nicholas Boso (9 AUG 2000)
    ├ Marion Boso (31 JUL 1978)
    └ Pier Paolo Boso (26 MAR 1981)
— Christl Carli (19 NOV 1949)
  + Konrad Folie (27 JUL 1951)
    ⌐ Jörgen Folie
    └ Hannes Folie
└ Liesl Carli (19 NOV 1949)
  + Werner Schrentewein (5 OCT 1947)
    ⌐ Eva Schrentewein (13 MAY 1972)
    └ Pietra Schrentewein (10 MAR 1976)

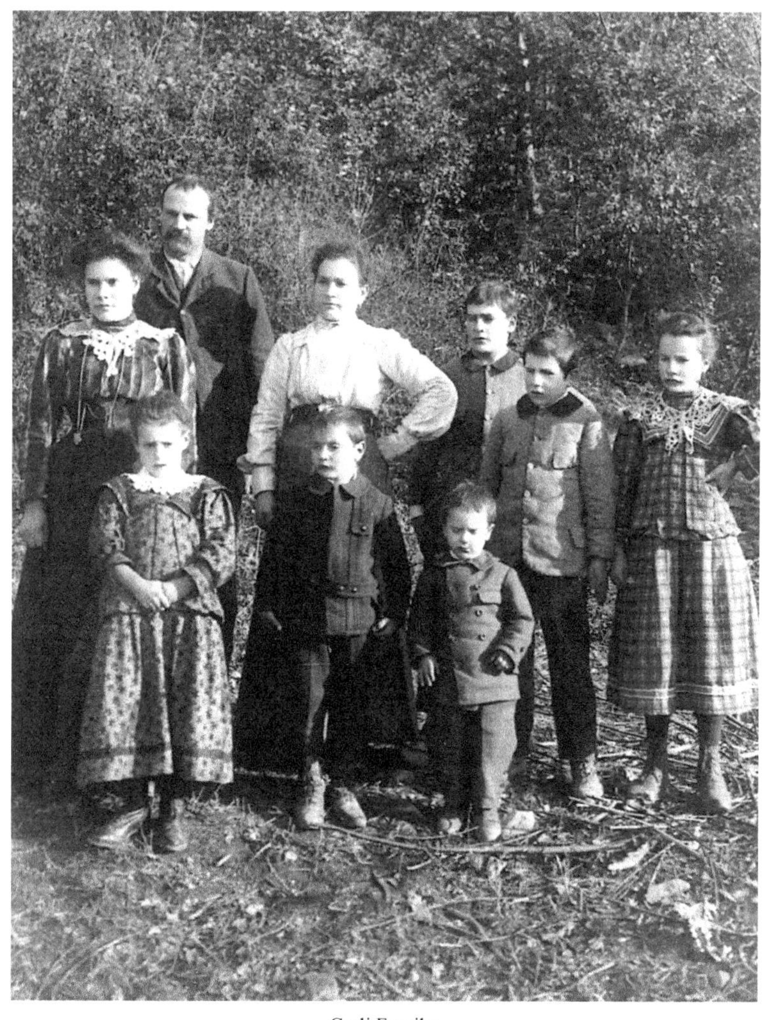

Carli Family:
(Back) Maria, Vigil Carli, Maria Tapfer, Johann, Vigilio, Katharina
(Front) Gretl, August, Engelbert

Index of Paintings
by Carla Carli Mazzucato

Index of Quoted Works

Other Books
about Carla Carli Mazzucato and her art

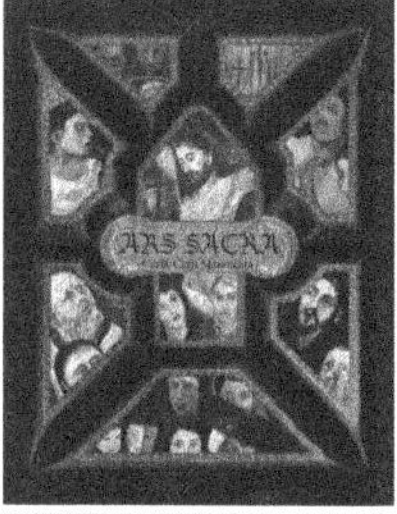

ARS SACRA
*a reflection on the Passion of Jesus Christ
in the art of Carla Carli Mazzucato*
2020

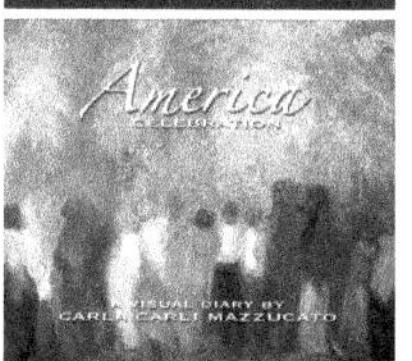

AMERICA: Celebration
*a visual diary of Carla Carli Mazzucato's
American journey*
2011

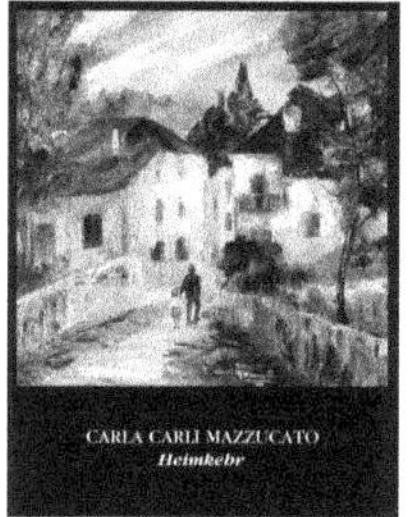

HEIMKEHR: Return to my Homeland
*landscapes and street scenes
of Carla Carli Mazzucato's hometown,
Appiano, Italy*
2001

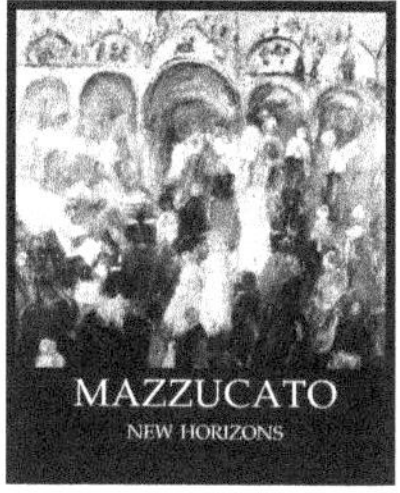

MAZZUCATO: New Horizons
*the art that established
Carla Carli Mazzucato as a leading
contemporary artist*
1994

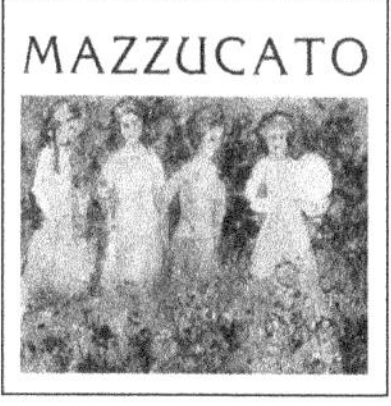

MAZZUCATO
paintings and poems
1987

available at — www.mazzucato.org/books.html

www.blusparks.com

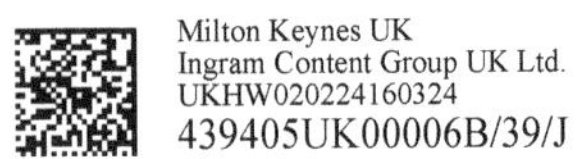

Milton Keynes UK
Ingram Content Group UK Ltd.
UKHW020224160324
439405UK00006B/39/J